THE
MARIPOSA
FOLK
FESTIVAL

THE MARIPOSA FOLK FESTIVAL

A HISTORY

Michael Hill

DUNDURN
TORONTO

Cover image: John Hartford, 1988, Molson Park, courtesy of Mariposa Folk Foundation, Clara Thomas Archives, York University.
Printer: Webcom

Library and Archives Canada Cataloguing in Publication

Hill, Michael, 1952-, author
    Mariposa Folk Festival : a history / Michael Hill.

Includes bibliographical references and index.
Issued in print and electronic formats.
ISBN 978-1-4597-3773-0 (paperback).--ISBN 978-1-4597-3774-7 (pdf).--ISBN 978-1-4597-3775-4 (epub)

1. Mariposa Folk Festival--History. I. Title.

ML38.O695M344 2017   780.78'71317   C2017-900033-0
                                                  C2017-900034-9

1   2   3   4   5   21   20   19   18   17

We acknowledge the support of the **Canada Council for the Arts** and the **Ontario Arts Council** for our publishing program. We also acknowledge the financial support of the **Government of Ontario**, through the **Ontario Book Publishing Tax Credit** and the **Ontario Media Development Corporation**, and the **Government of Canada**.

Care has been taken to trace the ownership of copyright material used in this book. The author and the publisher welcome any information enabling them to rectify any references or credits in subsequent editions.

— *J. Kirk Howard, President*

The publisher is not responsible for websites or their content unless they are owned by the publisher.

Printed and bound in Canada.

VISIT US AT

dundurn.com | @dundurnpress | dundurnpress | dundurnpress

Dundurn
3 Church Street, Suite 500
Toronto, Ontario, Canada
M5E 1M2

CONTENTS

Author's Notes and Acknowledgements

SPECIAL RECOGNITION MUST BE PAID to the contributions of many individuals to the telling of this story. The 1977 book *For What Time I Am in This World: Stories from Mariposa*, produced by the festival but edited by Bill Usher and Linda Page-Harpa, was my first source and starting point for telling this history. The work of Debra Sharp in researching and writing the history of the first two decades cannot be underestimated. Without my wife, Bonnie, who carefully clipped and collated newspaper articles, the job of telling the story from 2000 to the present would have been much more difficult and time-consuming. Sija Tsai's 2013 PhD dissertation — "Mariposa Folk Festival: The Sounds, Sights, and Costs of a Fifty Year Road Trip" — told a lot of the story from an academic point of view, and I am indebted to Sija for her careful and extensive research.

In the course of my research into the history of the Mariposa Folk Festival, I interviewed a number of people who played key roles over the years. I am most grateful for their time and input. Any quotations in the book that are not cited come from these interviews. Thank you to the following people: Doug Baker, September 14, 2016; Gord Ball, March 22, 2016; Pam Carter, August 13, 2016; Michael Cooney, March 2 and June 5, 2016; Ted Duncan, April 13, 2016; Richard Flohil, April 7, 2016; Gerry Hawes, August 25, 2016; Tim Lauer, March 22, 2016; Gordon Lightfoot, December 7, 2016; Owen McBride, September 18, 2016; Colin Puffer, March 27, 2016; Vivienne Muhling, July 29, 2016; David Warren, March 14, 2016; Ken Whiteley, November 2, 2016; and Ruth Jones-McVeigh, January 13, 2017.

Other individuals who have contributed to this work are Pete McGarvey, Sid Dolgay, Lynne Hurry, and Rob Sinclair. Special thanks to Anna St. Onge at York University's Clara Thomas Archives for her diligence, organization, and suggestions. Thanks to Gerry Hawes for his energetic and enthusiastic promotional work and suggestions. Thanks also to chief archivist Michael Moir and the staff of the archives for their support and help. Special thanks to the Mariposa Folk Festival board of directors for their encouragement and the permission to use archival material. I am also grateful to my editors (Dominic Farrell, Kate Unrau, and Cheryl Hawley) and the staff at Dundurn Press for their ongoing support and belief in this project. I am indebted to my friend Sonny Ochs for being my "pre-editor." Her suggestions and astute suggestions helped me in numerous revisions. And naturally, I dedicate this work to my immediate family — Bonnie, Erin, Stephanie, Adam, and Sam.

INTRODUCTION
Folk Music and Folk Festivals

AS THE SUN SETS OVER THE WESTERN SHORE of Lake Couchiching, a crowd of people — perhaps three thousand — sit in anticipation of the evening headline act. Already the day has been a blur of different activities. They've witnessed eclectic groupings of artists playing music based on a theme. These same patrons have bought T-shirts and CDs at the Emporium; they've listened with their kids to children's entertainers and made wildflower garlands at Folkplay; they've danced to Celtic tunes on the Bohemian Embassy Stage; they've had a beer in the Mariposa pub as they listened to some wailing blues; they've tried to play an autoharp at the Interactive Stage. They've sampled Jamaican patties, pad Thai, and good old-fashioned burgers along the food row. Earlier on the mainstage they've heard Le Vent du Nord, a Québécois group; Bahamas, a brilliant new singer-songwriter; Black Umfolosi, an enthusiastic troupe of dancers from Africa; and Family of the Year, an energetic folk-rock band touting their latest single. It's time for the big-name act. As the emcee announces her name, *the* Jann Arden and her band walk onto the stage. Cheers erupt from the crowd as the musicians launch into a familiar riff. This is the moment they've been waiting for all day. This is just a typical day at the Mariposa Folk Festival, something hundreds of thousands of people have experienced, and it's a magical experience, indeed. Canada's oldest and most famous folk festival has delighted so many and generated great memories for more than fifty years.

o o o

What is a folk festival? The answer probably depends on where you are and who the audience is. Perhaps the first question to answer, though, is this: what exactly is folk music?

Not surprisingly it is impossible to come up with a definition of folk music that satisfies everyone. Is it traditional music that carries on the singing and dancing traditions of Eastern Europe? Is it music akin to the Child Ballads of rural England? Is it Appalachian music sung to the accompaniment of homemade banjos? Is it the protest music of Woody Guthrie's Dust Bowl days? Is it the drumming and dancing of Zimbabwe or South Africa or rural Ghana? Is it a campfire rendition of "Country Roads" or "Four Strong Winds" or — heaven forbid — "Kumbaya"? Is it the modern songs of popular performers who play a mix of acoustic and electric instruments? The answer is yes, of course. It is all of these things and more.

For some, folk music has to have that traditional and authentic connection to the past and employ musical styles of long ago and far away. For others, folk has evolved to encompass any sounds that grew out of those traditional styles. Some believe it must be acoustic while others embrace the new technology and modern instrumentation that produces a form of music that can be embraced by "the people." In that case, for example, can hip hop be considered urban folk music?

In the 1940s folk music was popularly represented by Woody Guthrie, Lead Belly, or the Almanac Singers, all of whom produced a music that was simpler than the radio and dance hall music of the day yet deeply intellectual. In the 1950s the Weavers and the Kingston Trio popularized the genre with their chart-topping records, and they inspired thousands to take up the banjo and guitar to make their own folk music. In the 1960s Bob Dylan and the Byrds revolutionized folk, taking it in new directions and blending thoughtful songwriting with rock and roll; in the 1970s we had Gordon Lightfoot, Joni Mitchell, Cat Stevens, James Taylor, and John Denver, who ushered in an era of great singer-songwriters who were all based in the acoustic folk tradition. By the second decade of the twenty-first century, the proliferation of acoustic-based indie artists who embraced songwriting and new technology seems worlds away from the folk music scene of the early 60s, but one can argue that these young performers are producing folk music the way that Pete Seeger, Cisco Houston, and others did in the 1940s.

Folk music has been an agent of social change throughout the last century as well. To some, it is protest music, although that is far too narrow an interpretation to be valid. In the 1940s Woody Guthrie engraved his guitar with the message "This machine kills fascists." Peter, Paul and Mary performed at the 1963 Washington march where Martin Luther King gave his "I have a dream" speech, and they followed him to the Deep South for his non-violent marches of protest. Anti-war songs, such as Dylan's "Blowin' in the Wind," Phil Ochs's "Draft Dodger Rag," and Country Joe McDonald's' "I-Feel-Like-I'm-Fixing-to-Die Rag" were instruments in turning the American mindset against the war in Vietnam. Pete Seeger's thoughtful anthem "Bring 'Em Home" was recorded by Bruce Springsteen as recently as 2006 and carried the message that the troops needed to be brought back from Iraq, Afghanistan, and anywhere else the military and the politicians decided to send young soldiers. Seeger's "Banks of Marble" was revived during the brief Occupy Wall Street protest movement in 2011.

Folk music has never dominated the airwaves. Radio has traditionally embraced rock music and, in more recent decades, the brand that's come to be known as "new country." Similarly, television has focused more attention on the same kinds of music. It is mostly via live appearances that folk musicians get their material in front of people. And what better place than a folk festival to showcase that brand.

Folk festivals are, generally speaking, summer events where this brand of music thrives. Outdoor summer folk festivals (and those few "off-season" festivals) seem to be where this type of artistic endeavour can best be experienced. Sitting under a tree, looking out at water, and hearing acoustic-based music might seem cliché, but there is more than an element of truth to it. Some folk festivals try to maintain that traditional connection with the old ballads and styles of a long ago time. The Mill Race Folk Festival in Cambridge, Ontario, for instance, is programmed to showcase precisely those kinds of acts. Other festivals, such as Hillside in Guelph, Ontario, present acts that cross the broad spectrum of musical genres.

Folk festivals, in one form or another, have been with us in North America since at least the middle of the nineteenth century. German immigrants in Texas and in Pennsylvania held annual *Saengerfests* as early as the 1850s. Diverse "ethnic" festivals were held in the early twentieth century in places like Milwaukee,

Cleveland, Buffalo, and New York City. In 1932 the St. Paul (Minnesota) Folk Festival advertised that it would provide songs and dances from various nationalities and racial groups. The Canadian Pacific Railway staged a series of folk music festivals across the country between 1927 and 1931, in hopes of generating tourism business for the railroad and its string of hotels. Festivals in the southern United States, particularly in the Appalachian region, focused on traditional (i.e., banjo and fiddle) music, often banning any kind of amplification. By the time the Newport Jazz Festival spawned its offshoot, the Newport Folk Festival, in 1959, myriad folk music festivals had already been established around the U.S., and the concept seemed ready to grow and expand.

Sylvia Tyson, whose participation in Mariposa has spanned its entire history, talked about the early festivals and the evolution of the folk genre in the 1990 film *Mariposa: Under a Stormy Sky*.

> That era [early 1960s] was the beginning of social and political involvement. Those songs said something. There were stories to them. Maybe the stories were three, four hundred years old, but that didn't mean they weren't valid stories. And as soon as people started writing material, then they became even more valid because they were talking about you and me and what we were doing and what we thought, and that's because there was such a burgeoning awareness of social and political problems on college campuses at that point. I think that's why folk music became as popular as it did.[1]

Mariposa was the first popular and wide-reaching folk music festival in Canada. There had been other festivals over the years. For instance, the Miramichi Folksong Festival had been established in the 1950s before either the Newport Folk Festival in the U.S. or Mariposa in Canada. Yet it was Mariposa that fully developed the concept. Keying in to the popularity of folk in the early 1960s, Mariposa not only revived but revolutionized the folk idiom.

This is the story of the Mariposa folk festival through its financial ups and downs, its peripatetic nature, and its cultural contributions. It is the story of its founders, leaders, and volunteers. It is the story of the great — and sometimes not so great — musicians, dancers, storytellers, and poets. It is the story of a Canadian institution.

CHAPTER ONE
In the Beginning

CLUB PAVALON, MORE COMMONLY KNOWN as "the Pav," was an old-time dance hall situated on the edge of Couchiching Beach Park in Orillia. It had a reputation for bringing in great bands and was a popular hangout for teens, who would dance to the likes of Bobby Curtola, the Stitch in Tyme, the Downchild Blues Band, and the Guess Who. The Pav also doubled as a community meeting hall.

On a cold January evening in 1961, John Fisher took to the Pav's stage to address the local Chamber of Commerce about tourism and, specifically, how to promote it in small towns. Fisher had been nicknamed "Mr. Canada" for his enthusiastic and influential CBC broadcasts about Canadian culture and history. He would go on to be a key figure in putting on Expo 67 during the centennial year. But in 1961 in Orillia, he had come to town to speak about what would make Orillia a desirable tourist destination. Little did he dream that he was planting the seed of an idea that would lead to the creation of a Canadian institution — the Mariposa Folk Festival.

In the audience that night was Ruth Jones, a young, community-minded mother, who was a folk music enthusiast. She and her husband would often make the trek south to Toronto to hear the traditional and the new sounds coming from the coffee houses and folk clubs in the city. Ever since the Kingston Trio had topped the popular music charts with their 1958 hit "Tom Dooley," folk music had gained increasing popularity, especially with young people. The folk boom — some wags have called it the "folk scare" — was well underway in the winter of 1961. A number of folk clubs already existed in the city, especially in the Yorkville neighbourhood of Toronto. Ruth was intrigued by what Fisher said about the growing number of arts festivals around the country and how Orillia might benefit from staging something of that sort.

The wheels were set in motion. Several days later, as she lay in bed with a nasty flu bug and time to think, Ruth came up with the idea of putting on a folk music festival in town.

Orillia at that time was a quiet place of about fourteen thousand residents. Situated between two lakes, its summertime population allegedly doubled with the arrival of cottagers and nearby resort guests. Orillia's biggest employer was the Ontario Hospital School, one of the largest mental institutions in the country. That was also the workplace of Ruth's husband, Dr. Casey Jones. The rest of the town's economy was based on its moderately sized factories and depended upon the tourism business in the surrounding area. The sleepy demeanour was not all that far removed from the quirky fictional village of Mariposa that Stephen Leacock had described in his 1912 novel *Sunshine Sketches of a Little Town*. Leacock, a summer resident of Orillia, based many of his characters and events on real people and real incidents in the community. The book propelled Leacock into stardom as an international humorist, and it put Orillia on the map as the archetypal small Canadian town.

A few days after Fisher's speech, Ruth made a call to Pete McGarvey, a local broadcaster and a town alderman who was also interested in promoting Orillia as a travel destination. Only a few years earlier McGarvey had almost single-handedly saved Stephen Leacock's home from the wrecker's ball. By 1961 it had become a local museum and a tourist attraction, thanks to Pete's efforts and hard work.

"She had this glorious idea that we could stage a folk festival in Orillia that very summer. She thought that would be the dimension that John Fisher was calling for," recalled McGarvey. "I agreed wholeheartedly that it should be done; nobody else was doing it; the talent was near at hand; Orillia was, of course, a resort community accustomed to summer visitors; and we had plenty of places to show their talents — the Opera House, the community centre outdoors, or the Oval [the town's sports arena]. So that was it."[1]

The name Mariposa was suggested in tribute to Leacock's literary invention — his satiric jab at the Orillia he knew in 1912. Why he chose the Spanish word for butterfly has never been documented. He may simply have scanned his Ontario map and noticed that there was a Mariposa Township near Lindsay, Ontario, and liked the name. We'll probably never know. What we do know is that no attempt to mock Orillia was intended in the naming of the festival! Pete, Ruth, and her husband Casey all laid claim to having come up with the name. Ruth's notebook history credits Casey.

o o o

Ruth and her husband had been folk music enthusiasts for a number of years and they had an insider's knowledge of the folk community in Toronto. Ruth boldly and confidently approached many of her contacts in the city. An important group on that list was the Toronto Guild of Canadian Folk Artists. Among its somewhat radical left-wing members were people like Estelle Klein, who would eventually become artistic director of the festival, and Sid Dolgay, a member of the folk group the Travellers. Sid's band had recorded its own version of Woody Guthrie's folk classic "This Land Is Your Land" in 1955 and had a reputation as Canada's top folk draw.

The first meeting of the board of directors for the fledgling festival took place at the Jones home on Bay Street in Orillia. Ruth became president; Pete was elected vice-president, and Casey would act as secretary-treasurer. It was appropriate that Casey be treasurer: he contributed $5,000 of the Jones's own money, a sizable amount in 1961, indeed (the equivalent of about $40,000 in 2016).

The trio got the approval of Orillia town council and was even given a small amount of money — $250 — to help fund the festival. Ruth and her team solicited advice from what was then the only other modern folk festival in North America, the Newport Folk Festival in Rhode Island.[2] A date in August was selected, and even though it was still a snowy February, that summer weekend loomed ominously.

Much of the work and direction over the next few months came from Toronto. Under Ruth's leadership, an informal group of advisors from the city helped to bring in the acts, organize the minutia, and set in motion the procedures that would make her dream into a reality. In addition to Estelle Klein and Sid Dolgay, Syd Banks, who was a renowned television and music producer, helped out. Ed Cowan was asked to be the first producer of the festival and Ted Schafer was named the first emcee. Edith Fowke, host of CBC's *Folk Song Time* and a renowned folklorist in her own right, also chipped in. Edith — who was the quintessential expert on Canadian folk music at that time — pushed for an all-Canadian flavour. Ruth's brother David Major did a lot of the legwork "in the trenches," according to Ruth. Emerging musical star Ian Tyson used his early training as a graphic artist to design the first poster and the initial Mariposa logo. Many of the meetings were held in Ian's downtown-Toronto apartment. In his 2010 autobiography, *The Long Trail: My Life in the West*, Tyson makes mention of the fact that the poster for the first Mariposa Folk Festival still hangs in the kitchen of his home in rural Alberta.

Innumerable phone calls and hectic meetings took place in those months between February and August of 1961. Ruth and her helpers put a lot of wear and tear on their cars as they drove up and down the 125 or so kilometres of highway between Orillia and Toronto. Decisions were made on a lineup, on how to advertise and sell the new concept, and on where to actually hold the event. Numerous solutions had to be found for problems that no one had ever encountered before. Where would visitors stay? Where would they house the performers overnight? How would they recruit the necessary volunteers to man all aspects of the actual staging of the festival?

Ruth became something of a publicist for the festival as she travelled all over Ontario touting her new "baby." She gave numerous radio, TV, and press interviews and made the pages of *Chatelaine* and *Maclean's* magazines. In an unpublished manuscript Ruth recalled, "I arranged that all milk delivered to summer cottagers would have a promotional collar attached…. Every piece of mail that went through the Orillia post office for the month preceding the event got a special cancellation stamp. I travelled all over Ontario doing newspaper, radio, and TV interviews and made a trip to my hometown, Halifax, for a special media event…. We sent out hundreds of news releases — every one sealed and stamped by my four children, David, Bruce, Nancy, and Barb, while they learned and sang folk songs."[3]

Ruth sent out letters to people such as Pete Seeger, Theodore Bikel, Ed McCurdy and Alan Mills, inviting them to come and play at the festival. Few replied (Bikel, for instance, said he was "busy"), but she remained determined. Her goal was to teach Canadians about their own musical heritage, to give some of our homegrown musicians the publicity they badly needed, and to supply her hometown with a tourist attraction that was both exciting and wholesome. The lineup eventually took on an all-Canadian flavour, showcasing both established and new acts on the Canadian folk scene. The Travellers, Alan Mills, Quebec *chanteur* Jacques Labrecque, and fiddler Jean Carignan were among the established names hired. Younger performers such as Bonnie Dobson, Mary Jane and Winston Young, and the up-and-coming team of Ian Tyson and Sylvia Fricker were hired to draw the college crowd and show that folk had bright new faces to present to the world. Ruth asked Ian and Sylvia early in February, and both had responded enthusiastically.

There were definitely struggles. The Y's Men, a local service club, initially pledged $1,000 in exchange for the right to sell 750 tickets at a reduced price. A similar arrangement with the Jaycees, another service club, failed to materialize. Nevertheless Ruth remained optimistic and enthusiastic, as demonstrated by remarks in her journal: "They liked Finvola's tape — we are trying for LeBreque [*sic*] again! Oh — this thing is BIG!!"[4] Orillia's town council finally discussed and approved the event on May 1, and the Oval was rented for $150. Ruth even approached the army at nearby CFB Borden about a tent for the Oval grounds.

One of the key figures in the organizing and especially in the programming of Mariposa was Edith Fowke, though her contribution is often overlooked. Her input for the fledgling and later Mariposa Folk Festivals would be invaluable. She held strong views that Canadians should be exposed to traditional Canadian songs, and it was thanks to her that a number of traditional singers made their way onto Mariposa stages.

o o o

On August 18 the initial Mariposa Folk Festival was launched on the green space at the Orillia Oval. The festival's souvenir pamphlet described it as "Canada's FIRST National Folk Festival," but the designation of "first" can be debated.

The Miramichi Folksong Festival in Newcastle, New Brunswick, lays claim to being the first "folksong" festival and predates Mariposa by a number of years. Ruth had contacted that festival, but the only advice given was that they relied on grants from the New Brunswick provincial government.

1ˢᵗ **Mariposa Folk Festival/ August 18 & 19, 1961**

Caricature of Mariposa's first performers.

Purists would argue that neither festival can claim to be the *first* since there were a number of folk festivals — many sponsored by Canadian Pacific Railway — staged in places like Vancouver, Banff, Regina, Toronto, and Quebec City during the 1930s.

Whatever the case may be, the Mariposa Folk Festival was certainly one of the first, and its size and influence make it by far the most important folk festival in Canadian history.

From the beginning the festival, though smaller than it would later become, was a success, drawing large crowds. Its first home was at a site in Orillia known as the Oval. This area, home to Orillia's community centre and arena, was tucked between the imposing limestone Roman Catholic church, the local armoury, and modest, middle-class homes along the side streets. It served as the location for local trade shows and the annual Orillia Fall Fair, and it included a somewhat rickety set of bleachers for the local baseball teams and their fans (the baseball diamond was transformed into a concert venue for the festival, the stage an elaborate model of a medieval tent — a nod to Casey Jones's fascination with the pageantry of the Middle Ages). The entire property was surrounded by a secure high fence, likely a factor in selecting the venue when "nicer" but less secure parks in town could have served the same purpose.

Many years later Ruth Jones said,

> The first Mariposa Folk Festival was, understandably, one of the highlights of my life — a dream come true. The transformation of the ugly arena grounds in Orillia into a scene of enchantment — the central stage in the form of a Medieval tent, striped in buff and bright orange, flanked on each side with a small tent flying pennants. One expected knights to emerge for a jousting competition, rather than long-haired folkies with guitars and banjos. And the audience! Thousands of people from all over the country had swarmed to Mariposa for that magical weekend.[5]

A crowd of two thousand showed up for the initial Friday night concert at 8:30 p.m. Local radio station CFOR broadcast the opening "live." Pete McGarvey called upon Mayor George McLean, who was accompanied to the stage by a bagpipe fanfare. McLean welcomed the audience, extolled the virtues of Orillia, and called the festival a "focal point for all Canadian ears." The Joneses were called to the stage, and Ruth cut the ribbon to open the festival. The audience sat in their lawn chairs or on blankets and listened respectfully and intently to the evening performances. Hundreds of people then took part in a midnight jamboree that saw part of Mississaga Street, the main street of town, closed down. Participants danced to the sounds of Arc Records recording stars the York County Boys. On Saturday morning the festival offered films about folk music that had been selected from the National Film Board of Canada and the United States Library of Congress. A free children's concert was staged for those under fourteen. The afternoon program was dedicated to traditional Canadian musicians, selected by Edith Fowke. Rain kept the audience disappointingly small. An hour-long symposium on Canadian folk music was held, showing that from the start the organizers had lofty ideals and a plan to promote the intellectual side of folk music at the festival. It rained on Saturday, but that night's concert saw nearly twice as many people come through the Oval gates as the night before. An estimated four thousand people jammed the hockey arena, setting up their lawn chairs and blankets on the hard cement floor. They were treated to the likes of Ian and Sylvia, Bonnie Dobson, Alan Mills, and the Travellers.

The town, with a touch of caution, accepted the new enterprise. In those post-beatnik but pre-hippie early 60s, the relatively clean-cut crowd that came north from the big city was a new breed to the locals, according to Pete McGarvey. "Yes, they drank a little bit of beer. Some of them went down to the park and serenaded [the statue of] Samuel Champlain. But there was a very happy relationship between the townspeople and the concertgoers. By and large, they were a well-controlled group, there for entertainment and for enlightenment."[6]

The town, the visitors, and even the musicians saw the potential of the event. Jerry Goodis, one of the Travellers, was quoted in the local *Packet and Times* newspaper: "This could be another Stratford." He was obviously alluding to the success that the annual Shakespearean festival had become in Stratford, Ontario, where thousands upon thousands of visitors came each year from all across Canada and the northeastern United States. Could that happen in Orillia? Could Ruth Jones's brainchild parallel that of Tom Patterson's successful dream for his town? Jean Carignan was just as effusive. He told the *Packet and Times*, "The Mariposa Folk Festival is the greatest thing in folk music I have ever seen in Canada." Rich praise indeed.

o o o

The finances of the festival were a huge concern even before the event transpired. The admission prices were simply not sufficient to cover all the costs. At $2 for each concert and $5 for three, the organizers came up short. In the days before government grants were plentiful and generous, this shortage was a major problem. The performers were not paid extravagantly, yet money still ended up being owed for advertising, equipment rental, and legal fees. Dr. Jones had footed many of the bills using his family's personal savings and even going so far as to take out a mortgage on his lakeside home. He never recouped those expenditures. As Ruth and Casey looked back on the festival that fall and winter, they must have wondered what they'd gotten themselves into.

Street dance on Orillia's main street, 1961.

Many discussions that autumn and winter revolved around the financial state of the festival. If the Mariposa Folk Festival was to see another season, it needed two things: "up-front" money and better promotion. A saviour of sorts presented himself in the form of Jack Wall, a Toronto businessman who ran the Fifth Peg Coffee House in Toronto, among other things. Wall was a showman of the "Honest Ed" Mirvish variety. Known for his flair and daring business ventures, Wall planned to promote the festival as a "place to be."[7]

In February of 1962, Wall approached Ruth Jones with an outrageous plan. If the board of directors for Mariposa would sign over the rights to the festival to him, he would look after the bills that were outstanding, and he'd manage the upcoming festival. "We had nothing," stated Pete McGarvey. "We had run out of money. If there was going to be a festival, it would have to be done by someone of Wall's nature. Nobody else appeared." Wall bought the rights to the festival for $2! Ruth and her original cohorts maintained the artistic direction of the festival lineup. One other promise that the board of directors managed to get from Wall was an agreement that if there was a profit from the 1962 festival, then part of that money would go to a foundation to assist in research.

o o o

The second Mariposa Folk Festival began on August 10, 1962. Once again the Orillia Lions Oval was the site, and a crowd of over seven thousand people, many of them young university students, showed up to see what was virtually the same lineup as the year before, with a few notable additions. Ed McCurdy, who'd written the famous anti-war anthem "Last Night I Had the Strangest Dream," was what we'd now call a headliner. Winnipeg-born folk singer and radio/TV host Oscar Brand also brought his many talents to the festival. Most special of all, though, was the inclusion of the Tu-Tones in the lineup for the Sunday night concert.[8] The young duo comprised Terry Whelan and Gordon Lightfoot, two hometown boys who were considered "too commercial" to play at the inaugural festival. Lightfoot recalled what he and Terry were told: "We sounded too much like the Everly Brothers, which we actually took as a compliment. We were quite good — good harmonies and all that. We'd been to New York and had recorded some stuff. But we got to play the second year."

Lightfoot also pointed out that Mariposa was pivotal in his career, in that it connected him to management. Albert Grossman — manager for Ian and Sylvia; Dylan; and Peter, Paul and Mary — came to Mariposa that year with John Court, and the two were scouting for talent. Out of that appearance, Gordon (as a solo) ended up as part of Grossman's stable of artists. Some of his songs, most notably "For Lovin' Me" and "Early Morning Rain," ended up on Peter, Paul and Mary records. In that, Gordon feels Mariposa played a part.

o o o

There was considerable debate among the organizers and the public about whether or not the festival should be all Canadian and whether the emphasis should be on the traditional aspects of folk music. Ed Cowan, the publicity director of the show, commented that the festival performers had been criti-cized for ignoring "thousands" of purely Canadian songs and not being active in collecting those distinctive tunes. Denny Doherty, who would later be a member of the hugely successful The Mamas & The Papas, claimed that he and his group, the Halifax Three, were turned away from Mariposa because they played bars and were "way too successful" for the traditionalists in the crowd.[9]

Perhaps it was a sign of simpler times, but Ian and Sylvia not only per-formed on the festival stages Friday and Saturday nights, but also went to St. Paul's United Church on Sunday morning and played for the congregation.

In 1962 a remarkable innovation would alter or at least determine the course of most folk festivals across Canada and in parts of the United States. Estelle Klein, a soft-spoken but iron-willed woman with a wealth of knowledge about folk music and its evolution, had become part of the organizing group for Mariposa. It was her idea not only to present concerts but also to conduct what she called workshops. Her concept was deceptively simple. Blend groups or individuals in stage sessions where they talked, sang, or played music based around a common theme. When someone played a song, others were encouraged to join in either instrumentally or vocally. Over the years most Canadian folk festivals adopted the Estelle Klein–Mariposa model, a format maintained to this day. Mitch Podolak maintained that he learned everything he needed to know to start festivals from Estelle — significant praise coming from the founder of the Winnipeg and Vancouver folk festivals. Podolak was also instrumental in helping establish the Ottawa Folk Festival and the Stan Rogers Festival in Canso, Nova Scotia. Winnipeg, Ottawa, Vancouver, and the other leading festivals still assign their performers to workshops.

Another noteworthy innovation that year was to include "spoken word" as part of the festival repertoire. Veteran Canadian actor John Drainie was included in the lineup. Drainie had been a star on radio for years, best known for his portrayals of Stephen Leacock and his readings from the auth-or's work. So it seemed a natural fit to bring the Leacock impersonator to an Orillia/Mariposa stage and have him read from *Sunshine Sketches of a Little Town*. Pete McGarvey's past involvement in saving the Leacock home must have played a part in this decision. Promotional pamphlets for the festival in 1961 and in 1962 featured a write-up on the back touting the Leacock home as a tourist attraction, and 1962 was the fiftieth anniversary of the publication of *Sunshine Sketches*.

As part of their effort to increase revenue the board of directors (and Jack Wall, presumably) offered different packages for ticket-buyers. The price of admission for a single concert, for example, rose from $2 to $2.25. This was for advance buyers. The at-the-door price was $2.75. Discounts were given for group rates in an attempt to get some up-front money. With a substantial bump in the audience numbers, it was assumed that things would be in good shape financially.

All in all, the second Mariposa Folk Festival was determined by most of those involved to be a great artistic success. There were a few inflammatory articles in the local paper about the festival becoming an annual "beer-bottle throwing event at Champlain's statue," but most of those sorts of comments were thought to be coming from the curmudgeons who resented anyone having a bit of fun.

History repeated itself. By mid-winter of 1962 the money issues were causing some consternation with the organizers. Jack Wall had a questionable reputation for his business dealings. For example, he'd started a magazine called *Success* that had lasted only one issue. Now it seemed that not all of Wall's promises and assurances regarding Mariposa were being met. An immediate accounting of festival profits had been requested of Wall, but by Christmas that year he'd not produced a detailed report. Apparently he had not defrayed all the outstanding accounts from the festival's two years, yet he assured the board of directors that the money was forthcoming. By May 1963 he was still stalling, but the board had neither the legal nor financial wherewithal to do anything about it. They pushed on with no alternative but to put their trust in the Toronto entrepreneur.[10]

Little did anyone in Orillia or in Toronto know what was in store come the 1963 festival.

CHAPTER TWO

Year Three … Chaos!

THE FESTIVAL'S THIRD YEAR STARTED OFF promisingly enough. In the lead-up to the festival, it seemed Jack Wall had accomplished two things. Firstly, though he had chosen to keep details rather secret and hard to trace, he'd kept the festival afloat financially. Secondly, he'd managed to promote the festival as the "place to be," just as he'd proposed to do. As it turned out, he'd be more successful than almost anyone could have dreamed.

Wall may get a lot of the credit for the successful draw that the festival had become by 1963, but a number of other factors should be considered.

The two previous Mariposas had been artistically successful, showcasing some of the finest talent the art form had to display. Ian & Sylvia were about to become folk superstars (and I think we can use that word with folk in the early 60s) with their hit song "Four Strong Winds." Ed McCurdy and Oscar Brand were big names across North American folk circles, and the Travellers, with their version of "This Land Is Your Land," were practically household names in Canada. Bonnie Dobson was one of the country's singing sweethearts as well.

The 60s folk revival was at its zenith. South of the border Joan Baez and Bob Dylan were the queen and king of the folk idiom. Peter, Paul and Mary's version of "Blowin' in the Wind," Dylan's anthem for the civil rights movement, was nearing the top of the charts that summer. Other chart-topping folk songs (or at least songs presented in the style of folk music) included "Walk Right In" by the Rooftop Singers, "Puff the Magic Dragon" by Peter, Paul

The Travellers.

and Mary, "Tie Me Kangaroo Down, Sport" by Rolf Harris, and "If I Had a Hammer," Trini Lopez's version of Pete Seeger's great protest song.

There was also the fact that folk — and therefore Mariposa — was practically the only game in town. With only the Newport Folk Festival and the neophyte Philadelphia Folk Festival as rivals, Mariposa had the festival

Ian and Sylvia.

scene all to itself in Canada. Yes, there were folk clubs in most large cities, but an outdoor summer festival was not a common event in 1963. And the audiences were expected to be calm, peaceful, and musically astute. It was the days before the rock spectacles and overhyped tours that would take over the music entertainment industry a decade down the line. In the calm before the Beatles storm and the British Invasion, college audiences in particular were generally well-mannered and courteous listeners who came to concerts with the same kind of earnestness that jazz aficionados brought to a Dave Brubeck or Oscar Peterson performance.

Folk was weaving itself into other parts of the cultural fabric in 1963. In the United States, the ABC television network debuted *Hootenanny* nation-wide in April. The Limeliters, Bob Gibson, and Canada's (and Mariposa's)

Bonnie Dobson were among the first to appear on the show. The program's simple premise was to tape folk performers in concert at various college campuses throughout the U.S. In Canada, Oscar Brand's *Let's Sing Out* followed the same format and featured such guest stars as Eric Andersen, Phil Ochs, and Tom Rush. Both shows had loyal followers. Many of those young people in the television audience were also going to be the audience for summer folk festivals — namely Newport, Philly, and Mariposa.

Perhaps most important, at least to those of college age, was the association of folk music with the civil rights movement, particularly in the United States. When Martin Luther King made his famous "I Have a Dream" speech that August, he was not surrounded by rock stars. The crowd that lined the Washington Mall sang along to tunes by Mahalia Jackson, Odetta, Joan Baez, Bob Dylan, and Peter, Paul and Mary — folk music "stars." The songs that spoke to the issues of discrimination and racial equality were "We Shall Overcome," "If I Had a Hammer," "Only a Pawn in Their Game," and "Oh Freedom." All folk songs. The intellectual side of the folk boom was a draw at festivals, particularly Mariposa with its symposia and workshops. In analyses of twentieth-century music, folk music gets far less credit than it deserves as a medium of social change and as an intelligent, thoughtful expression of political, cultural, and social ideas.

As August of 1963 rolled around and Mariposa prepared to open its gates a third time, the buzz about the Southern Ontario festival was at an all-time high. Word of mouth, based on the previous two festivals, had spread.

Under Jack Wall's leadership, the publicity in Toronto had been highly successful in selling Mariposa as "the place to be." Ed Cowan, who had produced the first year's festival (and who went on to publish *Saturday Night* magazine), was the Toronto-based advertising and publicity director. Ken Danby, the high-realism artist famous in the 70s for his "At the Crease" painting, was the art director. Syd Banks, the producer of *Let's Sing Out,* was the artistic director while Estelle Klein looked after the symposium side of things. The lighting man for the '63 festival was none other than Chip Monck, who would go on to be the emcee at Woodstock six years later. If nothing else, Wall knew how to manage the extremely capable people who made up the Mariposa team.

The pre-festival promotion advertised the dynamic lineup that Syd Banks had assembled. Jean Carignan, Alan Mills, Malka and Joso, Jacques Labrecque, Bonnie Dobson, Ian and Sylvia (billed as "Canadian Stars in the U.S.A."), the

Travellers, Sharon Trostin (of later Sharon, Lois & Bram fame), Judith Orban, the Town Criers, Al Cromwell, and several others were authentic folk artists, known to fans of that sort of music. Most of these performers, including Ian and Sylvia, sang traditional ballads and songs that had been passed down over the years. A few original compositions were going to be heard that weekend. Ian had written, and the duo had recorded, "Four Strong Winds" although it was yet to hit the pop music charts. Alan Mills's original song "I Know an Old Lady Who Swallowed a Fly" was so traditional in style that most people did not realize it was his original composition. Bonnie Dobson had already premiered her signature song "(Walk Me Out in the) Morning Dew" two years earlier, and she had other originals in her repertoire to share with the 1963 Mariposa audience. The names — and the songs — were recognized by those who followed folk music and were a "draw" for the festival.

The merchants of Orillia were ready to welcome visitors of all ages and interests. Ads placed in the festival program far ahead of the event included many best wishes, "Mariposa specials," welcomes, and congratulations. Their outlook was generally sunny and positive. The same could be said of the majority of city officials and townspeople. Well, sort of ...

Orillia sits where small and narrow Lake Couchiching meets larger Lake Simcoe. Couchiching stretches about twenty kilometres north and empties into the Severn River at two tiny hamlets called Washago and Severn Bridge. The Silver Sleeve Campground at Severn Bridge was a relatively new spot at the time, and it advertised itself as "Canada's first rent-a-tent holiday camp." The place bragged about camping facilities, nature trails, playgrounds, and an outdoor tea garden. Its Mariposa program ad mentioned live entertainment and "the exclusive location of the jamboree and the all-night mammoth hootenanny, which will follow the Friday and Saturday night's Mariposa Folk Festival performances." Whether it was the Silver Sleeve's ad or word of mouth, young people poured into the campground, and it seemed, according to eyewitnesses, that many of them were there for the party atmosphere and not the folk festival itself.

All hotels and motels in town were jam-packed, and a call went out to local residents asking them to open their homes to the young festivalgoers. Many residents did just that.

Eight thousand advance tickets had been sold, but the town was quite unprepared for the hordes that descended. The downtown streets of Orillia overflowed with people, and even while the Friday evening concert was being held at the Oval, the main thoroughfares were completely jammed with cars. Chief McIntyre had all fifteen of his officers on duty, and they were reinforced by ten police officers from the local Ontario Provincial Police and RCMP detachments. Restaurants, showing a woeful lack of planning, ran out of food early Friday night. At first the only serious problems the police had to deal with were the traffic jams. A few inebriated folkies didn't seem like too big a deal considering how small a percentage of the visitors they represented. As it turned out, Friday night's inconveniences turned out to be just a taste of what was to come.

The organizers, led by Jack Wall, had enthusiastically promoted the event. Wall, who envisioned someday being able to buy a permanent site for the festival, pictured crowds of fifteen thousand people coming for the Mariposa experience. Based on the crowds that were flowing into Orillia for the third festival, it looked like it was well on its way — despite the poor weather.

Asked why the opening night crowd was so good in spite of the rain, Wall attributed it to two things: "The event was gaining national recognition, and also Orillians were accepting it and getting behind the venture" (as quoted in the *Orillia Packet and Times*, August 10, 1963).

Television crews from CBC and the American network NBC arrived in Orillia to chronicle the event, showing an eye for an exciting story and possible calamity. CHUM, Toronto's AM radio of choice for young people, sent a reporter as well. It was the largest contingent of media to descend upon the town since 1959 when the Queen had passed through during her Royal Tour.

The actual Friday night gathering was mostly uneventful. The concert grounds were packed by 7:30 despite the intermittent rainfall. And still the young people kept arriving. An estimated 5,500 people attended Friday night's concert, surpassing all expectations. Even more would have been there, but the highway north from Toronto was jammed. During the performances by Ian and Sylvia, and Alan Mills, the crowd sang along and cheered enthusiastically. The concerts ended close to midnight, at which point much of the crowd filed out of the Oval grounds to take cars or buses to the Silver Sleeve. A late-night square dance and jam was planned. The police patrolled the town's expansive Couchiching Beach Park, where one officer commented to the *Packet and Times* that it was "as quiet as a manse."

o   o   o

Saturday, although it started well, turned into a disaster.

A children's concert in the morning featuring Jerry Gray, Sharon Trostin, and Michel Choquette was well received. An afternoon workshop/lecture by Edith Fowke, entitled "How Folk Songs Wander and Change," was a highlight for those with an intellectual bent. Mayor Isabel Post, the local Kiltie Band, and a number of convertibles and motorcycles led a parade from the Oval to Couchiching Beach Park. The hootenanny held at the waterfront Aquatheatre was calm and orderly.

According to press estimates, well over twenty thousand outsiders had arrived in Orillia by Saturday afternoon. One group, the Black Lancers motorcycle gang, represented the unsavoury element that came for the party atmosphere and not for the music. The bikers parked their choppers along the main street but did little more than look threatening. They were under surveillance by a nervous police contingent anyway. The town had never seen such crowds on its streets and sidewalks. Couchiching Beach Park was overtaken by throngs of young people.

An estimated eleven thousand people crowded into the Oval green space for the concerts that evening. There were so many gatecrashers that men with baseball bats lined the fence at the Oval to keep out intruders. The field in front of the stage was extremely crowded. Spokesman Pete McGarvey told the audience at half time, "If you leave, you will not be allowed back in." Hundreds did leave, though, and they tried to get back in by climbing the high wire fence that surrounded the property. St. John's Ambulance reported that one girl fell and not only cut herself on a broken bottle but also broke her arm.

The crowd settled down to listen to the concerts, but the festival and the music had become secondary to the mass of restless young people. Those unlucky enough to find themselves at the back of the audience could not hear because of inadequate electrical speakers. So they started their own singalong at the back, something that irritated those within hearing distance. Tempers began to flare.

Meanwhile, a lot of things were happening a few blocks away on the main street of town. While the majority of the actual festival audience enjoyed themselves at the Oval — except for those at the back! — those who'd come strictly for the party atmosphere were wreaking havoc downtown.

At the end of the Saturday concert, "the concertgoers were asked to stay in place until calm had been restored downtown. Performers still on the grounds were hustled back to the stage and the music went on. As luck would have it, the Frats, Jamaica's leading folk song ensemble, arrived in town. They saved the night," said Pete McGarvey, who was one of the hosts that evening.[1]

Still, the show had to end sometime and there were few takers for the two singalongs that were planned at the Oval — one outside and one inside the arena. Instead, the crowds poured out of the Oval and down the hill toward the main street and the downtown area. The festival audience blended in with thousands, it seemed, who had come just to party.

Mississaga Street, Orillia's main business thoroughfare, became plugged with the young people who gathered there. In the words of the *Orillia Packet and Times*, "it bore the brunt of Saturday's rowdyism." The public drunkenness soon got out of hand and there were reports of fist fights breaking out in several places. One unsubstantiated story claimed that one young man broke a beer bottle and rammed the jagged edges into another man's face. Store entrances and doorways became public urinals. A group of kids began tap dancing on the roof of someone's car, and when the owner confronted the group, they threatened to overturn the car (and maybe the owner?). Passing vandals damaged a significant number of cars on the main drag and on neighbouring side streets. There were stories of autos being ransacked. Broken beer and wine bottles were thrown onto West Street and Matchedash Street, making driving on those side streets hazardous for cars.

Mississaga Street slopes fairly steeply toward the lake and there were some generous souls who set beer bottles rolling down the street to those waiting at the bottom, although the story seems fabricated if the street was as congested with cars and pedestrians as has been cited.

The police were woefully out-manned and outmanoeuvred. Chief MacIntyre told the *Packet* that a thousand cops could not have coped with the antics that went on. "Teenagers swarmed around a police officer as he tried to arrest a youth, and the youth escaped into the crowd. One officer checked a man in a sleeping bag on the street and came face to face with a gun."[2] The officer bravely confiscated the weapon, and its owner was arrested. A short time later, ten of the man's friends appeared at the police station to bail him out. When asked for the bail money, they went into a huddle, searched all their pockets and emerged with the grand total of sixty-nine cents!

The wild scene spread into Couchiching Beach Park, where scores of drunken youths climbed all over the world-famous statue of

Folkies serenading Champlain's statue in Orillia.

seventeenth-century explorer Samuel de Champlain, bathing it and themselves, no doubt, in beer. The oversized bronze statue became a target for beer
bottles. One intrepid partier climbed to the top of the more than ten-metre
monument and not only poured beer over the figure but also proceeded to
rub it down with alcohol.

Homeowners reported that their lawns were turned into toilets by party-
goers making their way from the downtown core to the city's biggest park. To
the north of the park, a narrow strip of bush separated the CNR from the CPR
railway tracks. That area was strewn with empty beer bottles, cases, and other
party detritus. Some enterprising individual in a red truck was allegedly selling
beer from the back of his vehicle for the astronomical price of $1 per pint.[3]

A throng of people, estimated in the hundreds, detained a police car before eventually letting it proceed. Three Air Force personnel from CFB Borden (a large military installation about forty minutes from Orillia) were apprehended and charged with theft. A barber pole was stolen from Tiffin's Barber Shop and ended up on the roof of a home a few kilometres away in the south ward of town. A bus that had been chartered by students from the University of Toronto was ransacked. Cameras and other personal items were either stolen or broken, and clothing was scattered along a wide swath near the park.

Some of the stories have an almost Keystone Kops flavour to them. Supposedly the police were nabbing people and placing them in the backs of squad cars, only to have the youths exit through the opposite rear doors. The tiny jail facilities in the Sir Samuel Steele Building — now the Orillia Museum of Art and History — could only hold a handful of offenders at a time, so the turnover was continuous in the basement cells, a constant revolving door. As new charges were laid, miscreants spent a few minutes in jail and then had to be released so that the next group of culprits could share the tiny cells.

Not one of the offenders nabbed by police was from Orillia.

The parking situation in the north end of town near both the Oval and Couchiching Beach Park was a shambles. Some streets were so crowded and jammed with cars that there was worry that a fire truck could not make it safely along the streets, if there were such a need.

Tales of sexual debauchery in the park and surrounding environs may be apocryphal but carry on to this day in the minds of townspeople who are old enough to have been at the scene or at least in town. Exaggerated stories were reported via newspaper teletype machines and allegedly spread from coast to coast.

Sunday morning in the town was a sorry spectacle. Couchiching Beach Park's many acres were strewn with garbage. There were bodies all over the place — some in sleeping bags, some simply in the clothes they'd been wearing when they fell asleep a few short hours before. Long lineups formed at the limited washrooms in the park, and some brave souls took early morning baths in the chilly water of Lake Couchiching.

At the Silver Sleeve, someone had allegedly made off with all the money in the camp's cash register, although the Sleeve's manager made no mention of it to the press on Monday morning. One entrepreneur, far ahead of his time, sold bottles of water at ten cents a quart. A photographer, trying to capture some debauchery, had been roughed up. Countless thefts of sleeping bags, radios, and suitcases were reported. Police claimed that teens as young as thirteen or fourteen had been drunk and disorderly. "I never saw anything more deplorable from the point of view of sanitation, morals, violation of the liquor [laws], and impossible traffic situations," said OPP Sgt. Ken Chalmers (as quoted in the *Orillia Packet and Times*, August 12, 1963). He felt that most of the festival-goers were upstanding but that a rowdy element had caused all the trouble. Chalmers went on, "There was a complete and wanton disregard for private property." Ruth Jones had advised that camping passes for that weekend only be sold to festival ticket holders, but apparently no one had heeded her warning.

o o o

This was not the first time that a festival had been the scene of riotous behaviour. The riot at the Newport Jazz Festival in 1960 had many parallels to what happened in Orillia in 1963. Over the July 1, 1960, weekend, teens and college-age students had arrived in Newport to find not enough places to stay, not enough food available, and stupendous amounts of beer — not to mention outrageous prices for all of those items. Add to that a small, overwhelmed police force and festival organizers who didn't know how to handle unexpected crowds. It was a recipe for disaster at Newport just as it was in 1963 at Mariposa. Newport city officials called in state police and the National Guard. Fire hoses and tear gas were used to disperse the unruly elements, even as Ray Charles and Louis Armstrong tried to perform inside the festival boundaries. It appears that Wall and his associates had not given much thought to a contingency plan for disorderly behaviour at the Mariposa Folk Festival.[4] Whether it was lack of awareness of the Newport situation or simple hubris, the MFF organizers had not learned from their Rhode Island counterpart.

In many ways the events of August 1963 in Orillia were a precursor — though less dramatic or traumatic — for what was to come later in the 60s. The political upheaval, anti-war protests, and general turmoil that coloured so much of the radical side of the 60s had yet to show itself much by 1963. It was still a time of respect for police and authority figures. Mariposa's troubles in its third year were all very minor compared to what was to come and bore little resemblance to the far more serious happenings at Woodstock and Altamont a few years down the road. Yet it may have signalled a loss of innocence for those who lived through the experience of having their small town overrun by youthful enthusiasm and overindulgence.

The political fallout from the weekend was immediate and decisive. In a general condemnation of the festival, its organizers, and the behaviour that had transpired, town officials effectively banned Mariposa from Orillia. The animosity of the townspeople was so entrenched that thirty-seven years later, when the festival eventually made its way back to the city in 2000, there were still naysayers and skeptics.

A headline over the editorial in the *Orillia Packet and Times* said it all: "Let's Make Sure That's the Last Folk Festival Here." The editor stated an opinion that quickly became the mantra of many, many citizens in town. In high dudgeon, he asserted that Orillia "cannot afford to harbor any event which will jeopardize this regular trade and cause cottagers to seek future accommodation in locations less subject to the inconvenience and disturbance that characterized the Festival weekend" (as quoted in the *Orillia Packet and Times,* August 13, 1963).

To say that the city officials were incensed is putting it mildly.

"We'll bar all future festivals," said Mayor Isabel Post, even though she also commented to the paper that she realized the trouble was caused not by festival patrons but by the riotous individuals who'd come for reasons other than musical entertainment.

Pete McGarvey, who wore two conflicting hats, was emphatic in his opposition to the holding of future festivals in Orillia. As Mariposa's publicity chair, he appreciated the overwhelming artistic success of the festival. On the other hand, as deputy reeve on the town council, he could not see any alternative but to send the event elsewhere.

"Culturally the festival was as successful as anyone could wish. But the public rowdyism and drinking by elements who have no interest in folk music anyway, spoiled it for those who came to enjoy the weekend," said McGarvey in the same article. Pete made the suggestion that Mariposa could perhaps set up at the CNE Bandshell in Toronto's Exhibition Park.

Mayor Post felt that the festival itself had been fine but that the "brawl" — her term — that followed had given Orillia a black eye. She worried about the detrimental publicity that the weekend events had generated. "Unless a tremendous change is going to be made, we cannot support another festival here.... It's not the fault of the festival organizers and police. They did an excellent job. I think the name Mariposa Festival now has a stigma the producers never expected it would have," Post explained to the *Packet and Times*.

Jack Wall, on the other hand, was quoted as saying the festival was a resounding success. He did hint, however, that the festival might have to change its format in the future. He also acknowledged that while there were commercial benefits to Orillia, far too many people had abused the hospitality and goodwill of the town. In typical Wall fashion, he kept his cards close to his chest and only admitted to the press that he'd meet with town council to discuss future plans. He was insistent that Mariposa would not move to any other Ontario town.

Mississaga Street grocer Vic Battalia unofficially voiced the concerns of many Orillia downtown business owners in a letter he wrote to the *Packet* a couple of days after the weekend. He reflected on whether or not the financial value of the festival was outweighed by the strain it had put on police services, the lack of respect the cops had faced, the looseness of morals, and the general lack of peace suffered by the community.

In a sidebar that speaks to the zeitgeist of that time and place, Royal F. Moulton, general secretary of the Ontario Temperance Federation (and yes, such an organization still existed at that time), had passed through Orillia on the Mariposa weekend and had seen teens imbibing. He called on the Liquor Control Board of Ontario to investigate the liquor and beer sales in Orillia that weekend and suggested that all outlets in the region should be closed if the festival was to be staged there again.

Within ten days the town council had passed a resolution opposing any renewal of the festival in town.

Adding insult to injury for organizers like Pete McGarvey was the fact that shortly after the noise died down, Jack Wall vanished. As much as $20,000 disappeared as well, but without proof and without books having been kept, no one could publicly accuse the entrepreneur of absconding with the funds. Whatever the case, many accounts went unpaid and the festival ran up a debt of approximately $9,000 despite myriad ticket sales.

Ruth Jones was upset by the fiasco that her beloved festival had become. In a 2013 interview at the festival, Ruth explained, "A lot of people came up from Toronto for 'party time' and they partied hearty. And they got the town council very upset — and rightly so.... It was not pretty."

o o o

There is an interesting footnote to the whole idea of Orillia banning Mariposa and fearing the invasion of the folk hordes. A little-known — or remembered — event took place in February of 1966, something called the Orillia Folk Festival. It took place in the community centre arena, the same basic location as the first three Mariposa festivals. The lineup looked incredibly like a Mariposa Folk Festival: Phil Ochs, Bonnie Dobson, the Allen-Ward Trio, Oscar Brand, and the Jim Kweskin Jug Band. The poster, with its leafy sunflower motif, looked an awful lot like a cross between Ian Tyson's initial Mariposa logo design and the logo that Murray McLauchlan would devise a short time later. There were Saturday afternoon workshops to go along with the evening concerts. It was all so suspiciously Mariposa-like that it raises questions: What had changed and how was such an event allowed to transpire? There was no hullaballoo over the event, no shunning of the folkies, no fear of riots or bikers, no municipal edicts moved by council to stop the event from taking place. Had things changed that much in three years? Were folk festivals now accepted as tame and safe in the new reality of Beatlemania? Looking back, it seems mysterious that Orillia would embrace another folk festival only three years removed from what the town considered a national embarrassment.

CHAPTER THREE

The Innis Lake Years

IF THE ORGANIZERS OF THE MARIPOSA FOLK FESTIVAL thought that 1964 would bring a change for the better, they were sadly mistaken. The town of Orillia, its peaceful veneer shattered (okay, maybe *shaken* would be a better description) by the events of August '63, no longer held out its arms in welcome.

In fact, two of the original movers and shakers had moved on by this time. Ruth and Casey Jones had parted ways, and Ruth moved to Toronto for a time before heading out to the west coast with two of her four children. Pete McGarvey faced a dilemma. In his role as a town alderman, he had been offended by the behaviour of visitors to his town. Yet he was also a founding board member of the folk festival. In March of 1964 he made his decision and tendered his resignation to the board.

With two of the original organizers gone, things were looking grim; however, a pair of enterprising individuals stepped forward. Randy Ferris, an Orillia native, was working as a DJ on radio station CKFH in Toronto.[1] He had a nightly folk music program from 11 p.m. to midnight. Having heard of Mariposa's supposed imminent demise, Ferris and his talent agent friend, Martin Onrot, approached the festival board in February of 1964 with several proposals. In something akin to a takeover, Ferris was the board president by the end of March, and Onrot was secretary-treasurer. Casey Jones remained as the only original member of the board for 1964, and James Murdoch rounded out the small group of directors. (Soon after, sadly, Casey developed leukemia, the disease to which he eventually succumbed.)

The task ahead looked daunting. There were only a few short months to turn things around, re-establish the festival's reputation, and mount a fourth event in the Orillia area.

"I didn't even particularly want to be the driving force, but for lack of someone else to do it, that was the way it was," said Ferris.[2] His first move was to persuade Estelle Klein to take on the artistic direction. She'd already established herself as a creative force with the festival symposia and workshops. Now Ferris wanted to give her the task of putting together a roster for the 1964 festival.

Klein initially refused. "I was so burned from '63 I said, 'No way!' I got very snotty. I said [to Ferris], 'I don't trust you. I don't trust anybody anymore. How do I know what you're going to do?' But he wore me down. I began to think, 'I really believe he's honest. I really believe he cares.' And so we started out again."[3] Ted McGillivray was listed in the program as artistic director, but it was essentially Estelle's show.

Joe Lewis, an associate at CKFH and manager of the New Gate of Cleve coffee house in Toronto, agreed to help Ferris as well. Lewis was a rabid folk music enthusiast with several long-running radio shows. His *Folk Music and Folkways* weekend broadcasts helped to popularize folkies like Stan Rogers and David Bradstreet in Southern Ontario at least. Lewis would also have a long-running connection to the festival as a fervent supporter of Mariposa.

Martin Onrot attempted to persuade the city fathers — and mothers — of Orillia that Mariposa should be given another chance. He met with representatives from the Chamber of Commerce, town representatives, and "interested parties" but was told in no uncertain terms that turning over the town to unwelcome guests was a non-starter. The *Orillia Packet and Times* condemned Onrot's efforts in a blistering and somewhat melodramatic editorial that implied that the revival of the festival in Orillia was bound to meet with "violent opposition" from many citizens.

If they couldn't set up in Orillia, Ferris and his assistants were determined to set up at least near the town. A 176-acre farm in Medonte Township, a predominantly rural municipality of independent farms and rolling hills to the west of Orillia, was leased and looked to have good potential. With Orillia so close, the town could provide the infrastructure needed to sustain the needs of the festivalgoers, assuming the merchants, grocers, and restauranteurs planned ahead.

The advance publicity didn't even call the event a festival. Instead it was advertised as the "1964 Concert Series *presented by Mariposa Folk Festival, Incorporated*, August 7th, 8th and 9th." Then printed in tiny font, much smaller than anything else on the page, it read "just west of" before going back to big lettering for "Orillia, Ontario, Canada."

Once again, a stellar lineup was ready to go: Buffy Sainte-Marie, Mississippi John Hurt, Gordon Lightfoot, Alan Mills, Sonny Terry and Brownie McGhee, and Jean Carignan. Workshops and symposia were scheduled.

Because of the deeply troubling events of the previous summer, there were jitters everywhere in the Orillia area. Many residents of Medonte Township felt uneasy about the same kinds of things happening there that had happened in Orillia in 1963. The Medonte Township council succeeded in passing a bylaw late in July requiring that Mariposa post a $200,000 bond of liability as well as a $500 rental fee. It also asked for

Gordon Lightfoot, Innis Lake.

$650 to be set aside for cleanup. Ferris and his team were given four days to come up with the money. Even in 1964 that was an outrageous amount, probably in the neighbourhood of $1.5 million in 2017. Mariposa had until July 31 to come up with the money. The festival was scheduled to open a week after that.

Ferris didn't have those sorts of funds. He also didn't have insurance for this kind of unexpected hammer blow. No insurance company would underwrite the festival after the 1963 debacle. His only recourse was to oppose the bylaw in court. He set the legal wheels in motion but, as would be expected, things didn't happen overnight. It wasn't until August 6, *the day before* the festival was to begin, the Supreme Court of Ontario heard the application for restraint. It was Mariposa's only glimmer of hope.

The judge ruled against the Mariposa application.

"The whole court proceeding took slightly less than forty minutes. I remember sitting in the court and listening to the judge's verdict, and I damn near sank through the floor. I had twenty-four hours to relocate a festival," recalled Ferris.[4] Yet he showed determination if nothing else. He went back to his Toronto office, called the other organizers, and told them about the judge's negative decision.

Up at Edward Durtnall's farm the stages were set up, wiring and lighting had been installed, and things were pretty much ready to go, but now the festival couldn't pay the township's bonds, and the court had ruled that Medonte's bylaw was legitimate. There would be no festival anywhere near Orillia in 1964!

Meanwhile, performers had begun to arrive in Toronto. Joe Lewis, with Buffy Sainte-Marie in tow, was besieged at CKFH radio station in midtown Toronto. The festival's tiny office on Bond Street was also a mob scene with ticket holders demanding their money back. Unfortunately, there was none to give. All the advance sales dollars had gone to paying for artists' fees and production costs.

Then someone came up with a solution that was at once brilliant and daring.

At that time Toronto's only professional baseball team was the Toronto Maple Leafs, the AAA International League affiliate of the Cleveland Indians. They were on the road that weekend, and someone at the Mariposa office — Ferris, Lewis, someone else perhaps — came up with the idea of contacting the baseball stadium to see if it could be rented. Maple Leaf Stadium, at the foot of Bathurst Street south of Lakeshore Boulevard in Toronto, was an imposing edifice, built in the style of Yankee Stadium in New York and well-suited for a minor league baseball team. A folk festival, though? Well, they'd see about that. Ballpark management okayed the desperate festival organizers and agreed to terms.

All the equipment needed to be shipped to Toronto from the Medonte farm site and set up at the stadium. More importantly, the Mariposa team had to get word out to the folkies that, yes, the festival was still on but it would now be held in Toronto at a baseball park. A media blitz was attempted but with limited success.

Friday night about five hundred people turned up for the first concerts. The sound was poor, it rained, and the temperature dipped to about twelve degrees Celsius. As the audience huddled under their umbrellas in the ballpark's outfield, acts like Gordon Lightfoot and Reverend Gary Davis gave them what they'd come to hear. In spite of everything Randy Ferris and his team had cobbled together a fourth Mariposa Folk Festival.

Estelle Klein's vision and artistic leadership were clear that year. She was determined to showcase not just Canadian acts but also American blues (Mississippi John Hurt, Sonny Terry and Brownie McGhee) and Native culture (Buffy Sainte-Marie, Isaac Beaulieu, and "Indian [sic] culture in Song, Dance and Handicrafts"). Gordon Lightfoot debuted a recently written number called "Early Morning Rain." An archival audio recording shows Lightfoot in fine form, his voice booming around the nearly empty stadium.

Reverend Gary Davis was a performer who had been "re-discovered" during the folk boom of the early 60s. It's a credit to both Estelle Klein and her unofficial blues advisor, Richard Flohil, that they brought him to Mariposa and revitalized a career that had started in the 1930s. His distinctive guitar style is said to have influenced the likes of Jerry Garcia and Ry Cooder. In a 2010 interview for a Mariposa Festival souvenir magazine, Gordon Lightfoot fondly recalled being placed in an afternoon workshop with Mississippi John Hurt and Reverend Gary Davis.[5]

Owen McBride, who has performed at probably more Mariposa Folk Festivals than any other individual, had a front row seat to see how Estelle Klein took over the programming reins of the event. Owen had been in the country only a matter of days when Estelle discovered him at a hootenanny at Don Cullen's Bohemian Embassy and hired him for the 1964 festival. She was particularly taken with his mastery of old English, Scottish, and Irish folk songs.

"Estelle was a unique person indeed, she had a real love for and under-standing of folk music. From the Inuit throat singers, to the Metis ring dancers, musicians from the Andes. She had this ability to make you feel you were the most important person in the room when she was talking to you. It was she who made my introduction to Canada so easy. Three days — arrived on Friday, sang on Sunday, went to a party on Monday and sang in a major folk festival the next July. I was 22 years old."

McBride went on to play most of the festivals from 1964 until the mid-80s. He also returned in 2010 for the fiftieth anniversary and made a guest appearance at the 2016 festival.

Buffy Sainte-Marie nearly missed the festival. After arriving from the U.S. and finding out that the Medonte council had put a crimp in the fes-tival plans, she'd been ferried around Toronto by Joe Lewis. Somewhere in all the hectic planning and chaos she slipped away and somehow got back to the airport. Joe Lewis scurried to Malton and found Buffy, seated in the departure area ready to leave town at any moment. He explained to her that the festival was still on. She resisted his pleas, stating that she had booked a flight to Saskatchewan to attend a powwow. She was adamant that she wanted to get out of Ontario, but Joe explained how desperate the organiz-ers were to have her stay in Toronto to perform.

Buffy Sainte-Marie.

Pete Seeger.

"Eventually we sat down and explained the desperateness of the situation. She started crying. We were being as pleasant as we could about it but as firm as we could, and eventually she came back to the city with us. She played the festival and got enormous headlines," recalled Lewis.[6]

As it turned out, she was the hit of the festival. At one point, she was called back to do four encores.

While they may have saved the festival from an ignominious collapse in Medonte that could have ended the story then and there, the organizers could not make it a financial success in Toronto given the obstacles they faced. Only about 3,000 people showed up for Saturday's concerts. The festival lost over $5,000 and had to give back about $900 in ticket refunds. This would not be the first or last time that Mariposa was in dire financial straits.

o o o

Year five, 1965, marked a turnaround of sorts for the festival. Although the music scene was changing and there were dark clouds on the horizon, interest in folk music was still strong, and the festival was able to benefit from that. The festival programs at that time shed light on the folk scene of the day, one that was, despite everything, still alive and well beyond the festival confines. Mariposa wasn't the only thing keeping folk music viable. Ads for venues such as the Riverboat and the Mousehole in the Yorkville area of Toronto included such names as Eric Andersen, Tom Rush, Jim Kweskin and the Jug Band, Odetta, Sonny Terry and Brownie McGhee, 3's a Crowd, Adam Mitchell, Michael Clark (of Byrds fame), and Jack Washington (later known to most folk fans as Jackie). Record stores such as Sam the Record Man advertised in the program and touted LPs by Peter, Paul and Mary, Gordon Lightfoot, Burl Ives, and the Kingston Trio.

Ferris recalls those days and wrote out some of his memories in a special segment of the 1985 program. He remembers having numerous telephone conversations with Pete and Toshi Seeger, who urged him to keep up the fight and save the festival. Randy believed that Pete's decision to appear at the 1965 festival sent a signal to other performers, and to the folk world in general, that Mariposa was a viable entity. "It practically guaranteed the festival's new stature and stability."[7]

Attracting such star power was part of the fight festival organizers engaged in as they struggled to maintain the viability of folk and the festival in a time of changing musical tastes. The Beatles had come along the year before, ushering in the British Invasion, and rock and roll songs like "She Loves You" were supplanting folk music on the pop music charts. Musical tastes were definitely changing, and the folk genre was increasingly being shunted aside. There was still plenty of interest in acoustic and traditional music, but the public's focus was really on a whole new wave of rock musicians. Many folk clubs had either closed or become venues to showcase rock and roll acts. Folk records were moved to the back areas of stores. Radio stations rarely featured hour-long blocks of folk music anymore. Even Bob Dylan, the reigning folk icon, was about to go electric at the Newport Folk Festival that year.

Mariposa reached a level of maturity in 1965, despite falling attendance and financial woes. With the successful artistic programming of 1964's festival and with an organizational team who were determined to keep it alive, Mariposa made a key move that helped to ensure its success. Ferris and

Lewis had been keeping their eyes open for a new site to hold the festival. A man named Murray Innis, who owned a campground about sixty kilometres northwest of Toronto in the Caledon Hills, offered his property for the festival. The site was on about a hundred acres of land with a questionable pond that had been dubbed "Innis Lake." Basically a converted cow pasture, the land was at least in a pleasant location and could handle a reasonably large crowd. Ferris signed a contract with the Innis family.

The next step was to secure the approval of the municipality. Ferris met with officials of the Albion Township council and found them surprisingly supportive. He also had many meetings with representatives from the Ontario Provincial Police. Both the council and the OPP wanted assurances that the festival could safely handle a crowd that might number well over ten thousand people.

"We met with the OPP interminably. We were down to the eleventh hour, going ahead on the assumption that, yes, we'd make it! I can remember quite consciously not telling the other people who were working on the project what the odds were against it going through."[8]

A private security firm was hired and Ferris put together a letter that detailed all the arrangements Mariposa planned: the port-a-potty company, St. John's Ambulance, and Tony's Industrial Catering. It even mentions plans to fill in groundhog holes on the property. The festival was slated to start August 6, yet by mid-July, the organization still hadn't heard whether or not they had approval to proceed. Ferris, in desperation, appealed to his MPP, Alan Lawrence, and to Bill Davis, the future premier of Ontario and the MPP for that area at the time, to see if they could grease the bureaucratic wheels. That afternoon — literally within hours of speaking with Davis — Ferris got a phone call from the OPP deputy commissioner wishing the organization all the best for the coming festival. As it turned out, the OPP were jittery about the potential for trouble. At the actual festival, there was a huge police presence with over ninety officers on site at a time.

Ferris recalled, "The okay was given not more than a month before the festival was due to go on. It had been a question of trying to keep myself pumped up and keep the rest of the people pumped up. I was sure the festival would be successful if we could just get the damn thing on without a hassle."[9]

Ferris knew the festival's recent history well and was not overlooking any possible scenarios. He went so far as to contact J. Edgar Hoover and the FBI requesting a copy of the U.S. Justice Department's publication *Prevention and Control of Mobs and Riots*. A response from Hoover himself resides in the Clara Thomas Archives at York University in Toronto.

That August weekend of 1965 was a turning point for Mariposa. The audience was orderly and mature, and the planning set a template for Mariposa and for most future folk festivals in Canada. The poster made it sound like a place that would be fun even without the name-acts on stage: a Mariposa canoe race, hootenannies, camping, swimming, and dancing were all advertised as part of the package. The festival was morphing into the entity we recognize today, with high-quality lineups, intelligent and thoughtful workshops, camping, and a fan base that returned year after year, expecting "more of the same."

The 1965 evening concert audiences were treated to sets by Phil Ochs, John Hammond, Gordon Lightfoot, and Ian and Sylvia. But it was the workshop settings that really set the tone for what folk festivals were to become. In relatively intimate spaces, the musicians explained their playing styles and their songwriting techniques and shared musical details that audiences never got in a concert.

Not only was the new format popular with audiences, but so, too, was the repertoire. Like Woody Guthrie and Pete Seeger, singers from the past who blended folk music with social protest, many of the modern folk singers also crafted sets filled with songs of protest. The war in Vietnam was beginning to take its terrible toll on America, and singers like Phil Ochs were astute enough to pick up on the tragedy early on. Phil's songs "Draft Dodger Rag" and "I Ain't Marching Anymore" delighted the sympathetic Canadian audience at Innis Lake.

The audience was also treated to another perennial Mariposa phenomenon: rain. Ian and Sylvia's opening night concert had to be cancelled due to rain and a power failure. These unfavourable elements would plague Mariposa for years to come.

If Buffy Sainte-Marie was the hit of the 1964 festival, then Joni Anderson (Mitchell) was the surprise hit of the 1965 event. A last minute insertion into the lineup, Joni introduced her classic songs "Circle Game" and "Urge for Going" to the audiences.

"I had first heard Joni at the Gate of Cleve," said Estelle Klein. "We [Mariposa] were doing evening concerts then and we were all filled up, but

Phil Ochs — the show must go on!

it was one of the few times I've ever made an exception. We added her for two nights. She sang those two songs. I can't remember what else she sang, but certainly those songs, and there was very good reaction. She sat in on a songwriters' workshop and she sang, of course, the same songs because she didn't have that many. A few people complained. They said, 'She's really nice but she's singing the same thing everywhere.' So when I invited her back the next year, I said, 'Joni, I really like what you do, but it would be nice if you could expand your repertoire a little bit.'"[10]

The serenity of the crowd — and the ingenuity of the organizing team — can perhaps be best demonstrated at the Saturday night mainstage concert. While Phil Ochs was performing, the power went out. (It had rained off and on all weekend, and Owen McBride recalls a car hitting a power pole.) Undaunted, several cars were arranged so they could shine their lights on the performer, and a stage hand with megaphone in hand stood beside Phil while he sang to the drenched but happy folkies.

Mariposa had found a new home and a calm, respectful audience out in the country. Innis Lake became Mariposa's base for the next three years.

Money remained, as it does to this day, a major issue in all decisions. Simply put, there wasn't a lot of it. Randy Ferris paid off many of the festival debts out of his own pocket. A pattern evolved. Set a small budget for the festival and work on credit until the gate receipts were in. Even the headline performers were paid only tiny amounts for their performances. Pete Seeger was paid a pittance for his appearance during the 1966 festival. Joni Mitchell was paid even less. Owen McBride explained, "In Estelle's day, performers, whether you were Bob Dylan or Owen McBride, were paid $175 per day. Mind you, they would fly you from wherever, [and] house and feed you. But that's what you were paid. So performers came for the exposure and the music. And the exposure was substantial."

The organizers devised one creative way to pay for the performers. Food rights were sold to the root beer and hamburger chain A&W. The local franchise owner in Brampton provided $5,000 on the condition that his outlet be the sole food provider for the festival. According to Joe Lewis, that was the seed money to pay the performers.

o o o

The lineup that year was stellar — at least by folk standards of the day: Carolyn Hester, the New Lost City Ramblers, David Rea, the Staple Singers, Tom Paxton, Bram Morrison, David Wiffen, Enoch Kent, Ian Tyson (solo), Joni Mitchell, Gordon Lightfoot, Doc Watson, and of course, Pete Seeger. And populating the workshops with those incredible names was one of Estelle Klein's strengths. Audiences were able to sit up close and personal for presentations of "Ontario Songs," "Blues and Gospel" (hosted by journalist and future artistic director Dick Flohil), "International Songs," and a workshop of autoharp, harmonica, banjo, fiddle, and mandolin players. Imagine the wizardry on display for the "Guitar Styles" workshop that featured Doc Watson, David Rea, Roebuck "Pops" Staples, and Ray Perdue!

Estelle Klein first introduced an aboriginal component to the festival in 1966. She scheduled an appearance by the Canadian Indian Dancers, with their repertoire of war dances, plus an eagle dance, hoop dance, and fire dance. It also marked the first appearance of folk rock at Mariposa when Kensington Market, with their electric guitars and huge amplifiers, played on the mainstage. (At that time, Dylan, the Byrds and the Lovin' Spoonful were top acts showcasing folk rock on the popular music charts.) It was all part of the evolution of folk music and what could be classified as "folk." Whether or not the purists approved, Mariposa — under Estelle Klein's leadership — was leading the way toward the acceptance of varying and new styles of folk music.

o o o

The comment that the 1965 festival had reached a level of maturity might have fit the event itself but that was not necessarily true of too many young men in the audience, in 1966. Ken Whiteley, a young volunteer at that point, recalls Joni Mitchell coming off the stage in tears. Joni was dressed in a very short mini-skirt and as she played, a cohort of yahoos heckled her performance with cries of "Take it off baby" and other misogynistic shouts. One can only cringe at the memory and hope that we've all come a long way from such behaviour at folk festivals.

o o o

Joni Mitchell, backed by
David Rea, Innis Lake, 1966.

Dick Flohil, later known better by his given name, Richard, was a journalist and blues fanatic who had been introduced to Estelle Klein in 1964. He had a wide-ranging knowledge of blues artists and styles and became her main source of information when she was selecting artists in that genre. Richard's advice eventually evolved into writing publicity and promotional materials. His contributions to the overall history of the festival cannot be underestimated. He would go on to become a board member and even artistic director in the late 80s and early 90s. Through Richard's excellent taste and eye for talent, Mariposa showcased artists such as Mississippi John Hurt, Son House, John Hammond, Howlin' Wolf, a young Bonnie Raitt, Bukka White, Big Walter Horton, Sonny Terry and Brownie McGhee, Reverend Gary Davis, and the incomparable Buddy Guy.

Innis Lake crowd and stage (albeit from the top of a port-a-potty!).

Richard had many tales to tell of his misadventures with some of these artists. At Innis Lake, such a remote location, there was no beer tent and no ready access to booze of any kind unless you'd brought your own and kept it hidden. Pops Staples (of the Staple Singers) was a dignified and soft-spoken man. Backstage, he quietly asked Richard to find him some whiskey. Richard complied, did a booze run to one of the local communities with a liquor store, and came back with the bottle of rye that Pops had requested.

Later that night Reverend Gary Davis staggered drunkenly onto the stage, slurred his words, made passes at girls in the front rows, and was so disorderly he had to be escorted offstage.

"Estelle was livid," said Richard. "Obviously, Pops had given the whiskey to Reverend Gary. But when the Rev returned to the stage on Sunday he was amazing. Actually, he was mortified that he'd fucked up!"

Buddy Guy, who has acknowledged the boost Mariposa gave to his career in the mid-60s, was another consummate professional when he played the festival. Flohil recalled how Buddy, who was known for his onstage antics, jumped onto what he thought was a different part of the stage but was, in fact, no more than a canvas facade. The guitarist, in mid-song, jumped through the cloth and crashed down onto scrap two-by-fours and other detritus. Richard and other shocked viewers rushed to Buddy's side only to find the bluesman still playing as he lay on his back amid the sawdust and dirt. A consummate professional indeed!

The festival was gaining international recognition. The print media noted that cars from as far away as California, Michigan, and Massachusetts were observed in the parking area. Thirteen-year-old banjo player Johnny Lanford came all the way from Oklahoma with his father and was quickly accepted by the performers who saw and heard the young man's prowess on his instrument.

o o o

In May of 1967 Randy Ferris sold the rights and title of Mariposa to his associate Tom Bishop for the grand total of $1,000. Randy felt he'd done as much as he could for the festival, saving it from near-ruin and turning it into a slightly profitable venture. He said, "When I left, I was quite happy and satisfied that the role I had to play in Mariposa was satisfactorily accomplished. It would only go on to be bigger and better, not in the sense of size or in artistic content, but just in the fact that it would continue to exist. Its future was no longer in doubt. Since that's what I had started out to preserve in 1964, I felt that my contribution was largely at an end. It was successful."[11]

Canada's centennial year, 1967, was one of nationwide celebration. Expo 67 was held in Montreal; new distinctive stamps, coinage, and banknotes were issued; the Centennial Train toured the country with cultural artifacts; and myriad local celebrations marked a youthful enthusiasm and national pride that extended across the nation. The strains of Bobby Gimby's "Ca-na-da" could be heard everywhere from sea to sea to sea, sung by a youthful dancing choir following Bobby, their Pied Piper. Television specials celebrated our culture and brief history, and the country seemed full of unbridled hope and optimism. It captured the zeitgeist of the time, at least for Canada.

Likewise, there was hope, optimism, and reasons to feel good if you were party to the Mariposa Folk Festival in 1967.

Tom Bishop, a Toronto businessman, took charge of the festival that year with an eye on making a profit. He'd seen Randy Ferris walk away with a bit of cash in his pocket, and Tom hoped to make the event a money-making venture as well.

By 1967, Mariposa had developed a "brand" and a reputation to go with it. Perhaps the predominant reason for that was the vision and imagination of the festival's artistic director. Estelle Klein had a keen eye for talent, and every year she hired many people who would go on to be big names in the entertainment industry. In addition to Joni Anderson, performers such as Leonard Cohen, Richie Havens, and Bruce Cockburn appeared at Mariposa long before they were well known to the general public. (They would have become well known anyway, but Mariposa was among their first big gigs.)

The artistic director also had a policy, which she would carry with her into the 70s, of treating her artists as if everyone were equal. Big star or newcomer, Estelle treated them the same and paid them the same — rather parsimoniously! No one ever played Mariposa to get rich in those days.

Estelle also continued to try and include all the various sub-genres of folk music in each festival. Blues, Aboriginal dance, gospel, bluegrass, singer-songwriter, Québécois, traditional balladry — all types of folk music were showcased. Newspaper critics were somewhat dismissive of this mind-set, and even some performers were a bit put off by the intellectual side of the festival. American songwriter Tom Rush said of the 1967 festival: "It's been too academic. It's really not a very festive festival."[12] Nevertheless, Estelle persevered with her pursuit of the intellectual side of folk music. And Tom Rush never played the festival again.

Around this same time, Estelle Klein began to develop a sense of what worked and what didn't work for audiences, based on some of her experiences visiting the Newport Folk Festival in Rhode Island. It was her idea to have "name" acts appear several times over the weekend and also to have several stages going at once, giving the audience choice and variety.

Beyond the festival gates, the mood of the times had changed somewhat. While south of the border, students were protesting the military draft and the ever-expanding war in Vietnam or dealing with race riots in the large cities, in Canada — and particularly at Mariposa — things were reasonably mellow and laid-back. The baby boomers were attending events like Mariposa, but rather than raising hell, they tended to sit back and enjoy. And in 1967 the organizers

Leonard Cohen, 1967, at Innis Lake.

gave them a great show. Leonard Cohen, Buffy Sainte-Marie, Tom Rush, 3's a Crowd, and Bonnie Dobson were among the artists presented.

The Buddy Guy Blues Band played Mariposa that year and Buddy seemed to have a very good time. In his autobiography, *When I Left Home*, he recalled, "Toronto was wild. I was wild … I jumped off the stage and had the fans carry me around like I had been elected president of the United States. I even climbed up the light tower where the operator had the spotlight and played from up there…. The fans screamed like I was the pied piper leading them to glory."[13] Buddy has been effusive in interviews about how Mariposa helped his career.

That proved to be the final year for Mariposa at Innis Lake. Bishop had a strong team to carry on, and they had tried some innovative things to bring notice to the festival, such as an outdoor preview concert at Toronto City Hall. The *Toronto Telegram* labelled the gathering "Hippies at City Hall." But cool temperatures and low attendance for the August 11–13 event in Caledon left the festival with a $3,500 deficit. In addition, the lease with the Innis family had expired. For a variety of reasons, it was time for Mariposa to move on.

CHAPTER FOUR

Toronto Island Years, 1967–1971

TOM BISHOP WAS INTERESTED IN making Mariposa a profitable venture, one that would make him and possibly others some money. The limitations of Innis Lake, north of Brampton, hindered that goal. It was arguably too isolated and too far from the city. There was inadequate infrastructure at Innis Lake and certainly no transportation network to get people there. Costs of moving equipment and personnel to the site were factors in the decision to pull up stakes. The lease had expired, giving Bishop an excuse to look elsewhere.

Tom and his team wanted to put the festival in Toronto, where there was obviously a huge potential audience. The baby boomers were coming of age and were eager to take in all forms of entertainment. Above all, they had money to spend and were more liable to spend it within Metropolitan Toronto than out in the sticks of Peel County. Bishop wanted to find a suitable venue in the city. While there were a lot of parks that could have served as a new home, one area almost cried out to be used for an outdoor summer festival. So Bishop, along with Estelle Klein, negotiated a deal with Toronto Parks Commissioner Tommy Thompson. Olympic Island, a short ferry ride across the waters of Toronto Harbour, was leased for the August 9–11 weekend in 1968. It was a beautiful setting: truly a peaceful, pastoral locale, the skyline of Toronto in the distance to the north and the vast waters of Lake Ontario to the south. Well-treed and immaculately groomed, the island offered idyllic conditions.

Bishop was quoted in *Billboard Magazine*, "We couldn't possibly think of a better site for both daytime activities and evening concerts, and it now appears we have discovered a permanent home for the Festival in future years" (April 12, 1969).

Planning a festival on the island presented some challenges. The ferry service to the island would have to handle thousands of ticket holders. Thompson assured the organizers that it would be capable — and it was. Performers and equipment had to be shuttled to the island using water taxis and barges — and they were. This added some cost to the bottom line, but by setting up so close to downtown Toronto, there was some assurance that bigger audience numbers could be expected. No longer would attending Mariposa require a trip to Caledon and the logistics such a trek might involve. Now the festival could be reached by Toronto transit and a pleasant ferry ride.

The 1968 festival expanded in scope. It became a full three-day event with daytime and nighttime activity. It was the first year that a crafts area, including wood carvers and potters, was set up. Klein reached farther afield for talent and brought in what are now called "world music" acts. For example, a dance troupe from India performed.

One of the key people Estelle brought into the fold was Michael Cooney, a versatile American performer whom she relied upon to advise about American acts. Thanks to Michael, performers such as James Taylor, John Prine, Leon Redbone, and Steve Goodman were hired by Mariposa as they first started out in their storied careers. Michael would play a long-term role in the Mariposa artistic selections. "I do remember that she was quite reluctant to hire Leon Redbone, but I talked her into it," Michael explained.

More than fifty musical acts were hired, but the media had some pre-festival criticism of the lineup. Where were the big names? Howlin' Wolf, Bukka White, Bill Monroe, and Gilles Vigneault were known to hard-core blues aficionados and knowledgeable folkies but were hardly what one would call big draws. Nevertheless, enough people came to keep the festival in the financial black. Over five thousand attended the opening night concerts, and an estimated fifteen thousand took in the weekend's activities.

One noteworthy change to Mariposa's corporate look — if we can call it that —was the change of its logo. Back in 1961 Ian Tyson had drawn on his training in the advertising field to design the first Mariposa Folk Festival logo featuring a stylized sun with rays emanating from behind it.

In 1968 Murray McLauchlan, an up-and-coming performer at the time and a Mariposa volunteer, used the skills he'd learned in the Special Arts program at Toronto's Central Tech high school to rejig the design into the smiling-faced sun that has been the iconic Mariposa symbol ever since. Not one but two of Canada's greatest songwriters applied their artistic skills both musically and with fine art to the Mariposa folk festival.

In 1969 the event date was changed to July in hopes that the weather would be more suitable to outdoor concerts and workshops. The actual organization of the event was becoming almost routine. According to Debra Sharp, author of the earliest history of the festival, "[It] had reached a point of unobtrusive ordering, and the smooth and easy progression of events set the pace for the years to come."[1]

The lineup was stellar. Joan Baez, Joni Mitchell, Ian and Sylvia, Taj Mahal, Bonnie Dobson, Doc Watson, and Oscar Brand were just some of the names festival attendees recognized. Daytime activities included such eclectic workshops as "Mountain Music of Peru," "Ragtime and Novelty Songs," "Blues Roots and Development" and "French Canadian Songs." "Instrumental Sessions" featured how-to-play lessons from such masters as Doc Watson, Amos Garrett, Bruce Cockburn, David Rea, and even Joni Mitchell — no doubt with her disparate guitar tunings.

Bruce Cockburn was a new and exciting figure on the folk stage. A mop of curly blond hair and round wire glasses framed a boyish handsomeness. His songs were mesmerizing. As he crooned his compositions, like "Going to the Country" or "Keep It Open," in his high and lilting voice, female audience members, in particular, looked at him in awe. Musicians were even more taken by the man's wizardry as a guitarist. (Rocker Eddie Van Halen is said to have been asked by *Rolling Stone* magazine, "What is it like to be the best guitarist in the world?" He responded: "Ask Bruce Cockburn.")

The CBC filmed many parts of the festival that year and aired it in September. Unfortunately, no copies of the film seem to have survived. The chronicle of an important cultural event has been lost. A newspaper clipping service did save a *TV Guide* write-up about the show prior to its airing in September that year. It sits in the Clara Thomas Archives at York University in Toronto as the only remnant of what would have been an interesting historical keepsake. The quaintly phrased description, from the September 26, 1969, edition of the *Winnipeg Tribune*, also featured a lovely photo of Joan Baez.

A glorious three nights and two days of music in the open air will be recalled by color television on Sept. 28 when CBC airs a special on the Mariposa Folk Festival. It happened in July on the greensward of the Toronto islands and before it ended 29,000 music lovers had listened in. In the words of one of them: 'It was a triumph of good feeling. You just couldn't imagine a more pacific gathering. Everybody was happy and relaxed — even in the pouring rain.' ... Nothing like some of the rough-housing involved in an earlier Mariposa Festival at Orillia.

The mix of name acts and unexpected workshop combinations became the model not just for Mariposa but for nearly all the folk festivals that sprang up in its wake. Folk festivals eventually popped up in Ottawa, Winnipeg, Regina, Edmonton, Calgary, Vancouver, Owen Sound, Canmore, Lunenburg, and many other places. They more or less followed the Mariposa model and have maintained that basic structure to this day.

Kudos for setting that trend go to Estelle Klein and her particular genius. Not only was she able to scout and track down artists on the rise, she found musicians who filled certain niches. She exposed the Mariposa audience to sounds and sights they'd likely never encountered elsewhere. She mixed unusual combinations of musicians from different cultures (and continents) in a blend that was well received and left festivalgoers wanting more. Many of the artists Estelle hired had huge repertoires of traditional material. If one performer sang a song about coal mining, for example, then another act in the same workshop might come up with another song that was about miners even if that had not been his intended next song. This kind of interaction and spontaneity made the workshop experience all the more interesting and unique. She also paired older, experienced musicians with younger performers so they might teach them some of the songs and demonstrate how to perform and interact with an audience. That kind of mentorship was important to up-and-coming musicians like Ken Whiteley.

o o o

In 1969 the festival was reaching out to become more than just a summer affair. In the autumn, the Mariposa newsletter talked of a concert series throughout the upcoming winter season and invited applications for a new songwriter evening concert series. In a co-sponsoring arrangement with the Toronto Musicians' Association, Mariposa made plans to hold an all-day event at a Toronto school in November. Estelle herself responded to audience comments about the site limitations, the difficulties with the ferry service, and especially about the choices of artists who'd played the festival.

o o o

The 70s brought some unexpected challenges, changes in attitude, and new directions for a new decade. The future has a way of doing that.

In August of 1969, the baby boomer generation shouted to the world "Here we are!" when nearly half a million young people descended on Max Yasgur's farm near Woodstock in upstate New York. In the universe of music festivals, it was a supernova that exploded with far-reaching implications. One repercussion was that when the hordes of people arrived at Woodstock, they overwhelmed the organizers to such an extent that the fences were taken down and most of the attendees were allowed admission for free.

"Free" was becoming a buzzword, especially among those who'd been reading Chairman Mao's *Little Red Book* or similar material, like Abbie Hoffman's *Steal This Book*. The "stick-it-to-the-man" attitude and anti-capitalist sentiments seemed to take on a life of their own for a brief time at the turn of that decade.

In the summer of 1970 an enterprise called the Festival Express set out across Canada with stops and concerts scheduled in major cities. The lineup included top rock and folk acts such as Janis Joplin, Eric Andersen, Ian and Sylvia, Buddy Guy, the Grateful Dead, and the Band.

At the very first concert, held at Toronto's CNE stadium, an estimated 2,500 young people tried to scale the fences in protest of what they saw as exorbitant ticket prices. A near riot ensued. Jerry Garcia, leader of the Grateful Dead, played a big role in calming the unruly mob by offering a free concert in nearby Coronation Park, where the Dead, Ian and Sylvia, the Good Brothers, and New Riders of the Purple Sage entertained.

The Calgary stop for the Express faced similar problems.

Comparable disturbances happened at a variety of paid events, including a Massey Hall symphony concert and a pop concert at the University of Toronto's Varsity Stadium. The youthful freeloaders didn't seem to realize that, whether they liked it or not, they were living in a capitalist society where they must pay for services, even of the musical variety.

The same kind of entitlement struck Mariposa that summer. The festival was once again held on Olympic Island. Although often referred to as Toronto Island, a small archipelago off shore from Toronto includes Olympic, Centre, Ward's, Algonquin, Muggs, and a few smaller islands. As many as fifteen hundred quasi-anarchists decided to storm the barricades at Mariposa that weekend.

Joni Mitchell, James Taylor, and David Rea were scheduled to perform on Sunday evening. Dozens of determined kids swam across the channel between Olympic and Centre Island in an attempt to get in for free.

"A Maoist group who were convinced that all music should be free arrived en masse at the gates of the Mariposa Festival screaming and yelling as they tried to crash through,"[2] explained Murray McLauchlan.

Michael Cooney, as one of the musical hosts, spoke from the stage about the incursion. "I was MC'ing that night; there was a LOT of consternation

Bonnie Dobson, Toronto Island, 1969.

Bruce Cockburn.

backstage. Someone in the audience shouted out about this is 'people's music' and should be free; I said, 'Half the performers at this festival are Native people; they make less in a year than your parents make in a month, maybe a week.'"

So much for the rosy view of the Woodstock generation!

Owen McBride, who was also emceeing that night, said that the incident was indeed "scary."

After a futile attempt to hold back the tide of interlopers, as at Woodstock the year before, organizers realized that safety had to take the place of profit, and they removed the barriers.

A similar gatecrashing took place at the 1971 Newport Jazz Festival, where young people, believing that the event should be free, jumped the barricades. But there was a price to be paid — if not by the 1970 festival intruders, then by the festival attendees in the years to come.

"I personally felt it was an insult for people to do that when we went to such lengths to keep our ticket prices low and to make our motives known," said Estelle Klein.[3]

Following the events of 1970 — which had featured such incredible musicians as James Taylor, Ramblin' Jack Elliott, Doug Kershaw, Odetta, and Perth County Conspiracy — Estelle and the organizing team decided to make some monumental changes to the format of the festival. Something was askew with the evening concert plan and needed to be remedied. The reliance on big names to draw crowds was taking something away from the workshops and symposium idea that had been Estelle's true focus since as far back as the festival's first year.

Because the Klein model meant bringing in a wide range of musicians from all the folk genres, many artists who were not suited to the bright lights of the mainstage were hired. Estelle wrote about all of this in *For What Time I Am in This World*, a book that was published in 1977. A potpourri of photos, anecdotes, interviews, song lyrics, and well-researched history, the book includes Estelle's pointed explanation of her philosophy and her reason for changing course for the festival after 1970:

> Mariposa audiences on the whole are pretty good, but a mass audience will not respond as much to an unaccompanied traditional singer as they will to a more familiar kind of music. So the performer, the unaccompanied singer, for instance, can't help but notice that it's perhaps polite applause. So I began to think that a) the evening concerts negated what I'd like to do and b) they made an uncomfortable situation for certain people. And you have a choice: you either make it uncomfortable or you leave those people out. Also I didn't feel I wanted to be left with a group of people who are easily acceptable known factors, as I think the public should hear more. And I didn't feel I wanted to discriminate against people who are very good and are stars in what they do. So how could you do it?[4]

It was a serious shift in policy and the ramifications could have impacted the festival's attendance and financial bottom line in the years to come. Yet the board of directors bought into Estelle's vision. Richard Flohil, Victor Page, Buzz Chertkoff — to name a few — agreed that 1971's festival would test a new manner of presenting the performers' concerts and workshops. There would still be individual concerts, but the workshops would be the focus during the day. For the first time ever, there would be no evening concerts at Mariposa. There were six stages set up amid the trees on Olympic Island plus a Native people's area and a separate craft area. Activities were jam-packed in a schedule between 10:30 a.m. and 8 p.m. on simultaneous stages. Dancing and singalongs were given more emphasis than they'd had in the past.

Despite encouragement for her vision from people like Pete Seeger and Michael Cooney, Estelle had her doubts and nervous, sleepless nights. Some musicians, agents, and even the press and long-time attendees questioned what Mariposa was becoming. Estelle secretly worried that she was going to "ruin the festival."

> I suddenly began to think, "Oh my god, what have I done? I've screwed this thing up — it's down the drain." But I didn't dare let any of those people think I had any doubts at all. They were weak and afraid and I didn't dare pander to that weakness. So I just kept saying, "It will work," and in the meantime my insides were in a knot. I never even

Gatecrashers on the island, 1970.

Stompin' Tom Connors, 1971.

communicated that to my own husband! I carried a tremendous burden and had a crack-up afterwards. I really began to be frightened that I'd ruined the festival.[5]

As it turned out, Estelle had nothing to worry about — at least from the point of view that she might have "screwed things up." An estimated ten thousand people arrived on the island each day and were presented with a scene that pleased nearly all of them. The thing about workshop stages was that they put an audience up close and personal with the performers. The side benefits fell exactly into Estelle's way of thinking.

> The audience was only a few feet away from them and the intimacy encouraged the listeners to accept new forms of music from which they otherwise might recoil. Coming to see Murray McLauchlan or John Prine, unsuspecting spectators would find themselves listening, entranced, to Jean Redpath.[6]

Much of what went on at Mariposa in the 60s and 70s was the brainchild of Estelle Klein — or at least due to her hard work. No other person in the history of Mariposa had more influence both within and beyond the organization. No one else ever had as much control over the finished product either. She was determined in what she wanted and would suffer no fools. In fact, some people found her manner with the volunteers a bit off-putting.

Vivienne Muhling, who could be described as a mentor to Estelle in the folk music business, recalled, "She could sometimes be quite high handed with volunteers and her husband when he was helping. I remember sometimes feeling uncomfortable with her 'That won't do' insistence … 'you have to do it the way I say.'"

Vivienne had first met Estelle through mutual friends in the 1950s. It was Vivienne who had both the foresight and the courage to book acts like Pete Seeger, the Weavers, and Josh White Sr. at a time when no one in either Canada or the U.S. would take chances on such "controversial" (read: communist) acts. According to Vivienne, Estelle asked if she could help with booking performers such as the Kingston Trio, and it was through this friendship that Estelle learned how to negotiate with agents, how to produce shows in Toronto, and how to use the media for promotion. For instance,

James Taylor, 1970.

the two women produced a show by John Jacob Niles at Casa Loma. In Vivienne's estimation, maybe the most important thing Estelle learned from her was the importance of helping each performer feel comfortable and important. That lesson would carry through her career with Mariposa. On top of all that, many of those who worked with Estelle admired her gutsiness. Vivienne admired Estelle's "ability to visualize that what George Wein [of the Newport Folk Festival] did in the U.S. could be made to happen here — not just individual concerts, but whole festivals — and major week-long concert events like the one in which she involved me when I first returned from New York — a week-long event promoting women performers."

Michael Cooney was instrumental in assisting Estelle with workshop ideas.

> We spent a *lot* of time thinking up ideas for workshops and which performers to fit into 'em. Once, because we had a blind Canadian singer of old country-western songs, we'd do a song swap of Hank Williams songs. We asked Steve Goodman and John Prine and one other person if they knew any. Each was all enthusiastic about it, said

they knew several. When the time came, it turned out
they all knew the first verse and chorus of the same three
songs; the Canadian guy had to carry the whole hour.[7]

It seemed that the new format of simultaneous workshops and concerts
but no evening concerts would be one that Mariposa followed in the fore-
seeable future.

The 1971 program was perhaps a reflection of the type of journalism
that prevailed in the early part of that decade. With influences ranging
from Tom Wolfe and Hunter S. Thompson to *Rolling Stone* and *National
Lampoon* magazines, many of the off-the-wall entries that comprise a big
part of the program had nothing specific to do with the festival: an article
about yurts; a Zap comic of dreamlike metamorphosis; an introduction
to macrobiotics. The program offered diverse reading for those waiting
between sets or on riding the ferry home. The concise biographies and
detailed stage schedule meant that the program served its rightful purpose. And who's to say that the eclecticism of the writing wasn't in keeping with the educational side of Estelle Klein's vision?

Artistic director and innovator Estelle Klein.

A sideline to the festival weaving its way into the Canadian cultural fabric was that on September 18, 1971, a song entitled "Mariposa" hit the *RPM* chart at number 35.[8] Written by Gerry Ralston, the lead singer and guitarist of Instant Ralston, it alludes to waiting for the ferry and singing songs in a "paradise to be free." It got as high as number 25 on the adult contemporary category the next week, charted in the first week of October, and then disappeared. It was not a hit record, but it did sing the praises — literally — of Canada's premier folk festival.

CHAPTER FIVE

The Memorable 1972 Festival

EVEN FOR AN ANNUAL EVENT THAT HAS BEEN running for well over half a century, the 1972 Mariposa Folk Festival stands out in the event's long history for a number of reasons.

It could be argued that that year was the height of the singer-songwriter in popular music. On top of that, so many of the top popular songs of 1972 featured songs or singers who could easily fit into the "folk" bins at record stores. *Billboard's* top ten for the year included Ewan MacColl's "The First Time Ever I Saw Your Face" as recorded by Roberta Flack; "American Pie" by Don McLean; "Alone Again Naturally" by Gilbert O'Sullivan; and Melanie's "Brand New Key." Other notables on the pop charts that year were the acoustically inclined "A Horse with No Name" by America; "Morning Has Broken" by Cat Stevens; "City of New Orleans" by Arlo Guthrie; "Mother and Child Reunion" by Paul Simon; "You Don't Mess Around with Jim" by Jim Croce; "Taxi" by Harry Chapin; "Play Me a Rock and Roll Song" by Valdy; and "Vincent," a lovely elegy to Van Gogh by Don McLean. In addition, musicians like James Taylor, Neil Young, Joni Mitchell, Kris Kristofferson, and Gordon Lightfoot were at the top of their game, releasing some of the finest work of their long careers. Canadian performers like Murray McLauchlan and Bruce Cockburn were hitting their stride with a couple of early masterful recordings. It was a good time to be a folkie. As well, Canadian content rules for radio and television were adopted in 1971, stating that a certain percentage of all programming had to be Canadian

Who says you don't dance to folk music?

written, performed, or produced. These rules helped the homegrown talent to be discovered and played, if not always respected.

Estelle Klein had settled on a format for the festival that seemed to work on several levels. She was providing a place for disparate artists to strut their stuff and show off their talents. She was not only bringing in entertaining performers but also doing her best to educate her audience in all the broad sub-genres of folk music. The organizers, the board of directors, and, most importantly, the paying festival attendees had bought into her vision enthusiastically.

Dave Bidini, in his perceptive book *Writing Gordon Lightfoot: The Man, the Music, and the World in 1972*, claims the events of Mariposa '72 might never have transpired had the Varsity Stadium show [where John Lennon, Eric Clapton, et al. had miraculously performed in 1969] not established Toronto as a place where the impossible was possible. The stars of Mariposa were likely drawn to the city for the same reasons as Lennon: the thriving music scene, entrepreneurs with access to the new money of old families, a generation of kids hep to new sounds and styles, and a lack of bullshit that tended to follow these kinds of large-scale happenings around.[1]

The stars did appear that year: Joni Mitchell, Bob Dylan, Gordon Lightfoot, Jackson Browne, Neil Young. And they were just visitors!

The actual festival lineup included Leon Redbone, Bonnie Raitt, David Bromberg, Murray McLauchlan, the New Lost City Ramblers, Bruce Cockburn, John Prine, Bukka White, Taj Mahal, Utah Phillips, Mike Seeger, the Original Sloth Band (Chris and Ken Whiteley plus Tom Evans), John Allan Cameron, Michael Cooney, Adam Mitchell, and Jean Ritchie. These artists — and plenty of others — had been organized by Estelle into workshops or titled concerts such as "War: A Common Heritage," "Ragtime: Cathouse to Concert Stage," "The Woman's Image in Song," "Scottish and Irish Traditional Songs," "Influences Of and On Bob Dylan," and "The Environment (What's Going On Here?)"

Friday's daytime events went smoothly and the crowd persevered through intermittent rain. In some ways it was a typical Mariposa weekend. Workshops and concerts began at 10:30 a.m. and continued throughout the day at six different stages until 8:30 at night. A note in the festival magazine told patrons that "all programs end at 8:30 p.m. Festival site must be cleared at this time."

Early Saturday eager folkies — mostly young — showed up at Olympic Island. The crowd swelled with each ferry that arrived at the island dock. The sweet smell of marijuana wafted on the breeze as joints were passed freely around the workshop venues. Even though the site was supposed to be an alcohol-free zone, John Prine managed to get himself "absolutely blottoed" to the point where he had to be rescued from possibly drowning in a garbage can.[2] Yet his stage appearances were sober and totally professional. The same was true of blues legend Bukka White. He loved his bourbon, and managed to amass and drink great quantities, but he held his liquor when it came time to get up on stage.

Bonnie Raitt, already making a name for herself at age 23, was as enthusiastic at the performers' hotel as she was at each Mariposa stage she played. According to those who were there, she led the late-night jam sessions with singing and picking. When her Saturday concert was shut down by a rainstorm, she invited those who stayed to gather around her under a tiny canopy. She played acoustically for the small gathering.

Colin Linden, a world-class guitarist and member of Blackie and the Rodeo Kings, attended his first Mariposa in 1972. He first met Bruce Cockburn and John Prine there and remembers seeing Gordon Lightfoot jamming with the Good Brothers on an island picnic table.

Lightfoot — as he has done many times at Mariposa — just showed up at the festival. Then at the peak of his recording career, Lightfoot was Canada's answer to international stars such as Bob Dylan. He played sold-out concerts everywhere in Canada, including week-long stands at Toronto's venerable Massey Hall. His most recent albums at the time — *If You Could Read My Mind, Summer Side of Life* and *Don Quixote* — stand up to this day as some of his finest work. The LPs had been released in the previous two years and had sold well in Canada and abroad. Gordon had played Mariposa many times in the previous decade, including a stint at the second festival in Orillia, and it seemed that he had a fondness for the festival and the type of music it presented.

The thing was, Lightfoot didn't come alone. Clad in a simple shirt, blue jeans, cowboy boots, and a headband was none other than Bob Dylan. Sporting the wispy beard he'd worn off and on for years, Dylan looks remarkably healthy and youthful in the photos from that year's event. Every folk and rock music fan knew his catalogue and his legend, and the fact that he was walking the grounds of Olympic Island sent a buzz through the gathered masses that July. He may have been on the island on the Saturday, but that cannot be confirmed. The mythology surrounding the man makes memories of his presence that weekend rather questionable.

"Dylan had come to see Leon Redbone," said Richard Flohil. Redbone was a unique performer who, much like Dylan himself, fostered a mystique about his background and his whereabouts. His music paid tribute to old standards and jazz from the twenties and was delivered with a distinctive guitar style

The Original Sloth Band, 1972.

and even more distinctive raspy voice. As a musician, he pushed boundaries in his performances, much like Andy Kaufman would do later in the decade with comedy. Redbone was known to come on stage, set up a record player, put on an LP and then walk off the stage, leaving the audience to wonder what was going on. He also was quite a card sharp behind the scenes in the artists' green room. Flohil recalled how Redbone cleaned out Ramblin' Jack Elliott, Guy Clark, and Tam Kearney in a poker game at the performers' hotel, the Town Inn, when they all played Mariposa in 1991.

Michael Cooney also recalled both Redbone and Dylan that weekend.

> Dylan came "incognito" but was easy to spot — he had a lime-green shirt and a red bandana around his head. He came to two "workshops" that Leon and I were in (probably called "Songs So Bad They're Good" and "Songs of the 1920s, 30s and 40s" or something). He must have really liked Leon because he mentioned him in a *Rolling Stone* interview shortly afterwards. Warner Brothers read it and called Leon and the rest is history. Leon told me I gave him his big break.

The organizers had known Dylan was coming. Flohil knew he was staying at the King Edward Hotel in downtown Toronto and relayed the news — at about 2 a.m. on Saturday night — to Leigh Cline, the technical director. Bob Dylan, *the* Bob Dylan, was coming to the festival. First thing Sunday morning Cline made his way to the festival site and called the board of directors to a hastily convened meeting. There was great concern that if Dylan showed up and wanted to play, it would cause pandemonium. After all, there was no longer a huge police and security presence at the peaceful and placid event. After an agonizing argument, the board's decision was made that, should he show up, Dylan would *not* be permitted to play.[3] Flohil, when interviewed by a TV crew, even denied that Dylan was there.

Ironically, Estelle Klein, who had so much to do with the growth and success of Mariposa, and who was normally the domineering presence at the festival, was not there that year. She'd done her organizing and scheduling, had assigned tasks to trusted individuals, and then had gone to Greece with her family on a much-needed vacation. It's interesting to speculate on what her advice would have been regarding whether to allow Dylan to perform. Given her recent decisions to keep the performances egalitarian, it's likely she'd have supported the board's decision. She was quoted a few years after that famous festival year in *For What Time I Am in This World* regarding the whole Dylan scene: "My feelings were it was blown all out of proportion. All performers are welcome as guests at Mariposa. I don't believe that any unscheduled performer should give a solo performance, and that's policy. But if they can be incorporated into a workshop where their music is valid, I would decide to do that."[4]

Dylan managed to walk the grounds of Olympic Island and Centre Island that day without being recognized too often and without being hassled by the crowds of adoring fans. (After all, this was Canada, where we don't normally mob or bother celebrities.) Bob Stevens, a long-time Mariposa volunteer, employee, and board member, recalled,

> I was working in hospitality that year. So I'm standing against a fence with Bob Dylan when he gets up and says, "I want to go see Leon Redbone." So I volunteer to take him there because Redbone was playing at the other end of the site, across the island. So I take him across this field

full of people thinking, "Wow, this is Bob Dylan here!" and nobody even bats an eye! He wasn't recognized at all, he was just another guy in an Indian shirt with a red bandana on his head.[5]

At about 5 p.m. Dylan and Lightfoot were about to leave the island, but for some unknown reason Dylan turned around and came back. People began to recognize the pair — probably Lightfoot first, then the more camouflaged Dylan. The crowd pressed around the two singers. Although there was no physical threat or anything of that nature, things could easily have gotten out of hand for the organizers. Dylan politely and quietly asked if he could get up and sing a song. The board's early morning decision was put to the test. Naturally, everyone at the festival would love to hear Dylan perform but there were six stages — seven including the Native peoples' area — and if this superstar were allowed to play, organizers imagined the mob scene as thousands of people abandoned all the other stages to come and hear Dylan. Who knew what kind of panic or mayhem might occur?

Richard Flohil remembered, "I think we responded with a fair degree of panic but on the other hand when you have 5,000 people chasing from one end of the island to the other after one small individual, panic ensues."[6]

Michael Cooney, as both a performer and one of Estelle's right-hand men, was the one tasked with telling Dylan he couldn't perform. "So they asked me to ask Dylan not to perform. I remember [in the 'backstage area' tent of one of the stages] that he never said a word; all the talking was done by some young jerk — his road manager? But he didn't play. (I'm not much of a party person so that night I didn't go to the party in David Bromberg's room at the hotel. Dylan did.)"

As Dave Bidini put it, "Had he played Mariposa, it would have been the kind of musical event remembered and noted for generations. Instead, the festival would end up denying the greatest songwriter of his generation a chance to take the stage."[7]

"I recall being there with Bob and Sarah, his wife," said Gordon Lightfoot. "We were acquaintances really, being part of Grossman's management stable. We saw Neil Young. And we would get together [both that year and at other times] at my place. It was kind of party central, as I was carefree and kind of footloose at that time."

Leon Redbone, 1972.

Dylan and Lightfoot weren't the only stars in town that weekend. Saturday morning Joni Mitchell had arrived without fanfare. Tagging along was someone who would end up joining her in the Rock and Roll Hall of Fame: Jackson Browne, writer of "Doctor My Eyes," "Take It Easy," and "Lawyers in Love." At that point he was just starting to make a name for himself, and he also happened to be Joni's boyfriend.

Some accounts of that famous festival state that Graham Nash, Joni's former boyfriend, was also there. Flohil did not recall seeing Nash on the island, but others claimed he was in Joni's party.

For the Saturday afternoon attendees, there was a big surprise in store. Murray McLauchlan was scheduled to play at 2:30 on Stage 6. He walked on stage and announced to the people who'd come to see him that he was giving up his set — for his friend Joni Mitchell. Naturally, the small crowd went wild, and as soon as Joni began to sing, hordes came running from all over the island as they recognized that soaring soprano voice. Joni played five tunes, including "You Turn Me On, I'm a Radio," and then turned over the microphone to Jackson Browne who sang three or four of his songs. No one took much notice of him, though, in the excitement of seeing and hearing Joni unexpectedly.

Neil Young, for whatever reason, also showed up unannounced the next day. His brother was a volunteer at the festival and a music journalist, so that could have been the reason. Maybe he just thought Mariposa was a cool place to be. His feet were firmly planted in both the rock and roll and the folk music camps, so it was natural for him to gravitate to a city that was hosting both the Rolling Stones and the Mariposa Folk Festival that weekend. Young was heavily into his folk persona at that moment in time, having recently released the acoustically inclined *After the Gold Rush* and *Harvest* LPs.

He and his wife, actress Carrie Snodgress, hung around the performers' tent most of the time. Bruce Cockburn was scheduled to play at four o'clock Sunday and reluctantly shared his time with his more famous counterpart. Young played his now-classic songs "Helpless," "Heart of Gold," "Sugar Mountain," and "Harvest." As with Joni the day before, Young's familiar voice pulled people toward Stage 4. Standing off to the side, listening intently, were Bob Dylan and Gordon Lightfoot.

Gordon Lightfoot chose to do things a bit differently, a bit more subtly. He joined the Good Brothers, a country-folk group from Richmond Hill, on a picnic table far from the stages and played acoustically for a tiny crowd of no more than thirty people. No hoopla, no threat of crowds out of control. Perhaps it speaks to the contrast between Canadian and U.S. stardom.

Lightfoot and Dylan chatted backstage in the fenced-off area for performers. A large and curious crowd gathered nearby but remained calm and respectful and didn't try to do anything out of the ordinary in order to reach the two folk heroes. Ray Woodley, an advisor to the board, had been escorting Dylan around and called the harbour police to take them back to the mainland. Richard Flohil recalled that Leon Redbone and Dylan made a memorable exit from the island aboard one of the police boats.

The Sunday concerts and workshops ended as scheduled at 8:30 p.m. and the audience members filtered back to the ferry dock. Even if they hadn't encountered or seen Dylan, Lightfoot, Neil Young, or any of the other interlopers, they went away delighted with the great music and superb programming that had been offered all weekend.

Not all was sunshine and hippie roses, though.

According to early festival historian Debra Sharp, "Although Dylan had not performed, many of the Mariposa performers were quite incensed. They

Michael Cooney and Owen McBride in workshop setting, Toronto Island.

felt the situation with Mitchell and Young was handled without discretion and that the upset Dylan had caused early Sunday evening was a great blow to the festival."[8]

The whole incident troubled Buzz Chertkoff, the festival president. He and his wife felt the whole festival had been hijacked and that he was in some way to blame for what had happened. Looking back over forty years later, the 1972 festival and its cast of legendary, unexpected characters seems at once cool, exciting, and memorable. But to Buzz it was problematic, insulting to the other performers — such as Cockburn — and he felt the organization had not handled it properly.

"I felt sick! I wanted to go home and bury myself. I felt the festival had suffered a real trauma," said Chertkoff later. "I wasn't totally satisfied myself that the problems of that weekend were handled well enough. That year I recommended that Estelle be president of the festival, and that would be an end to all the hassles. I'll never know whether anyone could have handled it better."[9]

Although some of the organizers felt the same way Chertkoff did, the festival was an artistic (and financial) success. Even without considering the contributions of the famous interlopers, the music produced that year by the musicians officially on the roster was stellar. Veterans Martin, Bogan, and Armstrong had played together for over forty years and pleased the audience with their high-spirited, engaging brand of folk blues; the Original Sloth Band bragged that they played nothing written prior to 1940, yet it sounded wonderfully new to 1972 listeners; John Prine, Bruce Cockburn, and Murray McLauchlan demonstrated singer-songwriter skills that would carry them to long careers; Alanis Obomsawin showcased Aboriginal culture to the predominantly city-bred and urban audiences; Bonnie Raitt, Leon Redbone, Taj Mahal, and Roosevelt Sykes gave the festivalgoers unique takes on the blues. By any standards, the 1972 festival would have been a success whether the world turned its eye on it or not.

The post-festival Mariposa newsletter was an interesting summation of that historic year. The editors noted that there had been considerable positive and some negative reaction to the musicians who'd appeared. Despite acknowledging the rain, mud, shortage of washrooms, sound bleed, loose dogs, and ever-unpopular ferry service, the audience was thanked and praised for coming through "with flags flying." The festival made money and was financially secure.

Somehow, the financial situation was tied to a promise for 1973 to have a "*quieter* festival than we held this year." The large crowds in 1972 had resulted in long lineups for food or the washrooms and longer waits for the ferry rides. Buzz Chertkoff, the president, promised, "Mariposa next year will attempt to limit its audience by an almost total lack of promotion." A decision was made to limit awareness of the festival to the newsletter, word of mouth, and very limited advertising. Later festival organizers could have looked back in awe and wonder at this unlikely dilemma. Too successful, so we won't advertise? Inconceivable for festivals in the early 80s and for the turn-of-the-century festivals back in Orillia!

It was clear that Estelle Klein was not happy about the disruption caused by crowd fervour directed toward the unexpected stars who'd shown up. She reiterated her desire to treat all the performers the same, no matter how large or small their fame and stature. She also did not like to think that she'd spent all that time programming stages and workshops, only to have some of them commandeered so that a few big-name artists could take over. Perhaps she'd already set in motion a plan as to the programming direction she wished to pursue in coming years.

CHAPTER SIX
The Toronto Island Years: The 70s

IN THE AUTUMN OF 1972 BUZZ CHERTKOFF did indeed hand over the presidency of Mariposa to Estelle Klein. She was truly the boss from that point on for most of the decade. The 70s was a time of relative stability for the festival, and Estelle Klein's vision was fulfilled during those years. She kept her finger on the pulse of each aspect of the planning, keeping in mind the ways everything could impact the performances. She was on top of every detail, from the food the performers were served to the technical specs on each of the stages.

She admitted in a number of interviews to being a powerful person:

> It's a dictator approach. You lay yourself on the line then. You have to be open to suggestions always and to ideas and learning, but at some point in the game, someone has to make a decision: yes, or no. And you accept that you will be criticized for that or commended. But they know who to praise and they know who to blame. And those are the conditions under which I will do any job. With programming, the final say is mine, and I'm willing to take the consequences.[1]

o o o

The festival had become a non-profit organization, incorporated under the laws of Ontario. No longer did one person such as Randy Ferris or Tom Bishop stand to gain financially from any profits. The Toronto Guild of Canadian Folk Artists took credit for the annual festival organization but laid no financial claims to the money made each summer. After the 1977 festival the board of directors changed the name of the organization to the *Mariposa Folk Foundation*, indicating that the Mariposa entity was much more than just a three-day summer festival.

For the next several years Mariposa thrived. A move to Centre Island (as opposed to Olympic Island) in 1973 gave the event room to expand. That year marked the first time that each workshop was recorded for archival purposes. Keeping a record of performances that would never be repeated was a brilliant move both historically and culturally. Now researchers and musical historians would have access to such workshop combinations as Murray McLauchlan, Malvina Reynolds, and Arthur "Big Boy" Crudup's take on "Song-Making" or never-to-be-repeated "Sentimental Songs" featuring Leon Redbone playing

Alanis Obomsawin and Aboriginal women.

alongside Steve Goodman. Many unique and brilliant performances (as well as occasional turkeys) were captured for posterity. A burden, though, was placed on future organizers to archive and preserve these recordings. Archival records were much in keeping with the intellectual side of folk, as envisioned initially by Ruth Jones and carried on by Estelle Klein, Edith Fowke, and others.

In 1974 over 80 percent of the tickets to the event were pre-sold by mail, and then the remainder of the tickets sold out in five days. Despite the rains that year, an estimated 24,000 people came through the gates. A hand-painted sign at the ferry dock announced, "Mariposa sold out."

At the same time Mariposa was thriving on the island offshore from Toronto, other folk music festivals were springing up around the country and south of the border. Most notable of all was the Winnipeg Folk Festival, which began as the brainchild of Mitch Podolak in 1974. An artistic success from the beginning, it went through growing pains and hard financial times, just as Mariposa had. Yet it flourished and eventually surpassed both Philadelphia and Mariposa in terms of total weekend attendance. Regina's folk festival predates Winnipeg as it was established in 1969. Home County in London began in 1973; Summerfolk in Owen Sound started in 1975; and Vancouver's first folk festival took place in 1977. All of them followed the model that had evolved at Mariposa, namely the mix of concerts and workshops, and all the artistic directors owed a great deal to Estelle Klein.

o o o

The 70s saw Mariposa begin a reaching-out process that took the festival's name and influence beyond the festival and out to a broader community in Southern Ontario.

For one thing, Estelle broadened her approach to what has since been labelled world music. Wanting to present a sampling of music from different nationalities, she formed what she called an ethnic committee, whose task was to look for musicians, dancers, and artisans who represented the ever-blossoming immigrant community in Toronto. In 1974 that group — headed by Ruth Pincoe — hired at least seven acts that fit that particular niche on the bill.

They went so far as to consult with the Smithsonian Institute in the United States about ethnocultural organizations. Many of the acts that were hired were dance troupes from areas of Eastern Europe, although there was representation from the Filipino, Chinese, Turkish, and Portuguese communities. Estelle and several other Mariposa volunteers were often called upon in the Toronto area to consult or advise about multicultural presentations. For example, a World Crafts Council event was held at Toronto's Science Centre in 1974, and both Estelle Klein and Marna Snitman were hired for that international assembly.

Not that everything always went smoothly! At times, the audience was not used to the so-called ethnic music or dance unless it was presented the way that they'd experienced it at Caravan, the multicultural festival in Toronto that featured costumes and food from other nations. Leigh Cline, an organizer and musician at Mariposa in those years, described a situation where he and some others were playing music true to the customs and style of Greece. "We were playing folk *dance* music actually. Because they don't separate the music and the dance. And the audience actually *hated* it. We got comments like, 'Well, when are you going to play the real thing?' It's like, 'This is the real thing guys.... This is the way they do it in Greece.' But — no. They were used to Caravan, and — and the other line we got was, 'Where are the costumes?'"[2]

The musicians themselves tended to be more open minded to the ethnic music and in particular to the instruments being utilized. David Rawlings, who played Mariposa in the mid-70s before going on to fame as the musical partner of Gillian Welch, recalled first hearing an instrument called a kora (a twenty-one-stringed African harp) while playing Mariposa. Those kinds of experiences were uncommon for musicians — unless they came to the Mariposa Folk Festival.

o o o

One way to encourage year-round interest in the festival was to publish a newsletter. Started in 1974, the newsletters were eclectic mixtures of "folk gossip," musical instruction, insight into the festival-building process, book reviews, ruminations, editorials, rants, cartoons, letters to Mariposa, interviews, and history. Interested readers were asked to subscribe, and the newsletters were mailed from the Mariposa office. Unfortunately, the newsletter published a "Farewell Issue" in November 1977. In her obituary column, managing editor

Marilyn Koop attributed the decision (to cease publication) to lack of sub-scribers. And she asked the all-important question: "why is this?" Was it really because the Mariposa newsletter couldn't compete when the women were looking at *Better Housekeeping*, the men at *Penthouse*, and the young college crowd at *National Lampoon?* That was Koop's argument. But perhaps the rea-son for the lack of subscription sales ran deeper. Could it have been that it was the shift in musical tastes, the fact the audiences didn't wish to sit in the rain at outdoor festivals, or that the entertainment dollar only went so far? Could it have been that having young children prevents one from participating in out-of-the-house activities, even if that activity provides a children's area?

Another way that the festival tried to reach out was through the sale of recordings of some of the performances from the festival. In 1975 and 1976 Mariposa issued LPs of the music that had been played that year at the festival. Both records comprised recordings taken directly from the stages. They were not studio recordings or doctored tapes sent from the performers' record com-panies but, as the 1975 album jacket boasted, "songs which have not yet been recorded and which may never be captured that way again. You will hear people making music together for possibly the first and last time and creating some-thing pretty special while they're at it. You will hear a very small cross section of what happened in June 1975." The next year's record featured such diverse artists as Steve Goodman, Taj Mahal, the Original Sloth Band, Rev. Pearly Brown, the Toronto Sacred Harp Singers, Archie Fisher, and Colleen Peterson.

A limited edition run of three thousand did not sell out, and some of the records were still for sale at the festival as late as 2009. That was not a reflection of the quality of the music — more a comment on the marketing of a unique and esoteric product.

In 1970, in an effort to develop new audiences for Mariposa, a small group of organizers began something called "Mariposa in the Schools" (although it was not officially named that until 1973). Estelle Klein, Klaas Van Graft, and Chick Roberts came up with the idea of sending performers to the schools — mostly in the Greater Toronto Area — where folk music could entertain the children, teachers, and parents and ultimately build a following for the summer festivals. The trio approached both the separate and public school boards with a proposal to put on concerts and workshops in schools during the daytime. At first the focus was on junior high students, but eventually the musicians ended up playing mostly to younger elementary school pupils. Securing a grant from the Toronto Musicians' Association Trust Fund helped to kick-start the enterprise. Further grants from the Ontario government each year not only helped to pay performers but also assisted schools in the costs of hiring. By 1974 dozens of performers were giving over five hundred workshops and concerts per year in classrooms and gymnasiums throughout Ontario.[3] The aim of the scheme was out in the open, as expressed by the authors of the festival program: the programs might turn schoolchildren on to folk music at a time when they were being bombarded with AM radio rock and roll; MITS, as the program came to be called, would also provide work for folk performers throughout the year. Finally, it would act as a marketing and publicity tool for the festival itself, showing the young audience what it could expect to hear at a Mariposa Folk Festival. Some of the performers who took their music on the road between festivals in those years were Raffi, Rick Avery, Chris and Ken Whiteley, David Essig, Grit Laskin, Salome Bey, Beverly Glenn-Copeland, and John Allan Cameron. Sharon, Lois & Bram were popular as individual performers in those initial years, both at the festival and in the schools. They would later team up to become the most popular children's entertainers in Canada.

Sharon Trostin and Lois Lilienstein, 1977, Folkplay.

This coupled nicely with the instituting in 1976 of an independent children's area at the festival. Estelle Klein asserted in the festival program that it was not to be considered a daycare centre, but more of a focal point for programming aimed at children. Coordinating the area were Sharon Hampson and Lois Lilienstein, with Skye Morrison leading the craft section. Caroline Parry helped as well.

Shortly before her death in 2015, Lois Lilienstein recalled, "We said, 'Let's have a children's area where we can program children's concerts, x number of hours a day, every day.' ... Estelle said, 'Go for it.'"[4] There was a stage set aside for kids' concerts and an area for play. The play area gave the youngsters opportunity for skipping ropes and playing marbles or hopscotch. It could also include learning a maypole dance, learning the spoons, storytelling, and quilting. The initiation of a children's area was a reflection of the growth of the baby boomers. Young people who'd maybe attended the festival in the 60s as young adults were now attending the festival as young parents. It made sense to entertain the whole family. In the audience survey that year, festivalgoers heaped praise on the festival for implementing this kind of activity.

As well as reaching out to children and parents with children at the festival itself, in 1979 the Mariposa in the Schools branch of the foundation produced a children's album entitled *Going Bananas*, which was nominated for a JUNO Award.

Something else that grew in size, popularity, and respect was the Native people's area at each festival in the 70s. Though it began as the rather awkwardly worded "Festival Arts Festival of the Native Peoples," the concept expanded throughout the decade. In the printed 1970 program, it was first described as " a unique gathering of Indian and Eskimo singers, musicians, dancers and crafts people." Front and centre in the organizing and presentation was Alanis Obomsawin, a singer, storyteller, and filmmaker from Montreal. Aboriginal people from all over Canada converged on the festival to demonstrate weaving, jewellery, and clothing. The Mi'kmaq, Cree, Ojibwa, and Haida nations were represented. A giant teepee marked the area. In 1971 César Newashish of Manawan Reserve near James Bay constructed a ten-metre canoe over the course of the festival and then donated it to the Royal Ontario Museum. Several of the programs in that era reflect the influence of Aboriginal culture — or were at least an attempt to demonstrate the importance of those cultures.

Some of the performers in those years were remarkable individuals with interesting stories to tell. (Then again, there are remarkable individuals at *every* Mariposa festival!) Steve Goodman and David Amram were paired together in a workshop entitled "Improvising Lyrics" at the 1974 festival. David recalled in his memoir, *Upbeat: Nine Lives of a Musical Cat,* that Steve loved to rap and scat sing, so he was a perfect fit for such a workshop session. The audience threw out suggestions to the performers and they in turn would make up songs on the spot using those suggestions. One of the ideas that became an instant song was a tune based on the story of *Moby Dick.* Flash forward a number of months, and David one day received a cassette tape from Steve with the song "Moby Book" on it. Amram was credited as co-writer with Goodman. Apparently someone at Mariposa sent Steve a recording of the workshop. Goodman then used what he and David had spontaneously improvised at the festival, tweaked it a bit, and produced a song that made its way onto Steve's 1975 album "Jessie's Jig & Other Favorites" — all because of a Mariposa workshop. In his definitive biography Steve Goodman: Facing the Music, author Clay Eals points out that about half of the song's lyrics and its entire musical structure came out of that innovation workshop at Mariposa.[5]

Musically, some years took on thematic approaches. The United Nations had determined that 1975 would be International Women's Year. In keeping with that initiative, Mariposa had plenty of female representation on the stages that year. Malvina Reynolds (who wrote the folk classics "Little Boxes," "Morningtown Ride," and "What Have They Done to the Rain?") was a highlight for the audiences. Other outstanding women performers included Sweet Honey in the Rock, Rita MacNeil, the McGarrigle Sisters, and Rosalie Sorrels. Workshop topics that fit the theme were things like "Strong Women: Purpose and Protest" or "Songs of Struggle and Change."

The 1977 festival focused on "the origins of North American folk music" and, of course, the lineup and workshops reflected upon the traditional and evolving nature of this musical genre. That year's presentations covered everything from Anglo and French ballads to Newfoundland, Irish, Spanish, and Scottish influences; Afro-American and Cajun songs to tales of the sea; Celtic dance and Caribbean theatre to pan flutes and Jew's harps; banjo and fiddle approaches, and songs of religious expression; and an entire stage was given over to Inuit or "North American Indian" [*sic*] culture and music. An entire stage was also dedicated to dance that year.

The craft portion of the festival evolved and changed significantly while the festival was on the Toronto Islands. It was first noted in the 1968 festival program that craftspeople were invited to come and demonstrate. Potters and wood carvers actually worked in front of audience members and demonstrated their handiwork in that way. By 1973 crafters had to apply to be at the festival, and they brought with them significant set-ups, such as glass-blowing kilns, potter's wheels, and hand-powered lathes. Luthiers and other instrument makers were naturally a popular attraction for a musical-minded audience. By the late 70s, a number of the craftspeople were conducting hands-on workshops and educational sessions for interested audience members. Some were participatory; some were instructional discussions; and some were demonstrations.

o o o

Government grants became important to the budgets of both the festival and its outreach activities. In 1975 the Government of Ontario instituted its first lottery, called Wintario. The goal of the Ontario Lottery Corporation was to fund community recreational events and projects with the proceeds of this first offering. Naturally Mariposa, and especially Mariposa in the Schools, fit that model perfectly. The Ontario Arts Council also began to issue funds to Mariposa to help with administrative costs. Ticket pricing alone could not sustain the festival. This reality was becoming more and more evident, and the board addressed it each year by applying for additional government funding.

A Wintario "matching" grant, where the festival and the government shared the costs, also helped the foundation to publish a book of anecdotes, photos, song lyrics, and a history of the event up to that point. It appeared to be a group effort of numerous volunteers who pulled together an eclectic and uneven picture of the festival. Called *For What Time I Am in this World*, it sold for $15 for hardback and $8.95 for paperback, rather steep prices in the 70s.

o o o

During the halcyon days on the island the festival ran like a well-oiled machine. As many as seventeen committees of volunteers planned, arranged, and managed the staging of the annual festival. Estelle Klein would meet with the area coordinators each year. "She was always trying to find ways to encourage people to do something better," said Ken Whiteley. "She had a group of people she talked to regularly."

Each year, just days before the scheduled opening of the event, electrical contractors and the Bell Telephone Company (there was only one telephone company at the time!) descended on Centre Island and strung their lines. Tents and port-a-potties were delivered to the island at assigned times. Stages that had been stored for the winter were taken out of mothballs and positioned in the island park. Cables, monitors, and scaffolds appeared miraculously. Over three hundred volunteers made the festival spring to life from nothing in but a few dozen hours. Then, only days after the festival was done, there would be no evidence that tens of thousands of people had been there.

Only Estelle Klein as artistic director and three office coordinators drew any salaries — and they were all considered part-time employees at that. The festival offices moved around Toronto in those years: first to 284 Avenue Road, then 329 George Street, 131 Roehampton Avenue, and eventually to an address at 525 Adelaide Street East.

The heavy load of not just programming but also overseeing the entire operation wore on Estelle Klein. By 1976 the years of managing such an enterprise had taken their toll, and while she kept the title of artistic director, she passed on the actual programming decisions to Ken Whiteley. She cited undisclosed illness as her reason for passing the torch. According to Whiteley, Estelle suffered an aneurysm in the late 70s and decided to mentor Ken on the fine points of artistic direction. It boiled down to giving him the phone numbers of performers and seeing what he could work out with each of them.

An experienced — though still young — performer, Ken knew the folk scene inside out. He'd been a member of the Toronto Musicians' Association since he was fourteen. As a multi-instrumentalist with the Original Sloth Band, as a soloist, and as a long-time volunteer or attendee (he'd attended his first Mariposa in 1964 as a teenager), Ken understood the task that he'd been handed. Under Estelle's guidance and with lots of advice, Ken assembled a stellar lineup and organized the artists into concerts and workshops.

Native Peoples' Area, 1978.

Inuit performers in traditional dress.

For the average festivalgoer, the change in artistic leadership was seamless. There were still workshops with themes like "Tunes, Stories and Songs of French Canada," "The Black Influence on Country Music," and "Diverse Banjo Styles." The intellectual side and the popular song melded well.

Steve Goodman, Jackie Washington, Atilogwu Afrika, Michael Cooney, the Friends of Fiddler's Green, Willie Dunn, Penny Lang, Alanis Obomsawin, Sneezy Waters, and David Wilcox (the Canadian one!) made up a small part of an eclectic lineup that reflected all the sub-genres of folk music.

And some of it was pure fun. Michael Cooney recalled one of his workshops with David Bromberg. "David Bromberg was fun," said Cooney in a 2016 interview. "Estelle used to put us together to do silly things, like 'Magic and Malarky,' in which David (who had once been an actual magician) did real magic tricks and I did silly fake ones. The finale was when he brought out his guillotine, chopped a cabbage in half with it, then I put my head in. After showing it to the audience he put down a newspaper to catch my head — the headline read, 'MAGICIAN SLIPS, MAN LOSES HEAD.' To finish up we played a few songs together, David doing the magic on guitar."

In his wonderfully hilarious memoir, Garnet Rogers shares his memories of meeting Utah Phillips and Archie Fisher at the 1977 Mariposa festival. Garnet, who was backing up brother Stan that year, was in a workshop with Archie, who showed Garnet a new style of guitar tuning, among other things. Garnet's recollection gives readers a look at the festival from a performers' point of view and, in particular, a view of Mariposa in that time period. In his words, "giants walked the earth in those days at Mariposa."[6] Indeed. People like Taj Mahal, Blind John Davis, Jean Carignan, David Bromberg, John Allan Cameron, Ramblin' Jack Elliott.... Not to mention Stan Rogers and Garnet Rogers!

Estelle and Ken alternated being in charge of the programming in the late 70s. In 1977 she was back in charge, but in 1978 Ken was listed as the "Artistic Director for 1978" while Estelle was listed under him in the credits as "Artistic Director for the Mariposa Folk Foundation."

In 1978 Ken may have created some magic, or history at least, in the field of children's music. Separately he booked Sharon Hampson, Lois Lilienstein, and Bram Morrison. Each performer was booked for a solo show in the Folkplay (children's) area. Lois was about to release her first solo record that

Taj Mahal.

September. The three had been performing around Toronto and Southern Ontario with Mariposa in the Schools, and all three were veterans of Mariposa. But 1978 at Mariposa was the magic moment: from that point on, the three musicians combined their talents and became a single unit. That year the trio borrowed $20,000 from family and friends to record their first LP as a trio: *One Elephant, Deux Éléphants*. It became the fastest-selling children's record in Canadian history and firmly launched the three performers on a musical path that led to popular television shows (*The Elephant Show* and *Skinnamarink TV*), JUNO Awards, UNICEF ambassadorships, and other honours.

In 1979 Estelle once again absented herself from the programming of the festival. That year she turned things over to Jeanine Hollingshead, who'd previously been an area coordinator. Jeanine, in turn, relied on the advice of Rob Sinclair, who had taken on the job of office manager. Tom Paxton, Stan Rogers, John Hammond, Robert Paquette, Colleen Peterson, and Ken Whiteley were among the entertainers hired. As in 1978, programming looked much the same when one examined the workshop titles and the activities that were offered. Estelle Klein's model seemed to run smoothly with or without her at the helm.

o o o

Something noticeable and troubling about the festival as it neared the end of a decade on Toronto Island was the decline in the audience numbers. Long gone were the days of Lightfoot, Leonard Cohen, or Joni Mitchell playing Mariposa and drawing youthful enthusiasts to the festival. Signs no longer announced that Mariposa was sold out. Perhaps it was a reflection of the musical tastes of younger people. The era of the singer-songwriter was being eclipsed by a more hard-driving and less intellectual style of music. Disco had been around for much of the decade, and punk was rearing its ugly but challenging head. Heavy metal and hard rock were establishing themselves with younger audiences, males in particular. Attitudes were definitely shifting and maybe not so subtly. Folk music — even its most modern forms as seen in the likes of Gordon Lightfoot, Bruce Cockburn, or Stan Rogers — was being marginalized. This shift in the public taste could be seen not only in the decreasing folk record sales but also in decreased attendance at events such as Mariposa. Huge stadium events for acts like Elton John, the Eagles, or Stevie Wonder were taking more and more of the entertainment dollar. But it was what it was, hackneyed though that expression may be. Those in charge of Mariposa steered a course, continuing to aim their ship straight ahead. It may have been brave, it may have been blind, or it may have been stubborn, but whatever the case, the festival stayed true to its roots — pun intended.

CHAPTER SEVEN

The Decline and Near Fall
of the Mariposa Empire

AS THE FESTIVAL ENTERED ITS THIRD DECADE of existence, things were vastly different from what they'd been in 1961 and even from what they'd been in the mid-70s. A few short years made a huge difference in a number of things. The crowds were down; being a "hippie" was passé; the attitudes had changed; the times and musical tastes were very different. Even politics were different — former actor and right-wing icon Ronald Reagan was about to become president of the United States. Folk music was no longer the popular choice of most listeners. It was not even the second choice for many people.

Mitch Podolak and Michael Cooney both agree, looking back, that most of the people who came to folk festivals were not really folk music fans. Mitch calls them "eventers" — people who come more for the overall experience. Michael feels that this was true of Mariposa as well; although he believes it wasn't as true of Mariposa as it was of other festivals since Mariposa drew people all the way from the U.S.

As the festival entered the 1980s, however, it was not drawing audience from either group in anywhere near the numbers it had in the past. So the festival had to alter its game plan. The venue and time of year for the Mariposa Folk Festival changed. Drastically.

In 1980 things in the folk world were not as secure as they'd been a few short years before. Advance ticket sales were so light, diminished from earlier years' numbers, that the board of directors made a radical decision in the early winter that year. They decided that there would be no summer festival

John Prine and David Bromberg.

Stan Rogers.

on the island.[1] Such was the fear that an audience would not show up that Ken Whiteley wryly mused upon the "Mariposa is dead" and "Mariposa is finished" sentiments in his foreword to the (eventual) 1980 program.

But it was Mariposa's twentieth anniversary and the organizers had great ideas to celebrate, whether they actually held a summer event or not. A kick-off party took place at the Brigantine Room at Toronto's Harbourfront Centre, near the foot of Yonge Street. There was cake (of course), a record swap, food, dancing, and Mariposa memorabilia on display.

The second celebratory event was given the elaborate title "20th Century Symphonic Music Folk Roots." David Amram,[2] an American musical jack-of-all-trades who'd played the festival a number of times and who had spread himself across folk, jazz, and Classical genres (and had even scored Hollywood movies!), was hired to conduct forty members of the Toronto Symphony and a group of folk musicians at a concert in legendary Massey Hall. Although the actual performance was amazing, according to attendees, it was played before a disappointing crowd of fewer than five hundred people in a hall that was meant to seat nearly three thousand.

It's unknown who came up with the idea of a "year-round festival" but the idea seemed to take hold with some of the organizers. "Mariposa Mainland" and "Mariposa in the Parks" were two concepts tried with varying degrees of success. Mainland events would be held at Harbourfront while the parks ventures would take place in a variety of city green spaces.

Toronto's Harbourfront complex was a project spawned in the early 70s, where industrial and warehouse spaces along the city's waterfront were converted to performance spaces, art galleries, and tiny specks of parkland. The locale was a good fit for Mariposa folkies and the two organizations co-operated that year to put on not only folk concerts but also dance demonstrations, workshop evenings, and crafts displays. The fact that Mariposa was a non-profit organization meant that it was able to book the Brigantine Room at Harbourfront for free. Tim Harrison usually scheduled one act per week between September and May, as a preview of the festival.

In conjunction with the Toronto Musicians' Association, Mariposa provided nine acoustic performances throughout city parks that summer. This was intended to be a year of laying groundwork for more of that kind of activity although, as it turned out, there was not much appetite for it.

Finally, the Mariposa team decided to hold a festival of sorts in late

September of 1980. The event was labelled the "Mariposa Fall Festival" with the word *folk* excised from the customary title. Although organizers denied that it was in response to a "loud hue and cry" that had gone up when it was announced there'd be no summer festival, Estelle Klein had supposedly come up with the idea of having a fall festival as much as two years prior.

"Estelle had long felt that the festival needed changes in its style, size, and format. While many of us waffled she emphasized that change was needed for growth. She felt that artistically and philosophically we were becoming static — we had grown comfortable with ourselves and were not expanding our horizons," said Daryl Auwai, editor of the 1980 program. "The dictates of economics, a more fragmented market, an energy-conserving public, and stiff competition for the 'disposable' (nice word, eh?) dollar helped underscore the Klein proposal."[3]

Estelle challenged the board and the advisory board to accept new approaches to the festival. Once again she yielded the actual programming to Ken Whiteley. It was a challenge for Ken and a tribute to his skills as an organizer and spokesperson, and as a folk musician, to put on a festival that looked like a typical Mariposa on paper, but in reality was totally different from anything that had been tried before.

Fred Penner, Sandra Beech, Enoch Kent, and Chick Roberts provided entertainment for the kids; Dan Yashinsky told his wonderful stories; the Frantics provided much-needed humour; David Bromberg, Downchild Blues Band, Mendelson Joe, Colin Linden, and Connie Kaldor were some of the performers who were already well known — or getting to be — in music circles. The 1980 festival, nicknamed "City Folk," took place indoors at Harbourfront, on Queen's Quay West, that November. The Brigantine Room, the Loft, Joe's Art Gallery — all part of one building — served as the stages while the café became the children's area. The theatre was used to show films, for some live music, and for the Frantics. As with recent outdoor Mariposa festivals, the stages ran from 11 a.m. until after 7 in the evening. There was something cozy and inviting about heading down to Harbourfront, going in out of the chilly breezes off Lake Ontario, and listening to folk music.

The 1980 festival, perhaps not surprisingly, lost money. Putting a brave face on things, the people in charge of keeping Mariposa going talked positively about leaving the isolation of the island, partnering with all sorts of groups in Toronto, and revitalizing the organization. But all the brave talk didn't make for secure footing either financially or otherwise.

Mariposa was facing a "crisis of spirit," as they called it in their first edition of *Mariposa Notes*. Shutting down the foundation was a real possibility. As a result, the directors convened a public meeting in January of 1981 to invite the folk community to air not only ideas and proposals but also grievances. Approximately a hundred people showed up. As a follow-up the board of directors held a weekend retreat in March to summarize and bring into focus the aims, goals, and future directions of Mariposa. There seemed to be two critical dilemmas: "go big versus go small" and "go pure versus go commercial." Nine goals were laid out for the organization. Many were blue sky, such as developing a Mariposa folk arts centre or becoming a national festival, but some were quite practical (holding a membership drive, offering help to inexperienced artists, producing children's concerts…).

o o o

As Mariposa limped into 1981, again no summer festival was offered that year. There seemed little call for a summer music festival that featured music not being played on the radio. In an effort to keep things alive and ticking on the folk scene, Mariposa did offer memberships, and with those came a newsletter called *Mariposa Notes*. A series of "Mariposa Sundays" family concerts was implemented.

Then, in the spring of 1981, the foundation received an earth-shaking setback. Estelle Klein, who'd been artistic director since 1964, tendered her resignation. Both she and her husband had been having serious health issues, and Estelle felt that she wanted "more time to pursue a wide variety of interests." She wrote a note of thanks to the board of directors, in which she talked of finally being able to look up from festival schedules and "notice the trees and flowers bloom." She intended to visit France, take courses in art history, and attend theatre.

Naturally, there were many tributes directed her way. After all, she was a nationally known figure in the music business. Her creative genius was applauded by the likes of performers David Amram and Enoch Kent. Organizers from other festivals were effusive in their praise as well. When John Prine (eventually) returned to Mariposa for the 1985 festival, he devoted his song "Souvenirs" to Estelle, telling the audience that she'd helped out a lot of performers during her days at the helm of the festival.

Michael Cooney recalled, "I think she was a genius at what she did. She sure worked hard at it. She got good people to handle various departments — Native peoples, crafts, etc. Estelle put all she had into the festival. Every year she'd almost have a breakdown after the weekend, and her husband would drag her off to Greece to recover. All-around great family, I must say."

Mitch Podolak, founder and artistic director of the Winnipeg Folk Festival and the most influential person in spreading folk festivals across this country, was a close friends with Estelle. They had attended the Newport and Philadelphia folk festivals together. "Estelle taught me nearly everything about folk festivals," Mitch has said repeatedly. (Although, in an interview on CBC Radio's *Touch the Earth* in the early 80s, he called Mariposa "dull and boring." Host Sylvia Tyson agreed!)

Gordon Lightfoot called Estelle a "mother hen to a whole lot of kids trying to make it. She offered encouragement and she'd often have get-togethers at her house in Rosedale. She was active in furthering the careers of people like Bonnie Dobson, David Wiffen, and others."

Ken Whiteley, who'd been hired as a musician by Estelle as early as 1969 and who would be mentored by her during his stints as artistic director, was lavish in his praise. "She was very good at connecting people, and exciting musicians with the possibility of the interaction…. She would bring an accordion player from Louisiana and an accordion player from Quebec and get them both excited about meeting each other. By the time they got to the festival they were all psyched and put them on stage together and they would just have a ball. It was this magic meeting of cultures that had things in common but hadn't talked for 150 years, 200 years."[4] Ken also felt that Estelle was somewhat frustrated in the early 80s by the fact that she was unable to roll out her vision of a "year long festival," and that this may have been a factor leading to her withdrawal from Mariposa.

Some spoke of her authoritative manner and used words such as "hard-nosed" and "tough" to describe her, but perhaps that's not such a bad thing. A woman running an important cultural entity — a woman running anything in the 70s, for that matter — had to exude those traits in order to be treated with a proper degree of respect. The simple fact remains that Estelle was a genius at what she did, and she was a major contributor to the musical culture of Canada.

o o o

By early 1982 the powers that be at Mariposa, sensing that July or August outdoor events had lasting appeal, had decided to restart the summer festival. While the sporadic Mariposa Mainland was a modest success and Mariposa in the Schools was going stronger that ever, there was a general feeling that a summer festival was once again viable. Executive director Rob Sinclair made no claims about the vigour of folk music in general, only that "Mariposa is healthy."

Well, some parts of it were, such as Mariposa in the Woods. Basically a folk music camp for adults, it was held in August in Aurora, Ontario, just north of Toronto. Ken Whiteley, Cathy Fink, Grit Laskin, and Michael Cooney were some of the performers who took on the roles of teachers and camp counsellors. Approximately fifty participants were offered workshops, how-to-play instruction, song-and-dance sessions, and — to enhance the camp feeling — swimming, hikes, and "vacation-style fun." The cost ranged from $270 to $360, a very reasonable sum even in the 1980s, as that included meals, rooms, and all program fees.

A festival was organized for June of 1982. The site chosen was at Bathurst and Lakeshore Boulevard, near the old site of Maple Leaf Stadium, where the festival had been hastily rescheduled and held in 1964. (The stadium was long gone, having been demolished in 1968 and replaced by an open park-like area.) Volunteers ratcheted into action once again. Sound equipment was rented; performance space was secured; artists were hired. The lineup, organized this time by Tim Harrison, was quite good: Nancy White, Chris Whiteley and Caitlin Hanford, Bim (Roy Forbes), Ian Tamblyn, Graham Townsend, Valdy, Stringband, Jane Siberry, Stan Rogers, Michael Ondaatje, Connie Kaldor, Figgy Duff, La Bottine Souriante, John Allan Cameron, and folklorist Edith Fowke. For the first time since the festival had left Orillia, the lineup was all-Canadian.

The festival may have been artistically sound, and it brought back a refreshed pool of volunteers, but financially things could hardly have been worse. Gate receipts for the festival itself were abysmal, in part because of the terrible weather that accompanied the actual event. At the annual general meeting for 1982–83, the festival posted an $80,000 net operating loss. The poor ticket sales and overspending on production costs accounted for the deficit. Mariposa in the Schools reported that their program lost $12,000 despite more than two thousand seemingly successful performances over the previous year. Something was obviously amiss. And there could be no festival in 1983.

David Warren, a board member and organizer at the time, qualified that in an interview by saying that there was a small event held at Christie Pits in Toronto that was labelled as a festival — but it was a combination of a small performance and a rummage sale!

o o o

The leadership seemed to be — to put it gently — a little muddled. Rob Sinclair was the executive director looking after day-to-day operations, but who was really in charge of the artistic side of things? Tim Harrison booked the festival and Mainland program; Lanie Melamed and David Kelleher looked after Mariposa in the Woods; Sandy Byer managed Mariposa Sundays; Liz Chappel and Bill Russell were in charge of MITS. But overall there did not seem to be one clear, strong voice as there had been in the days of Estelle Klein. It was a tenuous time for the festival, and Mariposa needed a singular voice, someone who could oversee all aspects of the festival. As a result there was chaos in the organization and highly dangerous deficit numbers despite the renewed enthusiasm and volunteerism that permeated the organization.

The festival — or rather, the foundation — stumbled into 1983. The office on Adelaide Street was reduced to begging for scrap paper, typewriter ribbons, pencils, and erasers. "Any donation in this direction would do a lot toward helping the office to keep down office cost," stated a plea in the winter edition of *Mariposa Notes*. That same issue mentioned Mariposa's first ever house concert and talked about Mariposa's 250 members. However, nowhere in the AGM minutes or the newsletter is there mention of the rancour and turmoil that had developed behind the scenes. Two camps emerged in those years: one struggling to keep the festival going, and the other believing the time had come to put the enterprise out of its misery. It would take a couple of years, but things eventually came to a head on that subject at the 1987 AGM when that discussion was put to a vote. (More on that in chapter 8.)

The most significant loss, if not first to go, was Mariposa in the Schools. While probably the healthiest section of the troubled organization, it was posting a serious deficit though it seemed to run so successfully. What was the explanation?

MITS worked — at least initially — in partnership with the Toronto Musicians' Association. In a "two-for-one" arrangement, if a school purchased one workshop, the union paid for the second. Schools benefited, the musicians benefited, and Mariposa could hope that it was growing an audience for the festival itself. The success of the program cannot be understated. It helped launch and maintain careers for Fred Penner, Eric Nagler, Raffi, and Sharon, Lois & Bram. It gave birth to a whole new genre of children's music that was sophisticated, eclectic, and wide reaching.

And it was all very simple. A performer such as Sandra Beech would arrive at a school, set up her equipment in the gym, and wait for teachers to bring their classes in, as if it were an assembly. Then she'd launch into a concert where she'd not only sing wonderful tunes to which the kids could relate, but she'd get many young pupils up using shakers and percussion instruments to perform along with her. Or a poet like Robert Priest would come to a grade-six classroom, for instance, and teach the students a variety of poetry techniques and styles. It was all wonderfully engaging and subtly educational.

Yet, as in the case of too many divorces, money became an issue between MITS and the Mariposa Folk Foundation. The relationship between the two parts of the organization soured. As MITS worked separately and successfully, the festival itself had fallen on hard times. Mariposa in the Schools received much more in the way of financial grants from government sources than did the actual Mariposa Foundation. Money from the MITS coffers began to be siphoned into the festival activities, much to the dismay of those running the educational side of things. There are unsubstantiated stories of personal finances being involved, with money going from MITS to pay off the festival's huge deficit. It's important to note that no money went into anyone's pockets from MITS — or from the Mariposa Folk Festival, for that matter. The crux of the issue was that MITS funds were used to pay festival debts. From the MITS perception of the partnership, that was unforgiveable. So in 1983 MITS split from the foundation and became its own entity, carrying on the work started by Estelle Klein and others back in 1969. The two organizations continued to share the same name and rely on many of the same musicians, but there was little co-operation in any other way. MITS paid a dollar a year to be able to use the name. In fact, like estranged spouses, the two groups would hear about each other but had little to do with each other over the next several decades in terms of contact. Some old memories lasted a long time. In 2009 MFF president Catherine Brennan and artistic director Mike Hill attended a fortieth anniversary celebration of MITS's long history in Toronto, but there was no renewal of the partnership, nor was there much communication afterwards. Some old memories lasted a long time.

Volunteers and the organizing crew kept Mariposa's activities going throughout the year, perhaps with an eye to having less reliance on the summertime festival. No festival was held in 1983, but in the early months of the winter of 1984 there were dozens of events that could be classified as Mariposa-related: a Mariposa Christmas party in December; a Mariposa birthday party in February; Mariposa Sundays concerts; Mariposa Open House; Mariposa song circles in various members' houses; weekly volunteer nights at the Adelaide Street office; a Mariposa "March Warm-Up" mini-festival; courses in crafts; musical instrument instruction; and folk dances. The festival and foundation still had very real presences in the Toronto arts scene, even if they didn't make the entertainment pages of the *Toronto Star*.

Even better news for Mariposa was that a major corporate sponsor had shown up just when the festival needed one badly. Things began to look up again.

CHAPTER EIGHT
The Barrie Molson Park Years

BARRIE, ONTARIO, IS A CITY OF about 130,000 people situated approximately eighty kilometres north of Toronto. Since the late 70s it has grown exponentially, thanks in large part to commuters who work in Toronto but prefer the less expensive housing of Central Ontario. One of Barrie's major industries in the early 80s was the huge Molson Brewery that sat beside busy Highway 400, the major artery linking Toronto and cottage country to the north. During the 1970s, Molson developed and expanded not only the brewery site but also land to the south, turning the land into a huge park and recreational area. Ever in search of opportunities to sell more of its product, the brewery saw that having space for concerts on site could promote tourism to the area and would further push sales. The Molson executives were on the lookout for opportunities to hold major events that would enable them to sell beer to thousands of people.

Conversely, with Mariposa on shaky financial ground in Toronto, the board of directors and the organizational team were perpetually looking for new sponsors and sources of funding. Private donations and memberships had helped to keep things afloat, but that model was unsustainable. With an accumulated debt of over $140,000 by 1983, the health and continuity of the festival were rather precarious. Debts were owed to staff members who'd been on payroll and to unpaid MITS performers. According to Rob Sinclair, executive director at the time, "the first priority of 1983 was to keep MITS alive regardless of the fate of the Foundation. A second corporation was created so that festival creditors could not access future MITS grants. To legitimize the new organization, especially in the eyes of the Ontario Arts Council, Mariposa had to struggle on: to collapse would have been viewed as a shell game."[1]

Molson had been a corporate sponsor in 1982. Despite the ongoing financial woes — or perhaps ignorant of them — the brewery must have felt there was something to be gained by supporting Mariposa in its attempts to regain a substantial audience. Add together summertime, music, young people, and beer. It seemed like a potentially profitable equation. Meanwhile the festival directors were looking around Greater Toronto to find a suitable place to hold the next festival, but nothing materialized. Earl Bales Park in North York was considered, but that fell through. So executives from Molson met with the Mariposa board of directors in late 1983 with a fairly straightforward proposal: what if the Mariposa Folk Festival became one of the events staged each summer at Molson Park in Barrie?

On the face of things, it made a lot of sense. Barrie was only a short drive north of the city and readily accessible from the highway. The park offered controlled access and necessary amenities, such as water, power, and washrooms. There was room on the huge site to easily accommodate camping, at least half a dozen widely separated stages, food areas, Folkplay (the children's stage), and parking. Barrie was a rapidly expanding city with an arts-friendly vibe, and there was bound to be a solid volunteer base for a music festival. With a corporate sponsor who was willing to foot many of the bills, Mariposa had little to lose. In the words of Lynne Hurry, a long-time Mariposa leader, "In 1984 Molson invited us to Molson Park in Barrie and we jumped at the offer."[2]

The mainstage was big, with a capital B.

Michael Cooney described the scene:

> An aircraft carrier–sized, concrete stage with a chain-link fence in front of it, to keep back the rabble which Rob and the rest were salivating over. I have learned from long experience that if you have 125 people in a room that holds 100, there will be more excitement, and people (and the newspapers) will say, "Huge success! Standing room only! Turned people away!" But if you have five hundred people in a room that holds three thousand, people (and

the newspapers) will say it was a flop. Better to crowd 'em in. The following year was Mariposa's twenty-fifth, and someone else ran it because they really wanted to use the aircraft-carrier stage. So the papers all said, "Too bad so few people came." (Probably the same five thousand people in an area that held twenty-five thousand...)

It's interesting to note that although the financial status of the organization was tenuous, there was still ample support coming from a variety of sources. A number of well-heeled patrons donated to the cause and were thanked in the 1984 program. In that list of people were interesting parties such as the Randall Ferris Foundation. Randy Ferris, the man who'd nursed the festival through the Orillia debacles of 1963 and 1964, seemed to have prospered, and he saw fit to make a donation to the organization twenty years on. Also in that list of patrons is Early Morning Productions, Gordon Lightfoot's office in Toronto. (Lightfoot and Ferris were also thanked individually by the foundation in 1984's "Festival Issue" version of *Mariposa Notes*.) Performers Brian Pickell, Joso Spralja, and Raffi were thanked for having "shepherded Mariposa through the financial abyss of the last two years."[3] Both the Canadian Folk Music Society and the Philadelphia Folksong Society donated money. The Ontario Arts Council, the Municipality of Metropolitan Toronto, the (provincial) Ministry of Citizenship and Culture (through the Wintario lottery), and the City of Toronto were also acknowledged for their ongoing support.

To put on the first festival in Barrie, the organizers pushed to get at least 250 volunteers for the various jobs that needed to be done. Sound, lighting, and audio-recording helpers were easily recruited, but the less glamorous jobs such as parking, security, gate sales, and site construction were filled more sporadically and perhaps less enthusiastically. It is worth noting that volunteerism was, from the beginning, a key to Mariposa success. One of those to come aboard in the Barrie years was the man who eventually became long-time technical director of the festival (and booker at Hugh's Room in Toronto). Citing the fun part and the enjoyment of working with others and experiencing new situations, long-time participant Colin Puffer said, "When I wonder about why volunteers do what they do and question what is in it for them, I think back to my Mariposa roots."

Demonstrating Tibetan rug weaving.

The actual festival, as it took place in 1984, was self-described as a "musical cafeteria with many delicious choices." It was indeed. In many ways, the model for that mid-80s fest was not all that different from what had been set up on Toronto Island in the early 70s or what one could experience when the festival returned to Orillia in the year 2000. It was a good model and did not need much tinkering or change from year to year. Or from decade to decade, as it turned out.

First and foremost were the daytime stages. There, audiences could listen to artists talking about their work and performing in "singarounds" based on themes. "Songs of the Legendary Carter Family" or "Midnight Hour Blues" were examples. Second, there were workshop sessions where participants could reasonably expect half talk, half music, as performers explained songwriting or everything you always wanted to know about the banjo, for example. Third, there were discussion sessions where the audience would be educated on topics like "How to Get People to Sing Along."

Molson Park offered acoustic areas in glades by a small stream, where musicians played without amplification for groups of no more than a hundred people. There was a dance pavilion where one could see demonstrations from cultural groups or learn Québécois step dancing or Morris dancing, or attend clinics on square dance or contredanse. That pavilion even offered programming entitled "After the Concert Dances," where you could dance under the moonlight until 2:00 a.m. or "until you drop."

The family and children's area — also known as Folkplay — was set up as a festival within the festival with not only a performance area but also lots of crafts and priority given to participation for the whole family. The emphasis on crafts was a big part of what made Mariposa different from many other festivals.

The craft area offered the audience opportunity not only to buy the wares that were brought in but also, in many cases, to actually work at making or assembling things. The hands-on experience was important to a number of the crafters and to many of their clients.

Even the camping experience was thoughtfully laid out. Campers were given the option of setting up their tents according to the type of music they liked. Bluegrass Valley, Blues Alley, and Ballad Hollow were three options offered. Depending on your musical taste, you could choose whichever area suited you. In addition, there was a big campfire singaround each night facilitated by Tim Rogers, a Calgary musician.

It's not unique to Mariposa, but the idea of singing along, no matter how talented or skilled one might be, is certainly a big part of the appeal of folk music and folk festivals. Pete Seeger is probably the prime example of a performer who encouraged everyone to join in. Mariposa went one step further. The Sign-Up-and-Sing Hoot Stage granted festivalgoers the chance to get up on stage for their fifteen minutes of fame. The open-mic' concept was not new but became an interesting and popular participatory activity for audience members.

If you have a festival that is sponsored by a beer company and you hold the festival on the beer company's property, it must follow logically that there will be a beer tent. Such was the case. The Order of Good Cheer Pavilion[4] was initially intended to be a drinking spot where one joined in the singing of British pub songs. Musicians such as Jackie Washington were designated hosts. The importance of beer sales to the festival coffers could never be overstated.

Ken Whiteley, an ever-present character in the Mariposa saga, was in charge of a unique venue at the first Molson Park festival. His realm was called the Cabaret Stage, which each evening featured a mainstage act performing in what was described in *Mariposa Notes* as an area akin to a smoky bar. Following the eclectic acts that performed each night, there were late-night jam sessions that gave the audience a taste of something different. Friday was country-themed, Saturday was given over to the blues, and Sunday night featured jazz. At a folk festival no less!

One of the stages was actually on the water, with a small stage built on the edge of a pond. Molson reluctantly agreed to allow it and according to the artistic director, Michael Cooney, it was generally a crowded area and "felt like a success." The atmosphere was the appeal as much as who was on stage.

There was a quiet area called the Ballad Barn where, after 11 p.m., one could listen to fine old ballads and the "real folk songs." There was no curfew on the performance times and the music went on until the late hours each night.

Finally, resident astronomer John Kenny offered something called "Starwalks," where festival patrons could have the opportunity to identify constellations and heavenly objects.

Such was the folk festival experience — Mariposa style — in the mid-1980s. Of course, Mariposa continued to be much more than just the summer festival. Despite the financial crisis in the organization, or perhaps because of it, there were an incredible number of activities going on beyond the festival itself. The volunteers must have been run ragged. The calendar for 1984 included the following: Sunday afternoon family concerts; an "Ontario hoedown"; evening concerts (featuring the likes of Pete Seeger); a *soirée québécoise*; a Halloween party; a Christmas party and dance; volunteer nights every Thursday at the Adelaide Street office; a winter outing at Molson Park; a Mariposa auction sale to raise money; a March "Warm-Up"; an all-night hootenanny; an office open house in May; and the formation of a baseball team made up of volunteers. Beyond all that City of Toronto activity, once again Mariposa in the Woods was held in August in Aurora.

o o o

Artistic direction of the festival was something of a revolving door in the 80s. Tim Harrison, Ken Whiteley, Michael Cooney, Ian Bell, Kate Murphy, Rick Bauer, Drago Maleiner, and Richard Flohil all sat in the artistic director seat. Despite the changing leadership, the festival retained its distinctive vibe and stayed the course, never bowing to pressures from outside to make it into a rock festival or something different from what Mariposa had always been.

After the lack of success Tim Harrison and his helpers faced, performer/board member Michael Cooney was asked to take on the job of putting together the lineup for the 1984 festival. Michael assured the board of directors that he could do it on a small budget, and he did. He claimed that he also learned that "performer fees aren't the big expense — it's travel, housing, food, etc."

The musical attractions were a who's who of the folk world. Among those who played at Mariposa during the Barrie years were Joan Baez, John Prine, Bonnie Raitt, Lyle Lovett, Roger McGuinn (of Byrds fame), Taj Mahal, John Hartford, Arlo Guthrie, Donovan, Tracy Chapman, John Hammond, Don McLean, John Hiatt, Jackson Browne, Loudon Wainwright III, Odetta, Melissa Etheridge, Eric Andersen, and Guy Clark — all international stars. A host of Canada's homegrown talent also appeared: Stephen Fearing, Kate and Anna McGarrigle, Jane Siberry, Garnet Rogers, the Barra MacNeils, Colleen Peterson, La Bottine Souriante, Prairie Oyster, Spirit of the West, Loreena McKennitt, Murray McLauchlan, Eric Nagler, Ian Tyson....

Often the performances and stage personas of these famous musicians can be summed up in one word or phrase by those who were there to experience their shows: Joan Baez — dynamic; John Prine — funny and serious at the same time; Loudon Wainwright III — engaging; Lyle Lovett — aloof and unengaged; Jane Siberry — eccentric; John Hartford — down to earth; Colleen Peterson — sweet; Ian Tyson — "Mr. Grumpy."

As it turned out, the move to Barrie saved the festival for a number of reasons. It provided a secure, permanent home for the summer event, but more than that it provided stability in terms of Mariposa's volunteer base and corporate sponsorship. While the financial wolf was still howling at the door in the mid-80s, things were marginally better than they'd been in ages. Each year the organizers felt confident enough to proceed with the next festival. There would be no repeat of 1981 when holding the festival was deemed impossible.

Morris dancers.

The 1984 festival had drawn about 7,500 people — modest numbers, on par with the very first festival held in Orillia. It did not solve any financial woes.

The 1985 festival was given a theme: "Out of the Past — Into the Future." The festival had been searching for a renewed mandate and that slogan seemed to fit the bill. Fingers were crossed that the event could at least return costs and not add to a growing deficit situation. Ian Bell was the artistic director of the 1985 festival but, for whatever reason, did not take on the task again for 1986. As a result the festival put out an advertisement in its November *Mariposa Notes* calling for applications for the position.

> The position will include planning and implementa-
> tion of the 1986 festival program and liaison with other
> Foundation programs as well as considerable manage-
> ment responsibilities. The successful applicant should
> have a strong background and experience in: folk music
> and folk arts, artistic program planning, demonstrated

management skills, financial control and planning, communication and interpersonal skills, committee coordin-
ation, working with volunteers.

Experience with or aptitude for the following would
also be an asset.

Corporate and government fund-raising, public relations and marketing.

o o o

Rick Bauer was the successful candidate chosen by the board of directors,
but he lasted only one year on the job. Perhaps the wear and tear of working
on an uncertain budget was one factor in limiting his tenure.

"The '85 festival was a landmark for us. It succeeded in re-establishing
the festival as an event to be noticed, it pulled an organization back together,
and I believe we cut our artistic wisdom teeth in the process. Although it
didn't exactly slay the financial wolf in the short term, it did show us how
it is possible to mount a major folk festival in this tough Southern Ontario
cultural zoo without losing our shirt — ever again,"[5] said board member
Rob Sinclair that November as he looked ahead to 1985.

That year's festival was a celebration of the twenty-fifth anniversary of the
event. It was held in late July and welcomed back both Ian Tyson and Sylvia
Tyson, who played the mainstage on Saturday and Friday evenings respectively.
Fans perpetually clamoured for the two to reunite musically, but that was not
to be, at least not at the festival that year. The special anniversary year was dedicated to Estelle Klein, "whose vision, dedication, and strength guided Mariposa
for more than a decade and a half. Mariposa and folk music in Canada owe her
great thanks."[6] Notable performers who helped with the quarter-century festiv-
ities were Murray McLauchlan, the McGarrigle Sisters, Garnet Rogers, Cathy
Fink, John Prine, Marie-Lynn Hammond, and Friends of Fiddler's Green.

The period was not without its drama. The 1986 festival lost $20,000,
despite the solid volunteer base, decent crowds, outstanding artists, and a generally well-run festival site. Worse, there was a $200,000 debt hanging over
the festival and no concrete strategy to pay it off. Grumbling set in among

some who'd been active in the organization, not the least of whom was former artistic director Estelle Klein. The board of directors actually split into two antagonistic sides. Estelle and the group on one side wanted to let Mariposa "die with dignity." Ken Whiteley was among those who sided with Estelle, and as a result, he feels he was blacklisted from the festival until his return in 2007, under a totally new board of directors and artistic director. On the other side were those determined to make the festival work and survive: Lynne Hurry, Rob Sinclair, David Warren, and a determined Ruth Jones-McVeigh, who trekked from her home in Ottawa to face down the naysayers.

Two annual general meetings were held as battle ranks formed among the membership. The first AGM was ruled invalid since insufficient notice was given to members. In those days (before email blasts), notice had to be placed in newspapers, and members had to be warned in writing of such meetings. Lynne Hurry and her supporters not only ensured the first meeting — dominated by the Klein team — was denied credibility but also rallied members who wished to keep the festival afloat and urged them to attend the critical second meeting. At the "real" AGM on January 29, 1987, Rob Sinclair assured the collected membership that the festival had secured funding from Molson for the next five years. Up front, Molson was donating $45,000, which would go a long way to paying down the debt the festival faced.

Sinclair had to explain how that deal had been worked out with Molson. The board of directors would retain artistic control, but the brewery would have a say in bookings for the night concerts. That latter part of the agreement would become a bone of contention in the remaining years at Molson Park. "With the increase in the deficit after the last festival, with a radically changed relationship with Molson or another fun [sic] source, the possibility of mounting another festival was pretty small," said Sinclair, as quoted in the *Ottawa Citizen* (January 29, 1987). We can assume Rob meant fund and not fun!

A vote was taken. Estelle and her cohorts were defeated by a membership vote of 257 to 73. The festival would carry on.

The question remains: what made the one-time director and her friends want to axe the festival and end its very existence? David Warren, while speaking of Estelle in laudatory terms, alluded to the fact that the woman had an oversized ego. "It had been *her* festival, but the big festival at Molson Park was no longer the hippie gathering it had been in the 60s and 70s. Also, the loophole that if you'd been a member of the board of directors you were a member for life became an issue with Estelle and her influential ex–board members." The huge and growing debt — which had seen employees go unpaid and volunteer dollars sucked in — was a key factor. David Warren also contends that the rancour over the redirection of MITS funds played a part in the contention that the festival should be discontinued.

o o o

Despite all of the drama, the festival survived and looked like it would continue — for one more year anyway. Drago Maleiner, the temporary artistic leader in 1988, probably summed up the situation with Mariposa best when he stated in the program guide, "It's been an exciting year trying to walk the line between art and solvency." In many ways that statement sums up the entire history of the Mariposa Folk Festival.

In its struggle to stay alive and maintain its dignity, Mariposa was party to a couple of helpful initiatives during these years that would have long-term influence. The number of folk festivals in Canada had grown, thanks largely to the success and example of Mariposa throughout the 60s and 70s. In October of 1985 organizers from all across Canada met in Toronto and agreed to form a national organization called the Canadian Council of Folk Festivals. Their objectives were laid out by David Warren, who acted as Mariposa's official representative:

- to establish a unified voice for folk music festivals
- to gain recognition for folk music as a legitimate art form with various levels of government
- to join with the literary, visual, and other performing arts in the ongoing development of Canadian culture
- to establish a national office
- to facilitate national and international tours
- to assist folk festivals in stabilizing their precarious financial situations by actively pursuing the establishment of ongoing operating grants from the federal government.

Charter members of the new organization were Calgary Folk Festival, Edmonton Folk Festival, Festival of Friends (Hamilton), Home County

Festival (London), Mariposa, Northwind Folk Festival (Toronto), Summerfolk (Owen Sound), Vancouver Folk Festival, and Winnipeg Folk Festival.

In 1986 Mariposa was involved in the formation of another such group: the Ontario Council of Folk Festivals. The OCFF held its first conference in November of 1987 to bring together representatives from the growing list of Ontario folk festivals. The networking, sharing of knowledge, and general sense of purpose were evident from the beginning. All the member festivals gained from the experience.[7]

At that time Mariposa also began a partnership with the Flying Cloud Folk Club in Toronto. The Flying Cloud was a small but enthusiastic group of folk music fans in the city who used a variety of venues, such as the Traditions Room at the Spadina Hotel or the Tranzac Club, to put on weekly shows. For a while the festival sponsored two evenings a month. Some well-known names and up-and-coming artists played those shows, with Mariposa's name often attached to them. For instance, La Bottine Souriante, Friends of Fiddler's Green, Enoch Kent, and Eileen McGann were featured acts who also played the festival at one time or another.

The dedicated people who sat on the board of directors through the late 80s attempted many things that would either grow the festival or at least sustain what was there. In 1986 they tried a small initiative called "Mariposa on the Streets," a fundraising activity. That September musicians busked on the streets of Toronto, capping the day off with a four-hour mini festival at the Hotel Isabella patio. Over sixty performers donated their time and money for the project.

Each year the directors went on a weekend retreat to, as Lynne Hurry said, "talk about, argue about, dream about and create a strategic plan to direct the operations of the Foundation."[8] The foundation managed to hire two staff members in 1986 and 1987 and pay for them through government grants. By 1988 two more workers were hired and paid with Mariposa's own resources. The board also set a goal to reach one thousand members by 1991; as of April 1990 they had reached nine hundred.

In an interesting nod to the past, Mariposa returned to Orillia for a one-night stand. The "Orillia–Mariposa Homecoming Benefit" took place in March of 1990. Sylvia Tyson and Garnet Rogers headed a small contingent of folkies who played at the Orillia Opera House. Unfortunately the evening's good feeling and great music did not sell out and the City of Orillia, MFF's co-sponsor, reported a loss of $1,500.

One of the rather innocuous things that was tried was altering the name, and hopefully the appeal of the festival. The "folk" part was dropped in favour of just calling it the Mariposa Festival. At various times the advertising and the program itself had labelled the event as the Festival of Roots Music. Did it widen the appeal? Did that draw in new audiences? There's no way to know. The full "Mariposa Folk Festival" did not reappear in promotions until the event returned to Orillia in 2000.

Electric guitars figured prominently in advertising. That kind of marketing imagery may or may not have changed perceptions of what was in store at the actual event.

In 1990, the final year at Molson Park, the festival was the subject of the documentary film *Mariposa: Under a Stormy Sky*. It was definitely an apt title as the '90 festival was inundated with rain. (The title was really a tip of the hat to one of that year's headliners, Daniel Lanois, and his song "Under the Stormy Sky.") It either rained or threatened to rain for the entire weekend. Rainy weekends had been more common than not during the Molson Park years. According to Lynne Hurry, pre-festival ticket sales for the 1990 festival approached thirteen thousand but gate sales were nil because of the unseasonable cold and wet weather. The film painted a definitive picture of the state of folk music and Mariposa as it entered a new decade. It also showed what it's like to run a summer festival in a lousy climate.

The film — broadcast on CTV and Bravo! in 1991 — gave a realistic picture of a rainy summer festival: lots of ponchos, Birkenstock sandals, tie-dyed clothing, marijuana, backpacks, cut-off jean shorts. But it also included archival footage of Mariposa festivals from the 60s, an interesting interview with a very young Estelle Klein, and insightful comments from the likes of Murray McLauchlan and that year's artistic director Richard Flohil. Said Estelle, "Folk music is the real thing. It's not something produced for the marketplace, for the most part. It's something that's come out of ordinary situations and ordinary people."

Sylvia Tyson, Joan Baez, Richie Havens, Murray McLauchlan, Emmylou Harris, Daniel Lanois, and others were shown in the movie, live either in archival material or from the festival in 1990. Murray McLauchlan's stage patter and one song were about the fall of the Berlin Wall that year. That certainly showed the contemporary relevance of folk music. Cindy Lee Berryhill talked about her background growing up and mixing the music of

Pete Seeger with that of the Buffalo Springfield. Buddy Guy talked of "passing it along," the *it* being the music he'd learned from blues masters. Richard Flohil, a blues aficionado if ever there was one, discussed how blues was accepted in the folk idiom and how even the electric guitar blues of Muddy Waters and Howlin' Wolf were all right in the folk setting.

It was interesting that Flohil, when interviewed for the film, commented, "We don't call it the Mariposa *Folk* Festival — haven't for years," and that they had stopped using "the F-word to drop the limitations that people see on that." Daniel Lanois added, "Folk music is changing all the time. It doesn't mean you're sitting on the back porch with a banjo anymore." Perhaps most telling of all was Murray McLauchlan's comment that "folk festivals have become the major place to hear alternative music. It's an alternative to pop radio; an alternative to pop culture … which is becoming more and more restrictive."[9] Perhaps Murray was being prescient, as the same thing could be said in 2017.

o o o

Stormy could also be used to describe the relationship between Mariposa and Molson. By 1990 the lure of a folk festival had been eclipsed by the likes of the more raucous and more profitable rock extravaganzas like Edgefest. First held in 1987 at Molson Park, the initial Edgefest had welcomed crowds of 25,000 people to hear the likes of Blue Rodeo and Teenage Head. In 1988 even more young people turned up to hear rockers 54-40. The event sold out. Then in 1989 Sarah McLachlan and the Tragically Hip drew such crowds that Highway 400 was jammed both north- and southbound near Barrie. The writing was on the wall. The folkies drew only modest crowds that included children and an older demographic. Rock acts and rock festivals guaranteed more ticket and beer sales. The different kinds of events didn't conflict in any particular way; there were plenty of dates open for all sorts of big events. But a seismic shift had occurred in taste and style, and Molson wanted to hitch their wagon to the more profitable and more popular rock shows. "Molson's offered to pay the entire fee for the Moody Blues," explained Mariposa's lawyer David Warren, "if we'd been willing to book rock acts." Mariposa chose to hire precious few of those, such as Jackson Browne in 1989.

"Jackson Browne is my Mariposa horror story," said artistic director Richard Flohil many years later. "His was a drive-by performance. He wasn't interested in any of the other acts. His most recent record had tanked so he wasn't a draw. His management had no idea what a folk festival was. They had the final say on who the opening acts could be and it wasn't until we mentioned Odetta that they agreed to the lineup." Browne, a high-profile activist and environmentalist, let his two tour buses run most of the day as they sat waiting for his performance. When asked to turn off the diesel-spewing vehicles, Browne's touring team members were belligerent and resistant to the request. They did eventually turn off the buses but only after quite an argument.

Molson was also turning its attention to other sectors of the beer-buying public. Sports, which had always been their major advertising focus, took precedence. Folk music was too laid back and not sexy enough, and a festival that wouldn't allow the suds company to hire who their executives wanted to hire was no longer all that welcome. M.J. Kelly, the 1990 executive director, admitted in the program that year, "Mariposa is still thought of as the 'love-in' that stereotypes the sixties." That was definitely not what Molson Breweries saw as a potential beer-buying market.

A chill had entered the relationship, and both sides were casting their eyes elsewhere. Molson's chose to end their sponsorship. Carrying a deficit of $45,000 Mariposa was once again homeless, thrown to the curb.

o o o

Throughout the "Barrie years" Mariposa had remained a de facto Toronto institution. The offices were on Adelaide Street, Lavinia Avenue, or Dundas Street East; the board of directors, hired staff, and most of the organizing leaders were Torontonians; the City of Toronto was a continual sponsor throughout the years, despite the fact that the event ran in Barrie. In newspaper reports and correspondence of many kinds, the festival was usually referred to as a "Toronto" festival. And perhaps most interestingly of all Mariposa had not been particularly embraced by the City of Barrie. A look at the programs from the late 80s notes that most of the supporters and friends of the festival were Torontonians and Toronto businesses. People and businesses in Orillia seemed to have as much or more of a presence on those lists as any Barrie residents, companies, or the municipality itself.

Mariposa in the Park was a Toronto follow-up to the actual event at Barrie. On a warm and sunny afternoon, as opposed to the cool and rainy festival of 1990, the mini festival was held at Christie Pits, a ballpark on Bloor Street. A mainstage featured Bob Snider, Brent Titcomb, and the Hard Rock Miners. The one workshop stage included acts like singer-songwriter Marie-Lynn Hammond, Rick Fielding, Tony Quarrington, Celtic musicians Brean Derg Muc, and the ever-popular Bobby Watt. While the one-day mini festival was not a huge and crowded affair, it was a sign that Mariposa could still be viable in Toronto despite fluctuating musical tastes and the competition for the entertainment dollar.

A "Mariposa Showcase in the Park" was presented at York University's gorgeous Glendon Campus in late July. Mariposa Country Dances were held bimonthly through the winter at St. George the Martyr church on John Street in downtown Toronto. Mariposa continued to sponsor Flying Cloud acts such as Robin Williamson (of Incredible String Band fame) and Guy Carawan at places throughout the city, such as the Tranzac Club, the Bathurst Street Theatre, and Trinity-St. Paul's Church. The festival had a very real and active presence in Toronto's cultural scene.

Don Cullen, who had been a constant presence on the Toronto folk scene since the 1950s, made a valuable contribution to Mariposa at this time. Don — best known as a member of Wayne and Shuster's television comedy troupe — had started a coffee house in the 50s called the Bohemian Embassy. It was there in the early 60s that he'd presented a very young Bob Dylan, Gordon Lightfoot, and a young lady from Chatham named Sylvia Fricker. Don also coached a teenage Mitch Podolak on the finer points of managing folkies. He managed to revive the Bohemian Embassy concept in 1990 and set up shop on Queen Street West. He dedicated every Wednesday and Friday to folk music with the name "Mariposa" featured on the Wednesdays. Norm Hacking and Rick Fielding were two of the artists featured. It was yet another case of Mariposa being a presence in Toronto.[10]

It took very little to convince everyone that Mariposa could and should be back in the city.

CHAPTER NINE
A Return to Toronto in the 90s

THE MARIPOSA INTERLUDE IN BARRIE had been full of ups and downs. With the disastrous late-June weather conditions of the 1990 festival and a lack of enthusiasm from the big corporate sponsor, the directors began to look for a new home. The current situation was simply untenable. Toronto was their first choice, and a number of venues were investigated. Then, in the midst of their search, Max Beck, the general manager of Ontario Place, approached the festival and asked if they'd consider setting up shop there, holding the festival early in September.

Ontario Place was pretty well a summer-only entertainment and exhibition complex taking up a sizable portion of the Toronto waterfront just west of the downtown core. Opened in 1971, it was operated by the Government of Ontario. Its most distinctive feature was a geodesic dome that housed the world's first permanent IMAX movie theatre. Interspersed on the grounds were restaurants, shops, a marina, and futuristic-looking pods that housed exhibits. As the complex evolved in the 1980s, the goal of the place was to draw in families for attractions such as the gigantic movie theatre and kid-friendly rides and activities.

With plenty of space — thirty-nine hectares — of mixed parkland and structures, Ontario Place had lots to offer. Power, washrooms, stages, ample parking, and access to transit made it a good place to put on a festival of any kind. With a Labour Day closing to the general public, Mariposa during that first week of September 1991 seemed like a good option. After some chilly late winter walks braving the icy winds off Lake Ontario, the board of directors and key coordinators agreed that a festival early in the off-season would be suitable. September 6–8 was booked and planning began for the first Mariposa back in Toronto since 1983.

Returning to Toronto had both advantages and disadvantages. Being back in the city, the potential audience was huge. Even if the majority were not interested in folk music, there'd be enough folkies to draw a decent crowd and plenty of others who would come because they enjoyed "events." There was a big population from which to draw volunteers. The offices — newly moved to Dundas Street East — were more convenient for the day-to-day operations and preparations. With so many extracurricular Mariposa-related events going on throughout the city core (dances, concerts, jams, etc.) the festival was very much alive and ticking in the minds of folk fans. The Toronto Transit Commission, with its network of buses, subways, and streetcars, made it possible for everyone to get to Mariposa events in the city without too much problem.

On the other hand, by the early 90s there were many, many more choices for where people could spend their entertainment dollars. The bar scene offered live music of every kind. Summer events in Toronto included long-established events like the Canadian National Exhibition (with marquee musical acts playing evening concerts). Tourist attractions like the CN Tower offered laser tag and other activities. The newly opened SkyDome (eventually renamed the Rogers Centre) was a major draw, offering sports for people to spend their money on. Street festivals, such as Caribana and the Beaches Jazz Festival, the Toronto International Film Festival (then called the "Festival of Festivals"), and myriad other events were scattered throughout the city and called for people to come and spend, spend, spend. Mariposa would be just another voice in an ever-increasing and noisy crowd. In recalling the competition between the modest folk festival and the increasingly popular film festival, Richard Flohil reflected on the disparity: "The Toronto media wets itself when the film festival is in town."

An interesting act that year, for a number of reasons, was the Barenaked Ladies. The band had sold an amazing number of cassette tapes of their songs, gaining some fame in the year or so before they landed a record. At Mariposa they played concerts and workshops to enthusiastic crowds. It was also noted in the program that Steven Page was the son of former Mariposa board president Vic Page.

Artistic directors of festivals are inundated with requests from performers, agents, and managers. Most ADs do not have the time to listen or respond to the plethora of submissions. Richard Flohil was the artistic director at the time and recalled that he never hired based on submitted tapes or records, with one exception in 1991. He received a host of audition tapes and listened to nearly all of them. Only two stood out and Richard hired both acts. One was a total disaster. The other was his most astute discovery: a young singer from a performing arts school in Buffalo, New York, named Ani DiFranco. The songwriter's career took off almost immediately. It was nice to know that Mariposa had given Ani a kick-start in the music business. It was not the first or last time such a thing had happened. One could argue that Joni Mitchell and Buffy Sainte-Marie had received the same kind of career boosts; although, in all honesty these talented people would have become big stars whether or not they'd ever played the festival. (Similarly, in the early 2000s, Sarah Harmer, Serena Ryder, Dala, Tegan and Sara, Matt Andersen, and Old Man Luedecke all played Mariposa before they were well known. The same arguments could be made for those acts.)

John Prine, Ramblin' Jack Elliott, Dave Van Ronk, Lucinda Williams, Guy Clark, Pops Staples, Jane Siberry, John Gorka, and Los Lobos were also on the bill in '91. They played on stages that were spread thinly across the massive Ontario Place grounds. The mainstage was the Forum, where audiences sat in a 360-degree circle around the stage. The crafts area took up much of the eastern part of the grounds while over at the western end, beyond the Cinesphere, were the Lakeside Stage, the Island Club, and the (not so) Secret Stage. The Dance Stage and Folkplay were rather idiosyncratically placed close to the retired warship HMCS *Haida*, a floating museum and historical site. It wouldn't have been friendly for the Mariposa organizers to ask their hosts to move the old navy destroyer!

Despite luring in eighteen thousand attendees over the weekend, Mariposa incurred another huge deficit by losing $37,000.

o o o

By the spring of 1992, a rather solid lineup was in place for the next Mariposa, again slated for Ontario Place. "One of the world's great guitarists" (as he was billed), Amos Garrett, was scheduled. Highly respected songwriters Bill Morrissey, Joe Ely, and homegrown Shirley Eikhard were booked. Unique acts were on the roster, performers like the Flying Bulgar Klezmer Band, jazz saxophonist James Galloway, Jackson Delta and Holy Smoke, a trio of street buskers. Ani DiFranco made a return appearance as did Tom Paxton.

That year the festival was scheduled for mid-June. The Du Maurier Downtown Jazz Festival was scheduled at the same time, so the two events held a joint free preview concert at Nathan Phillips Square, in front of Toronto's City Hall. It was an example of the creative forces behind both organizations trying to co-operate and share resources at a time when live folk and jazz music were struggling against the live rock acts, video screens, and disc-jockey mentality that so many city venues pursued.

Flohil admitted that his programming was "engraved in cheese." In the spring '92 issue of *Mariposa Notes*, he explained to the membership and any other readers what his job entailed.

> The main job is to reflect as wide a range of roots/folk music as possible. The AD has to choose artists who are superb in their respective fields, make sure that there is an exciting mix of new performers and proven veterans, make sure there are "box office" draws to bring a wider range of people to our event, that we have a significant number of Canadian artists involved, and that there is a fair mix of male and female performers.[1]

Weather, as was so often the case, played a particularly key role in the 1992 festival. June in Toronto is generally a pleasant and warm time of year with average temperatures of around seventeen degrees Celsius. Baseball season is in full swing, the leaves are on the trees, and the flowers are in bloom. Torontonians are happy to put thoughts of winter behind them, with the possible exception of professional hockey dragging on — though that never seems to happen with the Leafs. That year, however, a freak cold front hit Southern Ontario on the weekend of the festival and the thermometer plunged to a chilly six degrees. It was the coldest June since weather records began to be kept in the late nineteenth century. Hardly an enticing climate for an outdoor music festival! Brief wisps of snow swirled in the air at Ontario Place — already a chilly spot when the winds blew off Lake Ontario. Peggy Seeger, one of the performers, suffered from Raynaud's disease, an affliction where cold makes the fingers go ghostly white and causes pain and irritation. She had to be brought something to warm her hands every ten minutes — hardly something to be expected mid-June!

Despite the cold weather, the music was indeed memorable. Tom Paxton's witty version of "Wasn't That a Party" went over well. Eric Weissberg, one of the world's best (and best-known) banjo pickers, was part of a group called the New Blue Velvet Band at that time. His banjo stylings amazed the chilled audiences, who must have wondered how he moved his fingers so quickly in such icy weather. Tom Russell's rendition of "Navajo Rug," a song he wrote with Ian Tyson, had the romantics in the audience on the verge of tears.

Despite the great music, the chilly conditions meant that crowds for the "summer" event were, to say the least, underwhelming. Overly positive estimates put the crowd at about eight thousand. And because of such awful weather, the festival once again found itself in dire straits financially. The *Toronto Star* reported that the accumulated debt by the winter of 1993 was nearly $125,000.

One casualty of the frosty '92 festival was Richard Flohil. The organization was no longer able to pay him for his time and expertise, so rather than settle for the mere $2,000 salary he was offered for the following year, Richard resigned. A long-time mover and shaker in numerous capacities, Flohil would remain interested in Mariposa despite no longer being a part of the organizing team.

o o o

Credit must be given to the staff, the board of directors, and the volunteers in those lean years. The people who had been hired to work at the festival offices were never confident that their jobs would last for any length of time. The board struggled to keep the festival's vision and mandate, but it was responsible for fiduciary matters that would make any sane person lose sleep. Volunteers carried on their roles at evening events throughout the year, never sure whether there'd be another summer festival or not.

But there was. And for the 1993 festival a fresh approach was mixed with the historic. Olympic Island was once again the site for Mariposa's daytime activities. It had been fourteen years since the festival had taken place on the Toronto Islands, yet that was a place full of the fond memories so many people had of Mariposa and its halcyon days in the 70s. A decision was made to take advantage of that nostalgia and the comfort of a familiar setting. The innovative part of the '93 equation was the decision to put the nighttime activities in downtown, indoor venues. Workshops would take place during the day on the island and evening concerts would be held in (mostly) Queen Street West clubs — the Cameron House, the El Mocambo, the Free Times Café, the Horseshoe Tavern, the Rivoli, the Santa Fe, and the Tranzac Club.

Something else was new for the '93 version of the festival. A CD was produced using tracks donated by artists playing the festival. From the quaintly traditional "The Shores of Newfoundland/Traveller's Reel" by Tip Splinter to the world music of Giovanni Ruiz, the record gave a sense of what kind of music could be found at the festival and it was a way to "take the festival home with you." Valdy, Stephen Fearing, Anne Lederman, James Keelaghan, and Bob Snider also contributed recordings for the sixteen-song collection. This was a new initiative and generated some revenue for the foundation. Most of the festivals from that point on produced interesting and eclectic compilations like this.

The artistic lineup was an eclectic mix, as usual. David Warren headed a committee that worked at programming the stages with time-honoured folkies like Oscar Brand, the Travellers, and Guy Carawan; singer-songwriters like Roy Forbes, Marie-Lynn Hammond, Stephen Fearing, Willie P. Bennett, Chris Smither, Valdy, and Sylvia Tyson; blues artists like Colin Linden; plus the usual blend of Celtic, old-time traditional, bluegrass, and spoken word.

o o o

The 1994 festival continued the island-in-the-day and clubs-at-night format. Rain once again plagued the event. Lynne Hurry felt that the inadequate publicity and promotion that year also played a role in leaving the festival in deficit.

The festival, even well into the 90s, had retained a bit of the "hippie vibe" that one usually associates with the Summer of Love or Woodstock. The unmistakable perfume of marijuana smoke could always be found somewhere at the festival. Colin Puffer, who served as production manager and eventually as technical director of the festival, recalled an unspoken policy that almost went awry.

> When I was first involved with the Festival, there was always somebody in charge of "band favours" ... wink, wink. So, there was someone on site who could provide a joint if required. One Sunday evening, as we were tearing down stages, the unofficial Special Performer Services guy came up to me and asked, in a panicky voice, "Hey, Colin, have you seen my little green bag?!"
>
> "No," I replied. "What was in it which makes you so concerned?"
>
> "Three thousand bucks worth of weed," was the answer. [All figures in 1990s values.]
>
> The bag was nowhere to be found.
>
> Flash forward six months and I am talking to a U.S.-based agent about bringing a U.S.-based act back to Toronto for a Mariposa show. And she said, "You'll never believe this story."
>
> Her long-haired, patchouli-smelling act had driven back to the U.S. and passed over the Peace Bridge in their ancient VW van filled with guitars and luggage with nary a word from the dudes in the dark aviator glasses at the border. It was only when they started unpacking the van at home that they realized that they had a little green bag in the back seat.
>
> "Is this yours?" queried performer A.
>
> "Never seen it before," said performer B.
>
> Can you imagine how believable that would have been in the Sheriff Mike Amico shack? (Actually Mike Amico, who I remember from [Buffalo TV's] *Eyewitness News*, may not have been the drug bust dude at the time.)

Bottom line is that those un-named performers did enjoy their band favours and came back to Toronto, played a highly successful Mariposa gig, and reimbursed the Special Performer Services guy for the $3,000 bucks worth of his weed that they had smoked.

Gotta love those folkies.

The music, of course, was the most important thing offered at the festival, and Mariposa boasted the full gamut of styles and genres to experience. During the daytime on the island you could find great songwriting from the likes of Lynn Miles or Ani DiFranco or take in a Toronto Blues Society showcase. Concerts from the likes of Great Big Sea, Moxy Frivous, and Big Rude Jake drew people of all ages and tastes over to the multiple stages set up on Olympic Island. For the evening shows, your Mariposa ticket got you into venues like the Rivoli, the El Mocambo, and the Horseshoe Tavern to hear great musicians like Lori Yates, Dan Whiteley, Alpha Yaya Diallo, or Jackie Washington.

Jackie Washington was a throwback to a bygone era. The grandson of a slave who'd escaped to Canada via the underground railway, Jackie was a self-taught musician who was as funny as he was musical despite the fact that he'd lived and performed in an era when black people suffered the abuses of extreme prejudice and bigotry. At one point in the 50s, Jack (as he was called then) worked at menial jobs such as washroom attendant and shining shoes at Toronto racetracks. With the folk revival, he'd found a niche and ended up playing Mariposa a number of times.

o o o

The highlight of the 1995 festival was a tribute to Gordon Lightfoot. The weekend-long salute focused on the legendary songwriter's contribution to folk music and to Mariposa specifically. Several of the workshops during the day on Olympic Island were Lightfoot-themed: "I'm Not Sayin' — Story Songs in the Lightfoot Tradition" was one and "Travel Songs in the Lightfoot Tradition" was another. Artists as varied in style as the Travellers, Murray McLauchlan, Steve Gillette and Cindy Mangsen, and Eugene Ripper gave their takes on the great man's music. Gordon was honoured with the presentation of a plaque that read, "On the occasion of the 35th Anniversary Mariposa Folk Festival. The Mariposa Folk Festival honours Gordon Lightfoot, one of it's [sic] earliest and best loved performers. August 10–13, 1995."

The festival took place once again in a combination of outdoor and indoor venues. This decision was the result of a brave attempt to marry the traditional folk music setting with a growing trend among younger people to habituate the clubs and bars of the city core, most notably in the Queen West Village section of downtown Toronto. Was it successful? There are too many factors at play to definitively say whether or not the experiment succeeded. Attendance was so-so; press and television attention was negligible. The bottom line was that after two years of combining afternoon workshops on the island with "pub crawl" evenings, the festival was in debt to the tune of $70,000. The status quo was untenable.

CHAPTER TEN
Chasing Mariposa

AT THAT TIME — 1995 — the organization was led by Lynne Hurry, a determined, creative, and intelligent woman who knew how to get things done. Her support system included the likes of David Warren, Bob Stevens, Randi Fratkin, Dave Lang, Jeff Weed, Gord Magrill, Catherine Brennan, and others who had either been around the Mariposa scene for years or who had recently jumped in full bore. They were faced with a $100,000 debt that they hoped to eliminate through a fundraising campaign. With the summer event no longer viable in Toronto, and iffy anywhere else, once again a new home needed to be found.

David Warren believes it was Lynne who came up with the innovative concept that all hoped would save Mariposa. Using the spider plant as its model, the plan was that Mariposa could set up in several new locations throughout Ontario, put down roots (pun intended!), and then move on to set up a new festival elsewhere. Each location would then have its own organization, volunteers, and operational plan to sustain a summer roots festival in each location. That was the strategy, anyhow. On top of that, each community would be willing to put up money to encourage the endeavour and bring tourism to the region. It was, above all, a way for Mariposa to mount at least one festival with little money.

Three communities picked up on Lynne's idea.

In Orillia the festival benefited from the efforts of Tim Lauer, Gord Ball, and Don Evans, the so-called "three wise men." This trio of community-minded individuals had volunteered and worked at the local Arts for Peace festival. They knew a lot about music and a little bit about festivals. Arts for Peace was a one-day gathering in Orillia with music, crafts, dancing around the maypole, and other throwbacks to hippiedom. Gord and Don also played together in a musical troupe called ALEX, the Folk Band.

Tim, a life-long Orillia resident, had been ten years old when the first Mariposa festival took place in 1961, but as a friend of Ruth Jones's son Bruce, Tim had watched that first incarnation from a unique perspective. He'd been privy to the hectic action around the Jones household that first summer.

> An assortment of oddly dressed artists and musicians … just seemed to appear, sleep on one of the many couches, and then disappear. Ruth was the attraction I believe. She was outgoing, welcoming, and tolerant and would be the ring leader in issuing carte blanche invitations to this crew of motley artists.[1]

Tim attended one of the festivals in Barrie but for most of the 1990s he had watched from afar as the festival's popularity and success ebbed and flowed. He knew of the soul searching that was taking place in the Mariposa leadership as they tried to find a home, if not direction.

One day in 1995 while listening to a CBC radio item about the festival — which may or may not have mentioned Lynne's spider plant analogy — Tim was struck by an idea. He went to Don and Gord with the proposition that they consider "chasing Mariposa," the idea being to bring it back to its origins. (Gord admitted that his initial vision of an Orillia Mariposa would probably end up as a "dressed-up" Arts for Peace event.) It was decided that Tim would approach someone on the board of the foundation. He first spoke with Ann Smiley, who in turn introduced him to Lynne Hurry. Lynne had been president of the festival and its standard-bearer for the previous decade. "I am sure she fought through some pretty significant board, volunteer, and personal burnout to keep it alive," Tim said.[2]

A meeting was set up with several Mariposa board members from Toronto and an eager group of folks from Orillia. They met at Geneva Park, a YMCA conference centre just outside of town, and considered a number of scenarios.

"With negotiations lumbering along with Lynne as our main liaison and with the Orillia group blithely pushing ahead with visions of sole [proprietor] in mind, the franchise idea somehow seemed to fade away,"[3] said Lauer.

The two groups seemed to be at odds on a final decision. Lynne and the Mariposa board still wanted to grant "franchises" to several towns around the province; the Orillia team really wanted to bring the festival back to town but as the one and only incarnation.

Hurry reported that the Toronto group was impressed with Orillia's presentation. That seemed like good news and the implication — at least to Tim, Gord, and Don — was that the Sunshine City would be selected as the one and only host for 1996. A meeting was arranged with the mayor of Orillia, the local media, and interested community members.

Tim recalled the uncomfortable and somewhat confusing situation.

> The "three wise men" as we called ourselves — for what reason I don't recall — arranged that Lynne would meet the press, politicians, and others. I know that we were all assuming that Lynne was coming to announce that in 1996 there would be *one* Mariposa Folk Festival and it would be held in the one place it belonged, and that was at home in Orillia. This is the vision we had sold to the media and municipal council in advance of Lynne's visit.[4]

The three wise men invited Lynne to Orillia to make an announcement to the city that Mariposa would be coming home. So, it was something of a shock when Lynne, over coffee at a local bistro that morning, dropped a bomb. She reported that the MFF board had decided that, after much discussion, Orillia would receive one of three franchises — the others going to Bracebridge and to Cobourg. Three spider plant offshoots, if you will. Tim, Gord, and Don were floored by this announcement. The trio had sold the idea of Mariposa returning exclusively to its rightful home to the Orillia community.

On the spot, they asked Lynne not to mention the franchise idea and to simply communicate that she was in Orillia to look around, meet the interested parties, and then go back to her board in Toronto to make a decision.

"We also gave her the ultimatum that she could go back to the MFF and tell them that we were not interested unless it was Orillia and only Orillia," said Tim.

As Lynne toured the city that day meeting the press and creating a buzz in town, only the three not-so-wise guys knew that there was now very little chance of Orillia once again becoming home to the Mariposa Folk Festival.

Lynne went back to her board and in a short time they made a decision that they would set up festivals in both Bracebridge and Cobourg. Not Orillia. Tim feels that it was a case of a desperate and shell-shocked MFF board hedging their bets and planting multiple seeds, hoping that at least one would flower in the long term. The all-or-nothing approach "spooked a skittish board that was not interested in dealing with some rubes up-province who were already attempting to tell them what was going to happen to their festival, a festival that some of them had been coddling for decades."[5] Putting all the money on Orillia was too risky at that point.

An announcement was made in Orillia that the potential organizers had turned down Mariposa, citing the fact that Orillia would not be the exclusive home. The media supported the three wise men and their decision — sort of.

The *Globe and Mail* picked up on this drama and published an article that claimed the people who'd kicked Mariposa out of Orillia in 1964 were still around and still didn't want the festival back. Gord Ball wrote a letter to the editor (actually to both the *Globe* and the local *Packet and Times*) that countered what the paper had said.

> We are writing on behalf of the good folk in Orillia who recently tried to bring the Mariposa Folk Festival back home to its place of origin. In a poorly researched article by the *Globe and Mail*'s H.J. Kirchhoff about the future of Mariposa (Feb. 21), the author quotes an anonymous source ... who explained the failure of the Foundation to strike a deal with Orillia by claiming that "the people who kicked Mariposa out in the sixties are still around ... and they still don't want us there." A simple phone call to the people involved in Orillia (the *Globe and Mail* has our numbers) would have revealed that the return of the Mariposa Folk Festival was unanimously endorsed by Orillia City

Council, supported by the Downtown Management Board, and encouraged by the Parks and Recreation Department, the Chamber of Commerce, and the *Orillia Packet and Times* (February 25, 1996). Meetings which were organized to evaluate local grass roots support were well attended and spirited.… (signed) Tim Lauer, Don Evans, Gordon Ball for "The Mariposa Sour Grapes Committee."[6]

o o o

Leaving Orillia behind (for the moment), the Mariposa directors turned their focus on Bracebridge, one of the larger towns in cottage country north of Toronto. The community there enthusiastically embraced the idea of staging a Mariposa in Muskoka. In Lynne's words, "with two groups working toward the festival, one from Bracebridge and the other from Toronto, we faced blizzards, ice-storms, and traffic jams to get together and make the festival happen.… I was very impressed at the way the Bracebridge team took on the myriad of tasks needed."[7]

Mariposa had, for years, used the acronym FOG to describe the Festival Organizing Group. That year there was a B-FOG and a T-FOG (B as in Bracebridge; T as in Toronto) and each group brought expertise, skills, and effort to the process of putting on the summer festival. There was a hierarchy in each group, with members tasked with overseeing a different aspect of the festival. All worked together to help guarantee the smooth running of the event. The chair coordinated and set the agenda of meetings; a site coordinator would take care that all was prepared and managed on the grounds at Annie Williams Park; the production coordinator looked after technical needs and security; the hospitality leads managed accreditation and food for the performers; retail coordinators managed the craft section and food vendors for the public; volunteer coordinators rounded up and handled the dozens of people who offered to help out for free. There also had to be leaders who were willing to take on the tasks required in terms of marketing, fundraising, and publicity. And that was just the B-FOG team!

Bob Stevens led a group from T-FOG that looked after the finances, the artistic selection (made by a four-person committee that year), the beer garden, and the complex stage, sound, and electrical needs of the festival. For the first time in ten years, though, the foundation was working without paid staff and without a permanent office. Manny Drukier kindly loaned some space over the Idler Pub, but much of the work went on in people's homes. What equipment the festival owned ended up cluttering the apartments and houses of volunteers.

Meanwhile the spider plant was also working to put down roots in a different community to the east of Toronto. Cobourg is a pristine town sitting on the shores of Lake Ontario, about a hundred kilometres east of the city. While planning for "Mariposa in Muskoka" was going on, so was "Mariposa Festival By-the-Shore" at Cobourg. Again, two FOG groups laboured on the effort. The Toronto group was virtually the same — and kudos to them for taking on two festivals in one summer! Later FOG groups can only shake their heads and marvel at the work that must have involved. The Town of Cobourg seemed very supportive, just as Bracebridge was, and the mayor of Cobourg even travelled to the July festival in Bracebridge to both show support and to scope out the way things were run.

The Muskoka festival was a one-day affair in one of the town parks. The Festival Stage and the Olympic Stage were for workshops, and the mainstage saw concerts by the likes of Long John Baldry, Jackson Delta, and Friends of Fiddler's Green. A small acoustic stage was set aside for "local heroes," some of the region's musicians eager for their fifteen minutes of fame.

Cobourg's festival ran for two days, more in keeping with the Mariposa tradition. Part of the town's support was to get the whole community downtown with a sidewalk sale on the Saturday. A mistake — in director David Warren's opinion — was that so many concerts and workshops were offered for free that there was really no incentive for Cobourg's population to buy tickets. A third of the shows were conducted in areas where no admission was required.

The event in Bracebridge was a moderate success. The town — whose July and August population swells extensively with the nearby summer-cottage residents — embraced and supported Mariposa in Muskoka. The municipality saw potential for it to draw people to town. Cobourg, on the other hand, was less successful. Despite a remarkable artistic lineup (Tom Russell, Gillian Welch and David Rawlings, Martha

Wainwright, Fred Eaglesmith, Sylvia Tyson), the coffers were empty by the end of the weekend. Providing so much free music had come back to bite the organizers. Both towns had been warned that there could be as much as a $10,000 loss, but when it happened, the council in Cobourg interpreted it as a "betrayal" by MFF.

Coincidentally that weekend, there was a huge drug bust on the ferry that ran daily across Lake Ontario between Cobourg and Rochester, New York. Dope? Hippies? Mariposa? Guess who got blamed by some of the citizens for the illegal substance activity — although there was absolutely no connection! The spider plant in Cobourg withered and died almost immediately. It was a sad chapter in the Mariposa saga. Cobourg, one of the most beautiful and peaceful towns in Canada, would have been a grand locale for Mariposa (or a spin-off folk festival), but, alas, circumstances and misunderstandings conspired to end the venture after only one attempt.

Regardless of the repudiation by Cobourg, the Bracebridge festival seemed to have struck a chord. The town and B-FOG team were ready to take on the task once again for 1997. The featured performers were Moxy Frühvous, Lennie Gallant, Ray Wiley Hubbard, and the Burns Sisters. Perennial Mariposans Ian Bell, Anne Lederman, and Eric Nagler also played the various stages.

Foundation president Doug Baker's message in the summer issue of *Mariposa Notes* was forthright and informative. Doug spoke eloquently about the challenges faced by the organization and paid homage to the contributions of outgoing board president Lynne Hurry. He also mentioned the sizable archive collection housed in the Parkdale district of Toronto, where the foundation's new offices were also located. Doug later recalled,

> Those involved were a unique community, always changing, that came together with a love of Mariposa and its own culture. For a small example, the Mariposa folks from the 1990's all call each other by first and last names to this day: John Sladek, Dave Lang, Colin Puffer, Lynne Hurry, Bob Stevens, Mike Booth, David Warren, and on and on. The reason being, we all learned each other's names off our name tags. I loved it. I was hooked and I've worked every year since.

Lennie Gallant, Bracebridge.

Such sentiments are not uncommon among Mariposa volunteers through the decades.

The Woods was still an attraction for the hard-core folkies and was offered at Lake Rosseau College, July 31–August 5, 1997. The Laskins continued to manage it and even offered scholarships that year.

o o o

There was a great deal going on in the late 90s in the folk world. Some of it succeeded and some did not. Once the only folk festival in Canada, by its thirty-sixth birthday Mariposa had been joined by a host of other festivals that showcased the same musical genre and hired from the same pool of artists: Sunfest and Home County in London; Northern Lights in Sudbury; Collingwood's Celtic Continuum; Upper Canada Village Folk Fest at

Morrisburg; All Folks Festival and the Celtic Festival in Kingston; Hillside in Guelph; Stewart Park Festival in Perth; Blue Skies Music Festival near Sharbot Lake; Caledon Folk Festival; Mill Race in Cambridge; the Celtic Roots Festival at Goderich; Summerfolk Music and Crafts Festival in Owen Sound; the Ottawa Folk Festival; Eaglewood Folk Festival at Pefferlaw; Western Manitoulin Folk Fair; Peterborough Folk Festival; Festival by the Lake in Tillsonburg; the Wye Marsh Festival in Midland; and Octoberfolk in Brantford. This meant there was direct competition within the folk genre for the same potential audience. Some of the festivals were even on the same weekend as Mariposa! While some hard-core folkies were able to attend several festivals each year, it's probably safe to assume that most chose the one closest to home. Where one may have made Mariposa on the Toronto Islands a destination in the late 60s or early 70s, now if someone lived in Southwestern Ontario or Eastern Ontario it was no longer necessary to make the long and ultimately expensive trip and overnight stay to attend a folk festival. There was choice within close proximity.

That analysis doesn't take into consideration other kinds of competition, like the proliferation of new music, huge rock festivals, and tour extravaganzas that were sold to the public constantly. Live music was thriving in the city's bars and clubs. The demographics had changed too. Looking at photos of the Mariposa festivals at Innis Lake or Toronto Island, the crowd was predominantly made up of young people in their teens and twenties. By the 1990s, a good portion of that crowd had aged, and with that brought new mindsets to their entertainment purchases. Many had children, and the scenes at Bracebridge and Cobourg reflected an older audience with kids in tow. By the fiftieth anniversary of Mariposa, the audience survey told organizers that the largest demographic was between forty and sixty years old. Photos from that year confirm the shifting age demography.

Beyond all that, with computers and digitization becoming ever more prevalent, it was becoming possible to produce one's own records in one's own home and then get them out to the public. It was the early days of home CD production, but this possibility was becoming reality sooner than record companies expected.

Nevertheless, in the aftermath of the second Muskoka festival, there was optimism at the new Toronto Mariposa office on Queen Street West. The organization was looking forward to a third festival in Bracebridge. The

Stephen Fearing and Eric Andersen in Parkdale, 1999.

festival had actually made some money that year. With infrastructure in place, volunteers eager to go, and lots of support from both communities, there was little reason to doubt that Mariposa had found another home for the annual summer festival.

The 1998 festival in Bracebridge, as with the previous two, was heartily supported by the town. Its Parks and Recreation department took on a lot of the heavy lifting to put together the festival. Perhaps too much so, in that many of the volunteers and paid staff were worn out by the time the last festival in Bracebridge was presented. The festival came off without major hitches in 1998. In the words of former president Doug Baker, it was an "artistic success," which in Mariposa-speak means that it did not make money! The CD for that year's festival, produced by Baker, was a magical mix, with artists such as Stephen Fearing, Cindy Church, Clay Tyson, Long John Baldry, and Larry Gowan.

Festival chair Neil Hutchinson was optimistic about the next year, stating in the '98 program, "We've now become a festival with a reputation for great people, great venue and great music. We now hope to increase our reach — to build a year-round culture of folk music in Muskoka, and a solid foundation of artists, fans and volunteers who will come back year after year. Thanks for your help, thanks for coming and SEE YOU NEXT YEAR!" There was, however, little left in the tank for another Muskoka Mariposa. The disconnect of an organization still anchored in Toronto and a hard-working team nearly two hundred kilometres away proved unsustainable, even though the enthusiasts in the city and in Muskoka still wanted things to happen.

As the twentieth century neared an end, it looked as though Mariposa might simply fade away. Not that the enthusiasm wasn't still there. Those involved and those who came to the events were generally happy with the product, and despite the dwindling number of patrons, they thoroughly enjoyed the experiences. But without the resources to mount a full festival, in 1999 the organizers partnered with the Parkdale community to put on a "free event" at the Parkdale Village Town Square. Many of the components of a typical Mariposa were there: spoken word, crafts, children's activities, a beer garden, and a truly stellar musical lineup: Eric Andersen, Blackie and the Rodeo Kings, Rita Chiarelli, the Arrogant Worms, John Prince and a Piece of the Rock. But it was not really a traditional Mariposa Folk Festival. There wasn't even an official program! The *Parkdale Villager*, a neighbourhood newspaper, published the artistic lineup with some incomplete biographies interspersed with community news, restaurant ads, and a committee report on the local "ecomomic" [*sic*] development. Richard Flohil, an interested observer only, confirmed that the event was not really a Mariposa festival and "not much of an entertainment experience at all."

The Mariposa Folk Foundation, despite the energy still being expended by the likes of Bob Stevens and Lynne Hurry, seemed to have run out of steam, and this attempt at keeping the festival in front of Torontonians is no discredit to the volunteers, organizers, or the board of directors who struggled to keep the ship afloat. Nor is this commentary meant to cast aspersions on the citizens and organizers in Parkdale. The atmosphere in the city was just no longer conducive to mounting a three-day festival. There was little interest generated, and it's doubtful that the public was even aware that Mariposa still existed. Musical tastes had evolved over the years, and laid-back acoustic material could barely be heard amid the clamour of hard rock, hip hop, and electronic music. Mariposa's style of music was nowhere to be found on the radio, either AM or FM. Great shows like Sylvia Tyson's *Touch the Earth*, Murray McLauchlan's *Swinging on a Star,* or Joe Lewis's *Folk Music and*

Folkways were as passé as TV shows like *Hootenanny* or Oscar Brand's *Let's Sing Out*. Youth who'd been brought up on a diet of punk, heavy metal, and hip hop could not relate to what they saw as their parents' — or worse, their *grandparents'* — music. Even some hard-core folkies were turning their backs on what was being more commonly called roots or Americana.

Michael Cooney, very much a traditional singer, expressed that sentiment well. "I'm fond of saying, 'If you know who wrote it, it's not a folk song.' Many singer-songwriters are just low-budget pop singers, working the 'folk circuit' hoping to make it big. And I believe it shows."

Mariposa in the 90s had been on the road, moving from Barrie to Toronto to Bracebridge and Cobourg and back to Toronto. Being on the road can be a good thing. Just read your Jack Kerouac, Paul Theroux, or Bill Bryson. The foundation gave its festival customers a varied yet familiar experience. The organizers and volunteers had fun as often as they also had sleepless nights. The foundation itself probably learned a lesson or two on the financial, organizational, and artistic sides of things.

CHAPTER ELEVEN
Welcome Home Mariposa

IN LATE 1999* TIM LAUER CALLED Lynne Hurry to express Orillia's continuing interest in bringing the festival back. A second series of discussions ensued. This time things were more fruitful. No bridges had been burned following the failure to woo MFF in 1996, so the relationship between the Orillia group and the board of directors in Toronto was a positive one.

Gord, Tim, and Don were dispatched to Toronto. They met with MFF representatives at David Warren's Forest Hill residence. Lynne Hurry, Don Cullen, Sid Dolgay, David Warren, and representatives from the Parkdale business association listened to the Orillians give a presentation. (Tim and Don now had the added cachet of being city councillors.) This time they came to an agreement, and it was determined that Orillia would stage a singular Mariposa Folk Festival.

With the goal of bringing the festival home, in October of 1999 a new non-profit organization, Festival Orillia, was incorporated. Better known as FestO, the group's mission was "to stage an annual summer folk music festival in Orillia under the name of the Mariposa Folk Festival." A board of directors was set up.

A formal three-year agreement was signed between the two organizations and a date was set for the fortieth anniversary. It would take place at Orillia's Tudhope Park July 7–9, 2000.

---

* It was at this point in the story that I, Michael Hill, the author, became involved as a volunteer with Mariposa. As a result you may notice the use of first person pronouns (me and I) from time to time in the narrative.

If Lauer, Ball, and Evans were the heroic threesome to bring back the festival to its birthplace, then Gerry Hawes became an important fourth part of that team. Gerry, who was known around Orillia for his work as an executive assistant to local Member of Parliament Paul DeVillers, was recruited as the chair. "There I was, a guy who had never served as president of a not-for-profit corporation and had never attended Mariposa Folk Festival or any music festival for that matter, now serving as president of a fledgling not-for-profit that would produce Mariposa Folk Festival in Orillia in eight short months."

Gerry's skill set included organizing events and knowing how to navigate the political scene. The FestO board included Dennis Ball, Murray Cleland, Ted Duncan, Bruce Jones (Ruth's son), Marian Parrott, Margaret Pomeroy, Rick Purcell, and Joanna Rolland. The three wise men were also key members, of course. There was some discussion about the size and scope of the event, but according to Gord Ball, it was Gerry Hawes who pressed for the idea that they "go big or go home." Gerry realized right from the start that this wasn't just another local community event but a festival with provincial, national, and even international importance. It would require an amount of deliberation well beyond what goes into local planning.

Gerry Hawes described it in this way:

> I saw the pairing of FestO and MFF as a perfect marriage. MFF needed an enthusiastic partner with access to enthusiastic and dedicated volunteers, community support, and funding in order to realize their goal of reinvigorating the festival, and FestO needed the artistic, technical, and production expertise of MFF in order to successfully stage the big and complex event. The easy part was that everyone agreed on the same goal. We all wanted a successful return of the Mariposa Folk Festival to Orillia, and to cement a good future for the festival there. The hard part was the politics of getting the two organizations, and their respective volunteers, working together — which needed to happen very quickly. This challenge got sticky and difficult at times, and it burned up a lot of energy between Lynne and me, often involving difficult conversations.

Gerry Hawes credited Tim Lauer for being the "pragmatic contributor" who took the lead in making sure the site was within the Orillia city boundaries.[1]

Although not stated in the document, there was an assumption that the two groups — MFF and FestO — would eventually merge. As a starting point each board placed two members on the other's board of directors. It was also agreed that the festival organizing group would include representatives from both FestO and MFF — but "will report to FestO."

Not that everything went smoothly, by any means. Tim Lauer likens it to the Orillia group being in a boat and reaching a hand out to the drowning festival in Toronto. Desperate though they were, members of the Toronto group weren't quite sure if the Orillians were worthy of saving their beloved festival! During the negotiations Don Evans threatened to resign a number of times. Doug Baker remains emphatic that Orillia did not *save* Mariposa and maintains that the festival arrived back in its birthplace as a fully formed entity, a festival that had been started in Orillia but had been nurtured and developed into a national icon elsewhere.

At one point, early in the spring of 2000, a prominent member of the FestO board approached president Gerry Hawes with the news that the Mariposa logo and name were not properly registered. That person suggested absconding with the name and logo and cutting loose the group from Toronto. Gerry was alarmed that someone could and might do such an underhanded thing, and he quickly let Lynne Hurry know that the name and logo might not be fully protected. She made immediate calls to ensure the foundation was not undermined. Such was the state of affairs between certain members of FestO and MFF.

Gerry held Mariposa Folk Foundation president Lynne Hurry in high esteem.

> [Lynne] was big in stature and personality. She was impressively tall, well put together, authoritative, and direct, at the same time as having a warm, almost motherly personality. She and I hit it off right away. Lynne loved and believed in Mariposa Folk Festival and wanted nothing more than to see it get back onto a firm foundation.

Lynne Hurry, president of MFF.

Planning for the 2000 festival started with zero dollars in the bank and hopes that government grants, sponsorships, and ticket sales would make up the difference. The Mariposa Folk Foundation had virtually no money in their Toronto bank account, and on top of that they were carrying approximately $55,000 in old debt on their books. Most of that was later written off. FestO also had absolutely no money, as it was a new organization. The festival was about to land in Orillia, as the old song goes, "on a wing and a prayer."

Planning for the festival finally commenced in the winter of 1999–2000. Robert Hawke took on the daunting job of site manager; Dave MacMillan agreed to look after stages and sound; Ken McMullen contributed his talents as financial controller. Many of the Mariposa board members and the key electrical personnel, Jeff Weed and Jim Carnrite, were instrumental in the park layout. (Much of the set-up was determined by how easily the electricians could get power to the various stages!) Colin Puffer held the role of technical director and, as such, organized the stage managers, rented the musical backline (drums, keyboards, and amplifiers) and lent years of experience to what was really a brand new enterprise. As Gord Ball put it, they were all flying by the seat of their pants. Artistic selection was headed by Randi Fratkin, a Toronto volunteer. A newspaper ad in Orillia enticed hundreds of volunteers. Revival of the mother of Canadian festivals was on its way.

The Philadelphia Folk Festival chipped in by sending some money. Their philanthropic donation of $3,000 U.S. amounted to about $5,000 Canadian when the exchange rate was applied. In addition, a small group of advisors came north to lend assistance and guidance. An interesting sideline to that story is that when the Philly contingent arrived in Orillia days before the festival, they intended to camp, as they did every year at the Philadelphia Folk Festival. Unfortunately, no permission had been granted for camping in Tudhope Park except for the electrical crew, who were also doubling as "overnight security." After some hasty negotiation, the City of Orillia allowed the Philly visitors to camp in what was labelled "the VIP parking" area. It was the genesis of camping at the festival site — a long and not-so-smooth process that developed over the following years.

A Mariposa in the City was held in Parkdale in June of 2000 — programmed by Mark Crowe. (Bob Stevens had been behind the staging of several of the other city events.) Hoping to once again draw a crowd of about five thousand souls, the Parkdale Business Improvement Association thought they might bring some new life and class to a community that for too long had suffered a reputation for being the hangout of druggies and street prostitutes. The PBIA anted up nearly $20,000 to pay for the one-day event. Gord Ball and Tim Lauer walked Queen Street that day and saw that the small event posed no threat to the much bigger one being planned in Orillia. There was no artistic crossover and very little, if any, competition for the folk audience. The planning in Orillia was on a much larger scale and dwarfed the Parkdale effort.

Shortly after the festival in Orillia, Gerry and Lynne made the decision to end any future small Mariposa events in Parkdale. They thought that the small Toronto gathering was a diversion from the main goal of restoring Mariposa to its former glory. Plus, there was the fact that both events drew on many of the same volunteers, and to have the two events so close on the calendar was a drain on the human resources.

July 7, 2000, seemed to arrive in a hurry. A crowd of perhaps a thousand people gathered on the grassy slope in front of the mainstage at Tudhope Park that Friday afternoon. They'd seen the advertised lineup, and they were eager to take in a variety of musical offerings. The Travellers and Oscar Brand were there representing the "old days." Guitar whiz Chris Smither and the "full-throated" quintet Tanglefoot were recognizable names to true folkies. Stacey Earle, the Burns Sisters, and Heartbreak Hill brought a considerable country flavour while Moxy Früvous and the Arrogant Worms appealed to a wide cross-section of the ticket buyers with their eclectic and original music. Topping the bill was, of course, hometown hero Gordon Lightfoot. His name alone guaranteed a considerable crowd.

Three exhausted men looked at each other and smiled. The grins said it all. "We did it," said site coordinator Robert Hawke as he surveyed the hundreds of people sitting in front of him, "We actually did it!"

He was talking to Tim Lauer, who had led the festival organizing group, and me. I was one of Robert's deputies that year. We had met and planned through the winter months to bring together security needs, fencing, signs, tables, tents, chairs, traffic barriers, and all the minutiae of the event's infrastructure. From a seed of an idea, the group that was responsible for bringing the festival back to life in Orillia had accomplished their goal and the participants were rightly proud of their accomplishment. They had begged, borrowed, and ... paid for equipment. Snow fencing to mark the boundaries came from the local Ministry of Highways storage yard, free of charge as long as the organizers picked it up and returned it. Tables and chairs were rented from the local rent-all companies. Picnic tables were borrowed from the Huronia Regional Centre, Orillia's mental institution. (The tables couldn't be picked up until late Friday afternoon and had to be returned after midnight on Sunday night!) The mainstage was trucked fifty kilometres from Midland by Dave MacMillan. Generators came all the way from Toronto, as did a lot of the electrical cables and necessities, thanks to Jeff Weed and Jim Carnrite. Dressing rooms were RVs supplied by an area dealer. Items such as coffee urns and plywood scraps were brought from the homes of volunteers. Side stages and ticket booths were constructed off-site, disassembled, trucked to the site at Tudhope Park, and then reassembled in the days prior to the festival.

Thomas Wolfe wrote, "You can't go home again." In this case, he was wrong. There were outsiders who had said it couldn't be done. Many observers, both in the folk music community and in the entertainment business in general, felt that Wolfe's sentiment held true for the Mariposa Folk Festival. Gary Cristall, co-founder of the Vancouver Folk Festival, was quoted in the *Globe and Mail* a few weeks before Mariposa made its second debut in Orillia. "Folk music is about identity, and I don't know what Mariposa's identity is," he said. Looking at a lineup that included Oscar Brand, the Travellers, and headliner Gordon Lightfoot, Cristall felt that other folk gatherings — the Winnipeg Folk Festival, specifically — were doing a better job of bringing in the younger generation. Gary's comments were based on what he'd seen over the last few years of the 90s and may have had some validity, but each festival year brings a different lineup and flavour.

The same *Globe* article quoted the esteemed Estelle Klein, her opinions along the same lines. "It distresses me to go to folk festivals and see so much grey hair. Folk music needs a mix of audiences. If there's no mix, it's dying...."

The sentiments seemed off the mark. It was as if these people were not even giving Mariposa a chance to recapture the magic. How could they pretend to know who would come to the festival now that it had a new home?

Estelle chose not to make the trek to Orillia for the first Mariposa there since 1963. "I don't like sentimentality. I'm not given to nostalgia. I take what's important from the past and move on" (as quoted in the *Globe and Mail*, June 22, 2000).

Gerry Hawes recalled two interesting incidents from that first festival back in Orillia.

> In fact, I had never been to any music festival before in my life.... I had no first-hand context for what it would be like. By around 7:30 p.m. on the opening Friday evening there were perhaps fifteen hundred people seated in front of the mainstage (approximately several hundred more were in the pub tent). I was fretting because, as a newbie, this did not seem to me like much of a crowd for the vaunted Mariposa Folk Festival. Lynne Hurry was late arriving to the festival, and when she did get there I met her in the parking lot behind the mainstage. I led her around the stage to view the size of the audience and, when she saw it she explained, "Holy mackerel, I haven't seen a Friday night this big in years!" Needless to say, I felt very relieved after that.

On Sunday night Gordon Lightfoot was the headliner to close out the festival. Hawes, who was in his thirties at the time, met Gord backstage for the first time and introduced himself as "Gerry Hawes, president of FestO." Gordon was somewhat shocked, as he initially thought that Gerry was *Jerry* Hawes — Gerry's uncle — who'd grown up on the same street as Gordon in the 1940s. Lightfoot was taken aback at the thought that Jerry (with a J) hadn't aged over that time span. After they'd sorted out that relationship and connection, the two had a pleasant conversation with Lightfoot recalling Gerry's uncle, mother, and the old gang from Harvey Street.

o o o

There were a number of interesting parallels between the 2000 festival and the very first one that had happened back in 1961. First of all, as in 1961, there were many volunteers and even key organizers who, like the crew working under Ruth Jones and Pete McGarvey, knew little about putting on such a show. Raw amateurs were in uncharted territory and somehow managed to find success both times. Gord Ball's "flying by the seat of their pants" comment was apt in both instances.

As in 1961 the local community responded positively. The times had changed, there was little fear that there'd be a recurrence of the 1963 fiasco, save for a few aging and grumbling curmudgeons. One bone of contention with a few local residents was that with the festival set up inside Tudhope Park, the short section of the Trans Canada walking and biking trail that goes through the park had to be sealed off. On Saturday afternoon of the 2000 festival, Ted Duncan and I happened to be standing near one of the festival fences that blocked the trail. Signs had been posted farther down the trail to indicate that access was prohibited. A man and his family approached the snow fence barrier and began to curse and swear at the two volunteers, seething and nearly foaming at the mouth because he couldn't get through.

"I'm going to call the mayor and get this event banned," he said.

I replied, "If you want to wait a minute, I'll go get the mayor. He's having a beer over in the pub tent."

The irate Orillian, having set a very questionable example for his children, turned around and left, mumbling to himself.

The organizers in 1961 had improvised and pulled off a magnificent show by using basic common sense, some local expertise, a small amount of money, and lots of enthusiasm. That was true of the 2000 festival as well. The leaders in both cases were enterprising, intelligent people who knew how to get the job done. Tim Lauer and Robert Hawke knew how to get the best out of their volunteer crews, just as Ruth Jones and Pete McGarvey had done forty years earlier.

There were even parallels in the choice of the artistic lineup. In 1961 the Travellers had been the big name on stage. By 2000 the Travellers were no longer the same people (except for Jerry Gray) nor were they at the top of their game, but they appeared to raucous audience support. Gordon Lightfoot headlined the new millennium's first festival. Oscar Brand returned to Mariposa as one of the familiar names. Both men had played the second festival in 1962, so in some ways it was a homecoming

But a deeper examination of the lineups shows that Mariposa, while taking its peripatetic journey around Southern Ontario, had really not changed all that much in terms of its artistic vision. In 1961 the team of organizers handling the choices for the lineup set up their roster to include primarily Canadian musicians. It had been made up of well-known acts (the Travellers, Ian and Sylvia, Bonnie Dobson), francophone acts (Jean Carignan, Jacques Labrecque), bluegrass (the York County Boys), fiddlers (Al Cherney), children's concerts, and spoken word. As the festival evolved over its long history, the integrity of the artistic vision never deviated much from its origins. Estelle Klein had added more of a world music, blues, and Aboriginal presence later in the 60s and early 70s, and each successive artistic director followed her model. Looking at the 2000 lineup, it had well-known acts (Lightfoot, Moxy Früvous, Chris Smither), francophone acts (Entourloupe), bluegrass (Heartbreak Hill), fiddlers (April Verch), children's performers (Richard Knechtel, Magoo), and spoken word (Ted Roberts). Mariposa had come a long way down through the years but its original artistic vision remained.

One hiccup in the roster came with the selection of Oscar Brand. As a veteran of many Mariposas over the years, Oscar was a fine choice even as an eighty-year-old. What was problematic about his inclusion was the way he was hired. Someone from the original 1960s organizing committee approached Oscar with a promise of a fairly high fee. Randi Fratkin, the artistic director, had a budget of only $40,000 for the entire lineup and had to revisit Oscar's offer. He graciously accepted the lesser amount offered by Randi, understanding the festival's tenuous finances. It was then left to Gerry Hawes to let the person who'd made the unauthorized offer know that he had no authority to represent Mariposa.

Pat World, one of the volunteers whose job was to drive the artists around town, was charmed by Oscar's down-to-earth likeability. As Pat was driving Oscar from the performer hotel to the site, they passed Orillia's Goodwill store. "Oh, stop. I love Goodwill!" said Oscar. Pat turned the van around and waited while Oscar went inside to peruse the second-hand clothing. Sure enough, the old folkie came back out with a new (to him) jean jacket, smiling at the great bargain he'd found.

o o o

It seemed that everyone involved in the move north from Toronto was pleased with what they'd managed to pull off. In the simplest terms, the festival had been a success; people had come in the thousands; the artistic offerings were terrific; and a volunteer base had been established.

Doug Baker, who'd been president of MFF in the late 90s, looked at the move to Orillia this way:

> I think there was a great culture shift within Mariposa in 2000. The extant organizers and volunteers looked at it as moving to another site, for a little while or for a long time didn't matter. The allegiance and love was for Mariposa. Some Orillia folks looked at it as more of an acquisition or corporate takeover. Their primary allegiance and love is to Orillia. Don't get me wrong. Orillia is a beautiful town, and Tudhope Park is a perfect site for a festival. But musicians have been heard to say that a lifetime career ambition/desire/dream was to play some day at Mariposa. Sorry, but I have never heard any say it was to play in Orillia. And that iconic, mythical Mariposa was formed in the '60s and '70s.

Perhaps it's a logical evolution: difficult birth; wild, adventurous, travelling youth; acquisition of some age and wisdom; and then settling down permanently in a pretty place by the shores of a lake with some financial security.

CHAPTER TWELVE
Mariposa Gets Its Mojo Back

THE FIRST FESTIVAL BACK IN ORILLIA in 2000 was a success, plain and simple. The organization had succeeded in re-establishing its presence as a true summer festival. Mariposa had been dwindling away to nothing. The organizers, especially the board of directors, were still enthusiastic but somewhat burnt-out, and the volunteer base had practically vanished prior to the move. The audience had nearly evaporated as well in Toronto. The 2000 festival had revived the moribund event and transformed it from a Parkdale sideshow into what the festival had been decades before — a three-day event with multiple stages with a vibrant atmosphere. It seemed proper that the Mariposa Folk Festival should set up there once again and this time, with any luck, stay. What remained to be seen was if it could sustain itself in its hometown.

Thanks in a large part to Gordon Lightfoot's presence as the headline performer, the 2000 festival made approximately $40,000 that year.[1] Both the MFF and FestO boards were rightly proud of their accomplishment. The experiment to bring the festival home had worked out. The phoenix had not only risen from the ashes but come home to roost.

The challenge ahead was to build upon and sustain that initial success. Those familiar with successful folk festivals across the country — Winnipeg, Vancouver, Calgary, Edmonton, Lunenburg, Hillside, Owen Sound, London — could see that there was one significant factor in the success of their enterprises. Each community had embraced the festival in its midst. Businesses came on board as sponsors, the volunteers returned annually, the

municipalities saw the value in the festivals, and above all the wider community saw these events as their own. Mariposa needed Orillia to adopt it.
As the planners looked ahead to 2001, it appeared that the Orillia area was
feeling warm and fuzzy about the festival, but the proof would come in the
form of an even larger crowd attending the second festival back in town.

In the autumn of 2000 things looked good to the directors of both
FestO in Orillia and Mariposa in Toronto. There was money in the bank, at
least for the festival and the Orillia part of things.[2] The volunteer base from
the local community seemed solid; the site was incredibly beautiful and well
suited to the needs of the festival; the community, while not really fully on
board yet, was now aware of Mariposa's presence as an important cultural
institution that had come back to town; the format of the festival had been
reset and had adapted the structure started at Innis Lake, nurtured on the
Toronto Islands, and established so well at Molson Park in Barrie; the artistic
vision was true to the mandate the board had set years before — the preser-
vation of folk arts in Canada through story, song, and craft. Why wouldn't
the next festival be just as successful as the one in the year 2000?

So planning began. Meetings were held. Several government grants
were secured and sponsors began to pony up money. Then that money
was spent, in some cases without proper oversight: no one had to answer
for his expenses. Money went toward tents, office costs, volunteer shirts,
food, and badges, and it went toward site costs such as signage, rental of the
park, toilets, and golf carts. Sound equipment and lighting alone came in at
over $12,000. The artistic budget, which was $53,000 in 2000, surpassed
$100,000 the second year. Publicity was a massive expense as the organiz-
ers decided to spend a bundle. They earmarked $35,000 just for television
marketing and spent nearly $90,000 in total. That was a huge expenditure.
On the downside, the Royal Bank failed to renew its $10,000 sponsor-
ship. When ticket sales did not grow in the second year, the Toronto and
Orillia planners shared a lot of angst. Was Mariposa headed back into that
all-too-familiar deficit situation?

Gord Ball later admitted, "We spent like drunken sailors on shore leave."

The actual 2001 festival had its usual assembly of folk stars (Ian Tyson,
the McGarrigle Sisters, J.P. Cormier, Susan Werner, David Francey, Valdy,
and Gary Fjellgaard) and they attracted a large number of fans — casual,
devoted, and … rabid.

And who says that folk musicians don't have rabid fans? Ian Tyson had been around for well over forty years as a singer. He definitely had a following and was seen as a draw. That year at Mariposa, Ian had one follower in particular: a woman known to Ian's management followed the songwriter from venue to venue. They called her a stalker. (This was not long after a stalker had been repeatedly jailed for plaguing singer Anne Murray.) Whether the woman was mentally unstable or not was never revealed to the Mariposa organizers, but the security team had been warned. In fact, written into Ian's contract was the proviso that he be accompanied by security no matter where he went on the festival grounds. And the woman did show up. She caused no fuss until Ian's appearance as the closing act on Sunday night. As he was singing and strumming, she was shouting, "I love you, Ian" and other such comments, most of them during lulls in the proceedings. Then she decided to run up to the stage and climb over the barrier with the intention of getting up on stage with Tyson. One of the security crew chiefs actually had to grab her and physically hold her back. In the ensuing fracas, she threatened to have the volunteer charged for manhandling her. As it turned out, he was a police officer by profession, and he knew his rights and obligations in keeping order. He also knew the proper procedure for handling the trespassing woman. No charges were ever laid on either side, and when Ian returned in 2010, there was no issue. If his stalker was there that year, she sat quietly in her lawn chair and admired him from afar.

There were over thirty artisans, an on-site store (the Emporium), and an on-site restaurant called "Alice's Restaurant." (Thanks to folkie Arlo Guthrie for that inspiration!) The crucial factor, though, namely a large crowd, failed to materialize. The Friday night concerts on the mainstage played to a half-empty field. Saturday and Sunday were barely better in terms of audience numbers. Anemic ticket sales meant that the gamble to spend more and market widely had been a failure.

The result was a shortfall of $38,000 for the foundation.

Like a broken record, Mariposa was back to where it had so often been before. After one successful and profitable year, the next year it was back in the red. FestO hired a company called Charitable Alliance Corporation to work with organizers to generate funds in the immediate term and to establish long-term financial security. Miscellaneous strategies were put on paper, although not very many of them panned out. CAC proposed such things as targeting businesses and individuals "of influence and affluence." They suggested an annual appeal and membership campaign, raffles, appeals to service clubs, a "viable and exciting sponsorship program," and cultivating relationships with the Toronto media.[3]

A comprehensive list of Orillia business owners, medical professionals, and lawyers was drawn up with addresses and phone numbers. The intent was to call upon all of these individuals, send them letters, or show up at their doors looking for donations. Ted Duncan, who'd taken on the mantle of president of FestO, admits that he had "many sleepless nights. It was a long winter and we could have easily gone belly up." Ted, along with Tim Lauer, Gord Ball, and local businessman and city councillor Ralph Cipolla, worked tirelessly to keep things going. They genuinely felt that they could keep the festival alive if they could just make it to the next festival! Unexpected bills kept coming through the door. According to Duncan, Cipolla was able to secure a line of credit with the Royal Bank and that money was used sparingly to nurture the organization through the next few months.

A good example of the creativity employed by the organizers to raise money was a colourful meeting that took place in the Brewery Bay restaurant in downtown Orillia. A small fundraising committee tossed about blue-sky proposals. Perhaps it also demonstrates the desperation some were feeling. Among the ideas for getting money into the Mariposa coffers were snow golf; snow baseball; a spaghetti dinner; a reading of Dickens; a "main street tennis ball race;" a murder mystery evening; a cookbook of recipes by performers, volunteers, and politicians; a life-sized *Clue* game; Nevada tickets; a flower sale; a fish fry; a combined Octoberfest/folkfest; a benefit hockey game. Few, if any, of these ideas actually came to fruition, but it was a sign of the commitment and imagination that some local people had.

One ongoing activity that brought in a few dollars was an annual curling bonspiel, but that had limited appeal. It was mainly attended by hard-core volunteers, and not enough money was raised to make much of a dent in the deficit. Ted Duncan made cold calls to volunteers and community members alike in an attempt to drum up money from people in Orillia. Gord Ball recalled Ted telling the board at a meeting that if Mariposa was to survive, it very likely would mean that all of them — the board members — would have to dip into their own wallets. Many did.

Yet from FestO's point of view, Toronto's Mariposa contingent did not pick up the fundraising ball as perhaps they should have. In their defence it could be argued that the Toronto people had been through all this before. Many had contributed personal money and time over a couple of decades, and that well was likely running dry. One long-time volunteer was still owed over $5,000. In any event the Toronto business community was highly unlikely to invest in a festival that was taking place one hundred kilometres to the north.

An exception in this Orillia–Toronto dynamic was Lynne Hurry's connection to the Philadelphia Folk Festival. She worked her charms with her contacts and somehow convinced the Philly folkies to help out; they came through with a $5,000 donation. Ted Duncan believes that was a bit of payback for the fact that Philadelphia had come to Orillia to learn how to put on a festival back in the early 60s when the two organizations were just starting out.

The two groups — FestO and the Mariposa Folk Foundation — were about to come together as a unified force. According to the initial agreement from 1999, the three-year accord was nearly up. At respective annual general meetings in the fall of 2001, both FestO and MFF adopted harmonized bylaws as the first steps toward unification.

Meanwhile, planning forged ahead for the next summer event. A humbled and more financially cautious group planned and spent more wisely. A couple of subtle signs of the more conservative approach were to be seen in the 2002 festival.

The artistic budget, for one thing, was reduced by nearly half. That meant that there were few big names to be seen. Artistic director Randi Fratkin faced the challenge admirably and mixed the old with the new. Comedienne/singer Nancy White, Lynn Miles, Si Kahn, and Bobby Watt were familiar faces from bygone years, so they were certainly welcomed and recognized by ticket buyers. With a keen eye for outstanding young talent, Randi brought in a couple of dynamic up-and-comers in Serena Ryder and Sarah Slean. David Francey, on his way to becoming one of Canada's favourite minstrels, was hired. Sylvia Tyson's band Quartette played Sunday's mainstage. Forty years on, Sylvia still had the wonderful voice she'd demonstrated at the inaugural Mariposa in 1961. The Silver Hearts, a huge ensemble of young musicians from Trent University in Peterborough, Ontario, were unknown to the audience but quickly became (along with Serena) the fan favourites of the weekend.

The actual program guide for the festival was another sign that the organization was scrimping wherever it could. Instead of glossy, costly paper and a substantial number of pages, the 2002 program was printed on inexpensive newsprint and was limited to twelve pages. It was an understated nod to the fact that there was nowhere near as much money to throw into marketing as there had been the year before.

Steve Earle, the outspoken American singer-songwriter, was the Saturday headliner, and his fee alone ate up over half the artistic costs. He brought with him more than his history of drug and weapons charges. Earle's popularity with the notorious Hells Angels motorcycle gang was in evidence at the festival that year. As Earle took to the stage that evening, suddenly and seemingly out of nowhere, dozens of shaggy-looking men with full Angels colours appeared throughout the audience. They were there to hear Earle and support him, not to cause any trouble. Yet it spooked some of the organizing team, who found the alleged criminal element in their midst rather disturbing. Word of the motorcycle gang's presence went beyond the festival gates. Within minutes of Earle's set starting, dozens of Ontario Provincial Police officers were spread out around the mainstage area, but nothing happened other than the Angels glad-handing Earle at the end of his set.

That 2002 festival had run on the assumption that there would be a manageable $24,000 deficit. The Ontario government kicked in money, specifically with a $17,000 tourism grant. The federal government offered up a cheque for $36,000 to help with costs and for the hiring of an administrative assistant. Ticket sales turned out to be somewhat better than expected, and the festival actually made about $16,000 when all was said and done. Combined with carrying the 2001 debt, Mariposa entered into budget planning for 2003 with a deficit of "only" $7,400. While it's rather tedious to dwell on numbers from a long-ago festival, it underlines the fact that each year was completely unpredictable financially.

It came as a bit of relief for the Mariposa Folk Foundation when FestO and MFF merged. Sharing board members from both Toronto and Orillia and working with one common goal was not only a good thing but a necessary one in the long run. Equating Mariposa with Toronto — and especially with its history on the islands — was now ancient history. Orillia was beginning to embrace the annual event. Most of the volunteer base lived in town. The audience survey showed that 48 percent of the audience that year had come from

Orillia, up slightly from the 46 percent figure for 2000. The remaining 52 per-cent came from elsewhere in the province, the northeastern United States and even from as far away as Germany. Toronto — through numerous volunteers, FOG members, and audience, of course — remained a player.[4]

One concern among the organizers was the continual worry that the festival itself was not getting its fair share from the vendors on site. Borrowing a page from Summerfolk in Owen Sound, a decision was made to have patrons at the festival use only Mariposa's own printed scrip. The food booths would only be able to accept the festival money, not real Canadian or American currency. By doing so and not allowing real dollars to be used, the tallying and reconciliation would be more easily assessed to ensure that Mariposa got its cut from the food vendors. That involved lots of pre-event planning. The Mariposa money, as it came to be known, had to be printed in various denominations. A system of handling the dollars had to be worked out so that the vendors and the audience knew of its existence. A booth had to be built to ensure that people could readily exchange real money for the substitute. The audience had to be educated about this significant change.

The process, while well intended, became a giant logistical problem. Audiences did not like having to exchange real money for scrip. What would they do with the leftover funds? The FOG team found it just another detail to worry about. And when the results were tabulated, assessed, and com-pared to previous years, it became obvious that the food sellers had been honest, and there was no need to suspect that the festival was not collecting its share of the profits. The process was quietly dropped although for the next few years volunteers were handed $6 in MFF money to spend as part of their volunteer package. Even as late as 2016 Mariposa dollars were still being given out to sponsors, musicians, and VIPs at the festival.

By 2003 things were heading in the right direction. A successful Trillium grant application earned the Mariposa Folk Foundation a whop-ping $75,000. (Newspapers reported $90,000, but documents show other-wise.) Through the Trillium Foundation, the Government of Ontario gives out about $100 million annually to non-profit and charitable organizations around the province. Between five hundred and one thousand projects a year are helped in this manner. Quite often these grants are for infrastructure, and that's what Mariposa had requested.

Tudhope Park had once been a tourist campground, and some of the original but no-longer-functioning buildings still stood on site. Mariposa's Trillium application called for two things: renovation of an old washroom into an on-site storage facility for festival equipment, and an upgrade to the existing electrical service to the park. The City of Orillia, which stood to benefit from these capital improvements, was happy to oblige and partner with the festival, allowing the organization to dig the necessary trenches and renovate the derelict building. A local contractor, who was also an annual MFF volunteer, completed construction work quickly. No longer would most of the stages, electrical cables, and other festival paraphernalia need to be stored in a volunteer's barn twenty kilometres outside of town!

The festival, for the next couple of years, was in audience-building mode.

Mariposa was back in the game of trying to market itself year-round. Local concerts labelled "Mariposa in Orillia" and Toronto events called "Mariposa in the City" were ways to keep the foundation's name in the public eye and to present well-known performers such as Valdy or Friends of Fiddler's Green. In addition, the Tranzac Club in Toronto's Annex was co-presenting concerts with the Flying Cloud Club. Mariposa's name was attached to those endeavours. And a unique set of shows that featured emerging young talent, called "From the Cocoon," kept Toronto's folk community entertained in the summer months following the festival.

In April of 2004, FestO was dissolved and the festival once again became the primary mission of the Mariposa Folk Foundation's board of directors. Budgets grew cautiously and in small increments. For example, the artistic budget of 2004 was $90,000, an increase of about $25,000 over the previous year. The allotment for promotion and marketing was also gently increased. It helped that federal and provincial money kept coming. Casino Rama, located across the lake from Orillia, gave generously through its "Community Wellness Fund." Private sector sponsorship came in at about $77,000 and public sector financing was about $66,000. What few in the public seemed to realize was that without this kind of financial assistance, Mariposa — and most other festivals, for that matter — could not function. Gone were the days when one could mount an enormous and successful festival on ticket sales alone.

Then a few things happened that might have helped folk festivals gain a small bit in popularity.

In April of 2003 a brilliant satire of folk music appeared in movie theatres across North America: Christopher Guest's *A Mighty Wind*. Did it help or harm the folk festival scene? The film did a number of things. In some ways it affectionately took people back to the height of the 60s folk revival, but it also satirized a lot of the quirky and eccentric behaviour of some of the characters. The clever songs in the film were both quaintly familiar in style and at the same time embarrassingly — and purposely — mawkish. It also showed how so much of what came from that folk revival era became sanitized, commercialized, and so far removed from the original sense of *folk:* the world of Pete Seeger, Woody Guthrie, and early Bob Dylan. People who knew folk music could see the focus of the humour. Sandy McAllister, a member of the Mariposa board of directors at the time, stated — with tongue firmly planted in cheek — that she couldn't watch the movie because for her it was more of a documentary than a comedy! Those unfamiliar with festivals like Mariposa may have looked at this "mockumentary" and wondered if this truly represented what was being presented at folk festivals. Taking the film at face value would certainly not draw many new fans to festivals. On the other hand, the soundtrack sold well and may have spurred some interest in the genre. It was one of those things that cannot be accurately assessed in terms of its effects on ticket sales.

The promotion of folk music was also aided by the technology that was being quickly and earnestly embraced by young musicians. With a personal computer and a bit of tech savvy, a musician could record his or her own music and sound quite professional — with or without actual talent! With ease anyone could produce an album of decent quality, independent of record companies like Columbia, Capitol, or Warner Brothers. Young musicians turned to producing and distributing their own material, and such facility in getting their music to the public made it somewhat easier for would-be musicians to find an audience. This technology lent itself most easily to a singer with a guitar, resulting in a renewed interest in singer-songwriter music, if not in folk itself. Again, it's difficult to assess how many festival tickets this sort of renewed interest might have sold, but it's fun to speculate.

The 2004 festival, which featured acts like Murray McLauchlan, Mary Gauthier, Prairie Oyster, and Blackie and the Rodeo Kings, was the setting of a small but important historical event. On Sunday evening as things were winding down, a black limousine pulled up to the performers' entrance, and out stepped none other than Gordon Lightfoot. This was particularly remarkable because two years previously Lightfoot had collapsed with an abdominal aneurysm. Rushed to special hospital facilities in Hamilton, he went through numerous operations and was in an induced coma for over two months. Many thought he'd never survive, let alone perform again. As of 2004 he had not appeared on any public stage since his medical emergency in 2002. Yet here he was at Mariposa, guitar in hand, humbly asking if they'd mind if he sang a tune.

There had actually been some pre-arranging done behind the scenes. Gerry Hawes had a good relationship with Barry Harvey, Gordon's manager at the time. When Hawes phoned Harvey to tell him about the mainstage tribute to Gordon Lightfoot at Mariposa on Sunday night, things seemed to fall into place. Gordon was getting ready at that point to get back on stage and this might be an opportunity, as Gordon put it, to "test my will." It helped that Murray McLauchlan would be one of the singers doing Lightfoot covers, and Gordon emphasizes that Murray is one of his favourite performers. And so, as they stood backstage listening to Lightfoot's songs being played up on the mainstage, Hawes wondered if Gord would say a few words to the crowd since he had not performed following his multiple surgeries. "No, but I brought my guitar," Lightfoot answered. Telling his chauffeur to open the trunk of the limo, Gordon pulled out his six-string Martin and headed backstage.

Saying things like, "Stay in your seats. You're in for a special treat," Michael Wrycraft, the emcee that night, kept teasing the audience without letting the cat out of the bag that Orillia's most famous musical export was backstage. As Lightfoot stepped into the spotlight on the mainstage, the crowd erupted in spontaneous applause. He walked to the mic and began his appropriately titled song, "I'll Tag Along." The mainstage field, which seated several thousand people, was eerily quiet as they strained to hear Lightfoot's muted voice. His vocals lacked the old power and tone, but it didn't matter to the silent, rapt audience. For so many in the crowd, this was spine-tingling. It was enough that he was there, and the fact that he'd chosen Mariposa as the first step on his musical road to recovery was special to the festival crowd. The editorial in the *Orillia Packet and Times* the following Tuesday was effusive (July 13, 2004).

> Folk music is built on symbolism. Lightfoot has given the
> Mariposa Folk Festival two exquisitely symbolic moments
> since the event was reborn in Orillia.... He has imbued
> Tudhope Park — already a magical place — with a deeper
> magic. That has increased the value of the festival to
> Orillia and the value of Orillia to the festival. Like Gordon
> Lightfoot, the Mariposa Folk Festival is a gift.

The paper was referring both to his triumphant 2000 appearance that helped
the festival return to town and to this historic event, when Canada's most
famous and respected minstrel had returned to the musical stage for the first
time since his near-death experience two years earlier.

o o o

A couple of things came about as a result of the 2004 festival (which the
Globe and Mail called "middle aged" and "gentle"). With a bigger crowd
than many had anticipated, there was a good bit of money in the bank. By
August the treasurer, Martin Ward, was able to report that, with revenue
anticipated to be around $80,000, there should be enough money to cover
the accumulated debt of $65,000 and the $10,000 in unpaid expenses from
the recent festival. He hoped that Mariposa would be out of debt by the end
of the year and still have a few thousand in the bank.

At the same board meeting, the directors approved "in principle the hiring
of paid management staff, using a compensation model that mitigates risk to the
MFF." An executive director would be hired for the first time in nearly ten years.
It was a sign of the festival's success, but at the same time it was a financial risk,
in that there was not enough money in the foundation's bank account to pay the
person's salary straight up. He (or she) would have to find additional funding
sources through government grants and sponsorships to augment an ED salary.

A candidate was already waiting in the wings. Chris Mockler had
attended the festival for a couple of years. His wife, Ann Burgess, worked at
the Spotlight office in Orillia, where Mariposa shared office space with other
arts groups. She worked closely with the Mariposa FOG committee and the
board of directors. Chris was also a fine amateur photographer and had taken

pictures at the festival for a couple of years. He had a political background, having worked in various capacities with the New Democratic Party, and he knew how to navigate the halls of government. Being an NDP insider had also led to contacts with union officials, something that certainly fitted in with the ethos of a left-wing folk festival. This eventually led to a profitable sponsorship from the Ontario food workers' union (UFCW) and the inclusion of labour leader Wayne Samuelson on the festival's board of advisors. Above all Chris knew folk music and had a very enthusiastic, positive personality. He jumped into the job right away and reported efficiently to the board on his priorities and planned actions leading into the 2004–2005 season.

Lightfoot returned the following year to headline the festival. His health had suffered but he was on the mend. He'd been through numerous procedures to correct the damage done by the aneurysm to his stomach and diaphragm. He'd persevered and was ready to get back to touring North America — with a somewhat diminished voice but with that incomparable catalogue of songs. Joining him at Mariposa in 2005 were fellow songwriters David Francey, Gurf Morlix, Harry Manx, Lynn Miles, and Murray McLauchlan. Rocker Tom Cochrane headlined the show on Saturday night, and Fred Eaglesmith brought in a crowd of "Fred Heads" when he played on Sunday evening.

The big story of the weekend was the weather — yet again! Friday night was a calamity. The headline in the paper on Saturday, July 9, told the story: "Storm Sends Mariposa to Plan B." A freak wind and rainstorm hit Tudhope Park around 5 p.m., just as the mainstage schedule was about to start. The wind whipped away several small shelters and blew down tree branches, but worse, the driving wind, rain, and hail, which came in quickly and violently, destroyed some of the electrical equipment on the mainstage. Although the storm blew through within ten minutes, there had been scant warning and limited time to cover and protect the fragile electrical gear on stage.

Remarkably, other parts of Orillia were untouched by the storm. It was as if a small hurricane had decided to wreak havoc with Mariposa that Friday night but nowhere else. However, many patrons coming to the front gate were oblivious that the park had just been slammed by mother nature.

As audience and organizers alike emerged from whatever shelters they'd been able to find during the storm, things looked disastrous. As quickly as the storm had hit, the skies now cleared. It took only a moment to realize that there would be no mainstage show that night as there was no possibility of replacing the sound equipment on such short notice. But the ever-resourceful Mariposa organizing team had a quick tête-à-tête behind the scenes and came up with an inventive plan to both satisfy the audience and keep the show going. President Chris Lusty, executive director Chris Mockler, and artistic director Randi Fratkin made a quick and creative decision. They decided to move the mainstage show to the beer tent. The bar would have to be shut down since Ontario's archaic liquor-licensing laws wouldn't allow beer and wine sales to a crowd that exceeded the number mentioned in the licence. Also, no one was sure whether minors could be in the Mariposa pub while alcohol was being served.

Mariposa's beer sales had always fed a substantial amount of cash into the festival's coffers, but not that night!

A fence crew began to remove the snow fencing surrounding the beer tent in order to open up the area and accommodate a larger crowd. The tent walls were removed to allow sightlines from all angles around the large twelve-by-thirty-metre tent. Randi spoke to the musicians who had been scheduled in the beer tent that evening to explained that the mainstage acts would be taking over the pub stage. Emcees Tom Coxworth and Steph Hill were advised of the changes, and they easily adapted to the new venue on the other side of the park.

Power came back on about 6:30 p.m., an hour after the storm had hit, and by 7:30 p.m. the Paperboys, an act from Vancouver, were playing to a jam-packed crowd. Normally the beer tent capacity was about eight hundred people either inside the tent or in the small "beer garden" around its perimeter. That night there were probably about three thousand people crowded into the same small space to hear the mainstage acts on the pub stage. Serena Ryder, well on her way to stardom, showed what an outstanding songwriter she was. But even more impressive was her powerful three-octave range, mezzo-soprano voice. Sarah Harmer, the evening's closing act, sang her big hit "Basement Apartment." Then, in keeping with the fine folk tradition of being socially conscious, she played her "Escarpment Blues," a tune that spoke up about the environmental abuse of the Niagara Escarpment.

What started off as a disaster turned into a triumph. The lineup was geared toward a young demographic, and the audience proved to be very adaptable and enjoyed the unique situation. It was an adventure for audience and performers alike.

Tom Cochrane gave a rocking show on Saturday night. His presence had ensured good ticket sales, though many of the ticket buyers were rock and roll fans of Tom's and not necessarily folk music fans. Sid Dolgay, who'd been a performer at the first festival (with the Travellers) and an organizer off and on throughout the ensuing decades, said that in all his years with the festival, he'd never seen such a big crowd for an evening concert, at least not since the festival came back to Orillia.

And of course, with Gordon Lightfoot finishing the show on Sunday night, a huge crowd sat transfixed in front of the mainstage, all ears for their favourite troubadour. Lightfoot did not disappoint. Each song was familiar to the audience. In an interview with the *Packet and Times* a few days before the actual concert (July 5, 2005), Gord admitted audiences were being "forgiving" when he couldn't do the old songs like he used to, alluding to the effects of his stomach troubles on his voice.

"I know which ones I can't do so I leave them alone … the ones with long phrases, things like that. 'Hangdog Hotel Room' is one with really long phrases and we used to really like to play that, but I can't get in enough air. I'm learning how to split the phrases up now and that's all coming around."

During the Saturday night mainstage performance, a new feature of the Mariposa Folk Foundation was inaugurated. In a tip of the hat to the people who'd started Mariposa forty-five years previously, the board of directors decided to celebrate Ruth Jones and her colleagues from 1961. Arrangements were made for them to be honoured with individual plaques, and time was set aside for short speeches. Ruth Jones-McVeigh, David Major, Pete McGarvey, Ted Schafer, Ed Cowan, Sid Dolgay, and Dr. Crawford "Casey" Jones were the first to be named to the brand new Mariposa Hall of Fame. An appreciative audience gave the group a warm reception.

The festival seemed to be back on solid ground. Financially it was relatively stable, and artistically it had embraced a musical style, one that audiences came to expect and enjoy. Ticket buyers knew the type of experience they could expect even if they didn't know the specific names on the roster. The atmosphere of the festival, with its food row, artisan village, beer tent, many stages, and family Folkplay area was in some ways like a familiar rural fall fair. Yet there was also a sophistication and intellectual aspect to much of the programming. In the words of Richard Flohil, quoted on the cover of the 2006 program, "Mariposa's got its mojo back."

CHAPTER THIRTEEN
Consolidation in Orillia

BACK IN 1995, ON THE EVE OF THE national referendum on Quebec sovereignty, CBC broadcaster Jowi Taylor conceived the idea of constructing a truly national symbol, something that came from all parts of Canada and that would be able to tour around Canada. He called it the Six String Nation Guitar. Taylor travelled the country collecting bits and pieces of notable Canadiana. For example, he secured wood from the deck of the *Bluenose II*, some flooring from the schoolhouse that Louis Riel had attended, wood from the hockey sticks of Paul Henderson and Wayne Gretzky, gold from a Maurice Richard Stanley Cup ring, walrus tusk from Rankin Inlet, a piece of Pierre Trudeau's canoe paddle, and a morsel of wood from Nancy Greene's childhood skis. Most of the guitar's front was composed of three-hundred-year-old spruce from Haida Gwaii in British Columbia. Nova Scotia luthier George Rizsanyi put it all together in a fine-looking instrument that eventually earned the nickname "Voyageur." Jowi debuted the guitar on Parliament Hill, on July 1, 2006, and a week later brought it to Mariposa, where Stephen Fearing played it on the mainstage Saturday night.[1]

The 2006 festival saw an artistic lineup that included notable songwriters Fearing, Lennie Gallant, Danny Michel, Lynn Miles, and Ron Hynes. Feist made her Mariposa debut just before her massive worldwide hit song "1234" rocketed her to international stardom later that year. Bluesman Colin James rocked the mainstage on Saturday, and Celtic fiddler Natalie MacMaster dazzled the crowd on Sunday night. Soulful songwriter extraordinaire

Artisans' Village, 2004.

Ron Sexsmith closed the festival on Sunday evening. After Natalie's energetic and hard-driving set, his mellow sound was quite a contrast and a bit anticlimactic.

Along with these established acts, the festival also premiered a few up-and-coming acts. Early each festival year, well before the roster is hired, Mariposa announces that it will hold live auditions. In 2006 the auditions were held in the Orillia area in front of not only interested music lovers but also the artistic director and a committee in charge of finding potential acts. The auditions were limited to those who were not yet established, and the general feeling was that if you had produced more than two CDs, you were not eligible. From a huge number of applicants, typically about seven to ten acts were auditioned, and generally three were selected and offered a small fee to play at the festival. They were then given a place on the roster, marketed in festival advertising, booked into concerts and workshops, and basically treated the same as acts that had been hired by the artistic director.

The duo Dala, a mainstage act on Friday night in 2006, had gained notice through the Mariposa Showcase process in 2004. They'd shown up with the other applicants and absolutely wowed everyone in the audition hall with their flawless harmonies and sophisticated songwriting. At the '04 festival, audiences had loved them so much that they were brought back two years later. The pair took on legendary status with the festival organizers and audience in that Mariposa felt it had "discovered" them and had been the first festival to present them. Dala would go on to be the hit of the 2009 Newport Folk Festival, and they made a triumphant return to Mariposa in 2014. JUNO Award–winning banjo player Old Man Luedecke had similarly been "discovered" as a Mariposa Showcase act, and he too had gone on to earn praise for his music across the country following his appearance at the Orillia festival.

It seemed that nearly every year, a special song would resonate with the Mariposa crowd. Certain songs would play from the mainstage speakers or between sets at the beer tent and hit a special note with the audience. These "ear worms" made themselves known early each festival and carried well beyond the event itself. In 2003 it was David Francey's lilting "Red-Winged Blackbird," and in 2005 it was Murray McLauchlan's "Gulliver's Taxi." In 2006 the song that seemed to fill the air all around the park was Lennie Gallant's magnificent tune "Pieces of You." They were songs that people loved from the first moment they heard them, and the best part of coming to a festival like Mariposa was that you got to experience these kinds of things annually.

The 2006 festival would be Randi Fratkin's last as artistic director. A well-respected pediatric dentist in Toronto, Randi had become part of the organizing team for Mariposa when the festival was still in Toronto in the 1990s. She had a keen eye for new talent, especially songwriting. Long before they were well known, people like Sarah Slean, Serena Ryder, Sarah Harmer, Danny Michel, and Justin Rutledge had been tracked down and hired by Randi. She had a particular affinity, or so it seemed, for alt-country and Southwestern American artists like Stacey Earle, Tom Russell, and Gurf Morlix. She worked with a committee during the first year back in Orillia and then took on the job by herself for the next several festivals.

By 2005–2006, the board of directors felt, however, that Randi did not communicate often or early enough in the process. Around the boardroom table the directors felt they trusted her taste and work ethic, but they wanted a clearer picture of the performance roster before each festival. She was asked to report more often, more promptly, and in more detail. When Randi either refused or was unable to deliver on that requirement, she was given her walking papers. The fact that the actual notification that she'd been terminated was given via email and not by phone or in person did not sit well with Randi, with several board members, and with Randi's many friends and associates in the folk community such as Richard Flohil.

In order to fill the vacancy left by Randi's departure, the board turned to me, Mariposa's vice-president at the time, to head up an artistic committee. I was given the task of finding two other people to join me. Sandy McAllister, a knowledgeable long-time board member, and Amy Mangan, a young Orillia volunteer, became the other two-thirds of the committee. A decision was also made to bring in advisory members. Dave MacMillan, David Warren, Tom Johnstone, and Jenny Ball were also recruited to provide some outside advice on musical acts. In a well-meaning but rather naive gesture to make the artistic selection process more democratic and inclusive, the committee held an open forum in Orillia's council chambers. Members of the public were invited to give input and make suggestions. If nothing else it was a break from tradition and a change of pace. Yet, in reality, finding talent for the festival is a job that requires careful research, an astute eye for talent, and strong decision-making abilities — something that cannot easily be handled by three people, let alone dozens of advisors.

Once word got out about the programmer changes within MFF, via *Penguin Eggs* magazine and the Maplepost listserv, a lot of nasty words were sent Mariposa's way. A committee to select the artists? Firing someone of Randi Fratkin's calibre? There was outrage, resentment, and a lot of petty digs, and certainly no one bothered to compliment the festival for its choice of direction.

The first task for the new artistic chair was more of a foundation activity. The inaugural 2005 Mariposa Hall of Fame had been seen as a successful attempt to honour the past, so it seemed worth making a second stab at it. A plan to hold an event outside the festival, one that would stimulate interest and garner some media attention, was set in motion.

Ian and Sylvia had headlined the first festivals in Orillia, ensuring good audiences. They'd been the darlings of folk music all through the 60s, and Ian had designed the first poster and the logo. He'd also helped round up some of the artists, and both Sylvia and Ian had been involved in the nitty-gritty of pulling the festival together. As individual performers, they'd appeared a number of times at Mariposas throughout the decades. On top of all that, they were by now iconic musical figures in Canada, not only as a duo but also as individual singers and songwriters. A board decision was made to try to bring them together and honour them with inclusion in the Hall of Fame.

Don Cullen, a long-time volunteer with Mariposa and a comic actor known for his time with Wayne and Shuster, was also due similar honours for his contributions over the years. Don had also started the Bohemian Embassy in Toronto, which had nurtured the careers of many a Canadian folk singer, including Sylvia Tyson.

Calls to their respective agents were placed, and the idea was proposed to both singers. Remarkably, both assented to the honour and agreed to appear. A venue — Hugh's Room in Toronto — was arranged. I sent emails to a number of well-known folk, country, and rock singers asking for testimonials. Tom Russell mentioned he'd seen both Ian and Sylvia and the Beatles in concert in the 60s and that Ian and Sylvia were "better." Nanci Griffith praised the pair, as did Tom Rush, Eric Andersen, Ronnie Hawkins, and Leonard Cohen. Copies of the testimonials were printed on Western Union–like stationery to be presented like a telegram to each honouree along with a plaque. Copies of a 1963 CHUM chart, showing Ian and Sylvia's "Four Strong Winds," were placed at each table.

The actual event was a remarkable evening of tribute and entertainment. The Good Brothers, Aengus Finnan, Nancy White, Marie-Lynn Hammond, and Blue Rodeo's Greg Keelor took turns singing covers of the Tysons' musical catalogue. Gordon Lightfoot, who showed up to take in the proceedings, spoke articulately off the cuff about his early friendship and personal relationship with the pair. After an intermission Sylvia sang two of her great songs (including "You Were on My Mind"), and then Ian took the stage to sing two of his songs. For the first time in decades, the pair finally reunited to sing the author-neutral songs they'd recorded years before — "Old Blue," "When First Unto This Country" and "Texas Rangers." The concert ending song of the night was, of course, "Four Strong Winds." The capacity crowd in Hugh's Room was mesmerized, not only by the quality of the music that night but also by the historical significance. It was a reunion of Canadian folk legends that many thought couldn't happen. The couple had split up in the early 70s and had reunited once in the mid-80s. Diehard folk music fans had long wished for another reunion. The two hundred people gathered there that night witnessed a unique piece of Canadian cultural history, thanks to Mariposa's Hall of Fame.

o o o

The 2007 festival was a success and that, in part, vindicated the new artistic committee. Hawksley Workman, Susan Aglukark, the Good Brothers, the Sadies, and Dave Gunning were all established acts. Long-time folkie David Bradstreet, someone who'd been around since the early 70s, finally got to play at Mariposa. Genticorum and their distinctive Québécois sound had audience members up and dancing. Newcomers Cuff the Duke, Jill Barber, David Celia, and Amanda Martinez turned a few heads. Matt Andersen, a larger-than-life presence on stage, was clearly one of the audience favourites. His phenomenal guitar playing and his way of singing blues tunes exceeded expectations. (David Warren and I had seen Andersen the previous October at the Ontario Council of Folk Festivals conference in Ottawa, where he'd played a late-night set to fewer than ten people. We hadn't let the small crowd influence us as it was clear that this was a talent to be reckoned with.) Saturday night, Don McLean gave a thoroughly professional show running through his hit songs "Vincent" and "Crying." His show ended with an excited audience of thousands on their feet singing "American Pie," matching him note for note. The audience, both young and old, left the park on a high.

Don McLean, 2007.

Orillia's favourite musical son, Gordon Lightfoot, closed the show on Sunday night to enthusiastic cheers. No surprise there. If Gordon had walked across the water of Lake Couchiching, his appreciative fans would not have been surprised. Just as he took to the stage, the skies opened and a torrential downpour hit the park.

Other than the mini hurricane that hit the festival in 2005, it was the only time in all the years back in Orillia that rain had been much of a factor. When the festival had returned to town in 2000, someone — and no one has taken credit for it — had the foresight to look up historical weather records. It seems that the weekend after Canada Day, July 1, is traditionally a weekend when it rarely rains in Central Ontario. That sounded perfect for an outdoor festival, so the Mariposa Folk Festival in Orillia has always been scheduled for that particular weekend. Whether science or just coincidence, it worked for the festival nearly every year. So many August Mariposas in the past had been drowned out — as in 1990 — that it seemed like a wise decision to hold the event the weekend after Canada Day.

Lightfoot took to the stage and faced down the wind and rain. His manager, Barry Harvey, was apoplectic as he screamed at Gord from the sidelines to get off the stage. Barry and most of the MFF organizing team could see the danger of someone standing in pouring rain amid all that electrical equipment. Gordon refused to listen, soldiering on. As he began singing "The Wreck of the Edmund Fitzgerald," the crowd erupted in applause.

"We've got a job to do and we're going to do it, " he said at the time.

In an interview for this book, Gordon stated, "We were soaked and actually felt warm at that point anyway."

There were a couple of reasons for Lightfoot to keep the show going. He knew his audience was there to hear him, and he had developed a certain nostalgia for Orillia (and the Mariposa Folk Festival) over the years. A true professional, he wanted to deliver the show he'd planned for his hometown crowd.

Nearby Casino Rama had announced early in 2007 that Bob Dylan would be playing at the casino the same weekend as Mariposa. This was obviously a problem for the festival. The casino had been a sponsor of the festival since 2000, but its decision to host Dylan put it squarely in competition with Mariposa. Knowing the two songwriters were friends, I called Dylan's manager in New York (in my capacity as artistic chair) and invited the superstar to come to see Lightfoot's show.

The rest of the details are fuzzy. Rumours that Dylan might appear at any moment circulated all weekend among the audience and the performers. Everyone seemed to believe that that Dylan might drop in on Gord's show at Mariposa Sunday evening, after his own show at the casino had finished.

Unfortunately, the rain caused havoc. Many of those in Mariposa's mainstage audience were unprepared or not motivated to sit in the thunder, lightning and rain at Tudhope Park. A good number got up, raced to their cars, and began a slow exodus out of the park.

Tudhope has only has one way in and out. As a number of patrons' vehicles made their egress from the park that night, along came a white stretch limo from the direction of Casino Rama. It turned in to the park, the only car entering rather than exiting the place. Pulling into a small turnabout used by the buses, it stopped momentarily. The parking crew notified the backstage team, but just as they did, the big car edged into the exiting traffic and made its way back onto Atherley Road, the main route between Orillia and Rama First Nations reserve. Tom Johnstone and Kathy Cole, two Mariposa board members, raced to the limo to explain that no, the rain wasn't stopping the show, and yes, Lightfoot was still playing. They couldn't get to the car in time. It slipped away into the night. No one is positive that Dylan was in the limo, but the "what ifs" have become legendary among those who were there. A revisit (pun intended) of the 1972 festival? Many drool at the thought of Dylan getting up on stage at Mariposa with Lightfoot. Two great folk icons together would have made for a remarkable evening.

"Nice to know that Bob was hovering," Lightfoot joked lightly when asked about the story.

Lightfoot completed his show, facing down the wind that was by then blowing the rain horizontally. Lightning and thunder seemed to be every-where in the park, and while some patrons picked up their chairs and left, many sat obstinately refusing to leave so long as their ultimate folk hero was on stage playing. Finally, as he completed his entire set, he gave the cus-tomary Lightfoot bow and headed off stage. As he stepped off the stairs, he stopped and tilted his guitar — water poured out of the sound hole!

Despite its damp finish, the weekend ended on a positive note and things looked rather good for the weekend. Ticket sales had gone up by nearly 25 percent. The iconic names and other great performers were also to be celebrated. Also, more than five hundred volunteers had devoted at least twelve hours of their time over the weekend. The artisan and Folkplay areas were popular destinations. Most of all, the general vibe of the event made it welcoming and organizers felt positive and secure about Mariposa's future.

o o o

Securing the past was another story. Since the beginning of the festival, those in charge of the festival had saved items and memorabilia. Pete McGarvey, for instance, had kept handwritten notes from the first board of directors meeting. Since 1973, recordings of workshops had been carefully collected. Programs, photos, contracts, letters, T-shirts, and buttons had amassed and were being housed in the basement of an old police station on Queen Street in Toronto. Someone had to decide what to do with the material. For instance, some of the audition and workshop tapes were liquifying inside their containers and had to be quickly converted by an expert to a more secure format or they'd be lost forever.

The board of directors acted quickly. Calling upon the services of a professional archivist, they had the material in the Toronto basement assessed. The archivist looked things over and said, without hesitation, that the treasures housed there were worth "millions." Then she pointed to the rusty pipe suspended by a rusting support and stated, "That's the main sewer line in this very old building." The look on her face told the story: Get all of this stuff out of here as quickly as possible!

The board debated the subject for several months. Orillia seemed like the desirable location for Mariposa archives but no facility existed that could properly care for the material. One proposal was to take it to the local Orillia Museum of Art and History, but that institution had neither the budget nor the expertise to care for the delicate material. Mark Bissett, the local editor of the *Orillia Packet and Times* newspaper, offered a room in his office building to house the archives, but again, the fragile stuff would not be in a climate-controlled facility. Finally, York University in Toronto was proposed. York had a renowned music program and an archival department within their library that is world-class. They could give the festival's goods the proper care it needed so badly, and an agreement was reached.

Given Mariposa's role as a player in Canada's musical history, York was happy to take on the task of salvaging the tapes, pictures, and other material. A team moved all of it from the Parkdale storage to the Keele Street Campus on the north edge of the city. David Bradstreet and David Woodhead performed at the small ceremony to publicize the move of the valuables to a secure and permanent site. The long and short of the archival move was that York, with its archival expertise and its reputation as a research centre for music, was an ideal partner.

o o o

With the festival's legacy safely stored, the organizers could focus on the future. Mariposa's growth and independence in Orillia was obvious that autumn when the festival moved to new digs on the main street of Orillia. With a need for meeting room and hopes of using the office space for concerts or presentations, a search was made for available storefronts in the downtown core. It was deemed important that the office be a visible presence in town. Dala appeared at the gala opening and treated a packed house to a free concert, a preview of what the office could provide for the community and for Mariposa.

The new office became a base not only for MFF but also for the Orillia District Arts Council (ODAC), an arts support group. The local arts council was invited to share the space at a very reasonable and generous rental rate, which meant that the two groups could continue to share both facility space and human resources. It was indicative of Mariposa's change of fortune that it could lend space to other struggling arts groups. The Orillia Jazz Festival, the local spring blues festival, and other community organizations made media announcements and held meetings in the Mariposa office. For a while the Stephen Leacock Associates, the group that managed the annual Leacock Medal for humour writing, met monthly in the office. A number of employees filled the ODAC desk, usually on a part-time basis, and long-time Mariposa volunteer Bernice Haley was there to tend the front desk daily.

"Bernie," as she better known, was an eccentric character but one of the "faces of Mariposa" around downtown Orillia. An indefatigable volunteer, she would arrive at the office each day to answer phones, sell tickets, and generally schmooze with anyone who came within talking distance of the office's front door. Her energy belied her sixty-some years. Sometimes her quirky sense of humour got her into hot water. A young group from Newfoundland was hired for the festival one year, and Bernie, with her typical lack of political correctness, made a faux pas when one member of the band phoned the office. "Well dere b'y. It's good to hears from ya …" Bernie began. She spent much of the conversation talking in what she thought was a gentle rib at the famous Newfoundland way of speaking. The young caller, on the other hand, was not impressed and made it known to the Mariposa board that Newfoundlanders didn't care for the old stereotypes. Bernie was chastised for her gaffe but was able to laugh it off, as she did so many of her encounters with authority.

o o o

Looking ahead to the upcoming 2008 festival, Mariposa's local success even entered the world of satire. The *Orillia Packet and Times* columnist Colin McKim wrote a gently mocking article about Dylan's "failure to appear" (May 16, 2008). He listed some of the big names that would not be coming to Mariposa: Joni Mitchell, Leonard Cohen, Willie Nelson, Richie Havens.

> "Anyone who missed seeing Dylan last year will have the same opportunity this year," said festival promoter Clint Mockturtle…. When Sarah McLachlan heard Jann Arden wasn't performing at Mariposa under any circumstances, her agent called immediately to make sure Sarah was confirmed as a no-show. Even Céline Dion and Anne Murray have contacted the artistic committee to say they won't be caught dead here.

You've reached some measure of success when outsiders feel they can publicly rib you.

An eclectic lineup was gathered for the 2008 festival. In a stab at expanding the youth audience and drumming up interest, Mariposa launched its first-ever kick-off concert on Thursday night, the eve of the actual festival. Serena Ryder, who'd just won the JUNO Award for "Best New Artist," gave a dynamic concert that was reasonably well attended. Asking folk fans to shell out an extra $30 after they'd already purchased their weekend tickets may have been a questionable move, but it did not seem to hurt the attendance on the weekend.

Greek-Canadian guitar whiz Pavlo, Nova Scotia's Joel Plaskett, Dala, Loudon ("Dead Skunk") Wainwright III, and Hayden all made appearances over the weekend. Sarah Harmer was the Sunday headliner. Taj Mahal headlined on Saturday night, playing a very loud electric blues set that was quite a contrast to his acoustic "Fishin' Blues" or "Long Tailed Cat" days on Toronto Island in the 1970s. J.P. Cormier, Connie Kaldor, Cheryl Wheeler, and a new discovery — the Good Lovelies — were hits for the audience that weekend. John Wort Hannam and Corb Lund brought an Alberta-country sound and Alex Cuba dazzled with his Caribbean-flavoured tunes.

A quirky twist to the staging that year saw Guelph area singer-songwriter James Gordon bring his houseboat, the solar powered *Eramosa Belle*, to the festival. He docked it close to mainstage and then allowed the other performers to use its roof as a floating stage. A small grassy area, protected by shade trees, gave the patrons a new take on looking out over the water as you listen to music.

Also that year, Serena Ryder made a special unannounced appearance in the beer tent, which surprised and thrilled the people sitting there. The idea of "surprise guests" was attempted at Mariposa for a few years and saw Danny Michel, Joel Plaskett, Ron Sexsmith, Jim Cuddy, and Greg Keelor all show up unannounced. It may not have sold extra tickets, but it certainly caused buzz among the audience both during and after the performances. Patrons speculated on who might appear, with whispers each year that maybe Dylan or Neil Young would show up.

The local media was effusive in its praise of the 2008 event, recognizing that the festival had become an institution and also recognizing the fact that audiences for Mariposa now trusted that the lineup would be exciting, even without Gordon Lightfoot and other big-name acts!

As artistic director, I tried to generate some of the same magic of the previous year. Hearing that Pete Seeger was touring through Ontario with grandson Tao Rodríguez and Guy Davis the same weekend as Mariposa, I contacted Pete's agent and sent an invitation to come and visit but not necessarily play. Pete responded that he was unable to attend but turned the tables: he invited executive director Chris Mockler and me to be his guests at Hugh's Room the night after the festival. As it turned out, that was the last concert appearance by the legendary eighty-nine-year-old folkie in Toronto.

In a meeting with the folk legend just prior to his concert, Pete told me he remembered Mariposa at Innis Lake and complimented the great job Estelle Klein had done all those years before.

That year there was an attempt to start a program teaching folk arts on the two days prior to the festival. It certainly fit with the foundation's mandate. A committee was pulled together to hire artists who would give lessons to adults in things like creative writing, photography, storytelling, and dance. Four sessions would cost a participant $120. The purpose was to create a community of artistically minded people who would attend folk school prior to attending the folk festival. The downtown Orillia campus of Lakehead University was rented to accommodate the classes, and word went out to Mariposa's mailing list. Modelled on the immersive "Celtic College" concept that worked so successfully at the Celtic Roots Festival in Goderich, Ontario, it was founded on the hope that Mariposa audiences would come to participate in the folk arts forum and then stay for the weekend. Alas, there was little response and a disappointing turnout despite some talented instructors.

As 2008 turned into 2009 any visible change in Mariposa was negligible. The concert series hummed along, the office was usually open each day for ticket sales, and occasional news leaked out about the artists who'd be coming the following July. Yet behind the scenes there was turmoil. The two people who were the daily face of Mariposa, Bernie Haley and Chris Mockler, each faced different issues. Bernie was diagnosed with cancer and although she coped well with the illness, it did affect the workload she could handle at the MFF office. Chris Mockler, still heavily involved in the backrooms of the NDP, resigned in March. His resignation left a large hole in the organization, but it was not insurmountable; volunteer board members took on many of his responsibilities. Since much of the 2009 festival planning was already in place by late March, the loss of the executive director was manageable. Chris eventually landed in Ottawa as an assistant to one of Jack Layton's "Orange Crush" MPs.

In May, to mark the tenth year back in Orillia, Mariposa threw a thank-you concert in downtown Orillia during one of the annual street sales. Children's entertainer Magoo and several local folk musicians served up original songs for free. It was a way to thank the city for the support it had given the festival since its return in 2000.

o   o   o

Buffy Sainte-Marie headlined the 2009 lineup. The Aboriginal songwriter and activist had been the star of the 1964 festival and returned over the years to showcase her unique warbling soprano voice and original songs. She acknowledged the impact of folk music and its relevance in an interview with the *Orillia Packet and Times* (June 17, 2009).

When asked the question, what's there to sing about in 2009, she answered,

> Same as always — everything.... Folk songs usually last because they're about something that future generations can understand: war, peace, love, hate ... classic themes.... Something like "Universal Soldier" I very deliberately wrote hoping that it would last for generations and cross languages and countries, and it's still appreciated now, 40 years later.

Steven Page was the Saturday night headliner that year. The son of former Mariposa president Victor Page, Steven had recently been in the news. Being busted for cocaine possession had sullied his reputation a tad, and he'd gone solo, splitting from long-time bandmates the Barenaked Ladies. Page acknowledged his past with the festival as he commented to the local media that Mariposa in the early 70s had been a family time for him, a place where he was introduced to many kinds of music — from Pete Seeger to Taj Mahal. He also mentioned that the 1991 Mariposa Festival had been a jumping-off point for the Barenaked Ladies.

Other notable acts in 2009 were JUNO and CFMA (Canadian Folk Music Awards) winners Le Vent du Nord, local bluesman Ronnie Douglas, Valdy, Daniel Lanois, the Dixie Flyers, Enoch Kent, and Luke Doucet. As usual the workshops were deemed by many to be the best part of the festival. Spontaneous, never-to-be-repeated combinations thrilled the audiences as they gathered at each of the stages scattered throughout the park.

At one point the Good Lovelies, a musically brilliant trio of young women in their mid-twenties, were paired with long-time children's performer Fred Penner. The young ladies were almost giddy in the presence of a man whose television show they'd all watched as toddlers. Fred was enjoying renewed success because of just such a phenomenon. Like Ernie Coombs, TV's Mr. Dressup, Fred was being rediscovered and appreciated by the young adults who were now ticket buyers at concerts across the country. In a way it was freeing for Fred that he could now perform "adult" material for an audience he'd cultivated when they were preschoolers. Fred's concert on the mainstage that year was cheered on by appreciative young patrons.

An effort at an arts education program was attempted once again. Renamed and rejigged, "ArtsU" was aimed at the same audience, and this time it actually succeeded — if nothing else, it actually took place. A class on inventive photography was a hit with the participants. The focus was on creativity, and the few who participated came away pleased. The hope was that this scheme to attract the artistically inclined to Orillia for the days prior to the festival would develop and grow.

One of the biggest, best, and most influential innovations to come along in years had nothing to do with the music. Partnering with the local Twin Lakes Conservation Club, Mariposa implemented some serious changes to the way the water and any waste materials were handled.

With crowds in excess of twenty thousand people over the course of a weekend, it's easy to imagine the amount of plastic, garbage, and compostable material that could be generated. Board member Aaron Howes led an initiative to make the festival "greener and cleaner." Howes's father, Warren, headed up the local conservation club and recruited members to help out at Mariposa. In a drive to eliminate plastic water bottles from the site, Warren met with local water-store owner Paul Baker. Over a period of several months a water-dispensing station was developed. It could be attached to the municipal water supply, but with an added UV filter. The idea was for Mariposa audience members to bring their own containers that they could fill for free at the water dispenser. Baker estimated that the crowd would probably use about ten thousand litres of water but advised that if it were especially warm on the weekend, customers would draw as much as forty thousand litres from the water station. In greening terms, that meant the elimination of that many plastic bottles.[2]

On the composting front, there was another remarkable change. All cups, containers, plates, and utensils used at that year's festival were made of compostable, corn-based material. Vendors were permitted to use only that material so that everything could go into the compost bins placed strategically around the park.

One vendor tried to use his own cups and plates made from non-compostable material. Word got back to the greening committee quickly, and a small army of eco-warriors descended on the vendor to set him straight. A threat to toss the food-seller out of the park soon convinced him of the need to "go green."

The Twin Lakes Conservation Club members did sterling duty as volunteers, sitting near the garbage, recycling, and composting bins and directing people where to place their refuse. The festival's attendees, not surprisingly, bought into the new changes without complaint — folk festival audiences tend to be of the environmentally aware mindset. The festival board and organizers were understandably happy with how well the greening efforts had gone and were thankful to the local volunteers who'd implemented such a good plan.

As the festival looked ahead to a big celebration of its fifty years of existence, the organization seemed healthy, economically secure, ensconced in a beautiful setting, and accepted as a local "happening" and economic engine. After ten festivals back in the city of its birth, Mariposa had re-established itself as a place to be, just as Jack Wall had envisioned as far back as 1962. The mother of all festivals in Canada, it had regained respect in the folk music community, and it seemed on track to continue down a successful road.

CHAPTER FOURTEEN
The Fiftieth Anniversary

A simple thing about human nature is that we celebrate anniversaries, especially when they have a nice round number. The tenth, the twenty-fifth, the fiftieth....

There's no particular reason that a fiftieth anniversary should be considered any more special than a forty-ninth, but people do. Be it a birthday, a marriage, or a festival, the celebration of an easily divisible number, like fifty, is seen as something special.

The Mariposa Folk Festival was no different and for its fiftieth incarnation the board of directors felt that there was something to celebrate as the planning began. The old girl had lurched from one venue to another, moved town to town, and survived weather disasters, near riots, financial woes, a movement to disband, increased competition, and myriad changes in the public's musical taste. The list of challenges seemed endless, yet the festival had continued. In fact, by 2010 Mariposa was in relatively good health and enjoying stability. Ten years earlier it had staggered back to Orillia on its last legs and had somehow been revived, thanks in no small part to dedicated volunteers.

Planning started early to make the 2010 festival a special event in Orillia, if not provincially and nationally. After all, Mariposa was the "original folk festival" in Canada. This was the model that other festivals had followed. This was the one that had featured nearly every big name in the genre. This was the one that pioneered the workshop concept. For performers there was cachet in having played at Mariposa. James Taylor, for instance, had been urged to play the festival in 1970 by his then-girlfriend Joni Mitchell for a fraction of his usual fee, just because it was the cool place to be. For audiences, there was a certainty to the quality of what you could expect each year.

The festival had much to be proud of in its past and celebrating its fiftieth anniversary was, indeed, something to be happy about, but in truth the festival continued to be on tenuous grounds. Each year money came from the Ontario Arts Council, the Canada Council, and smaller government granting agencies whose mandate was (and is) to help cultural events such as Mariposa. Funds were forthcoming each year for this non-profit organization although that process had risks — sometimes grant applications were turned down or the amount received might be much less than what was requested. Reliable sponsors, such as Casino Rama, ponied up a good chunk of money each year as part of their contribution to the local community. Contractors Rental Supply, or CRS, was a dependable and extremely co-operative sponsor that generously donated fencing and equipment each year for the set-up of the event. Unions, such as the UFCW or OPSEU, gave each and every year to the cause. Few ticket buyers understood that ticket sales alone could not sustain what the festival had become. Without the grants and sponsors, the festival would be drastically reduced in scale and probably not survive.

The community of Orillia had embraced the festival since its return to the city, and other local organizations began to tie their strings to the Mariposa kite. The Streets Alive Festival of Banners, for example, was an arts incentive in Orillia. Local artists painted banners that were subsequently hung throughout the city's downtown and eventually auctioned to patrons, with the proceeds funding the next year's activity. For 2010 Leslie Fournier, founder and chair of the event, determined that the theme would be the Mariposa Folk Festival and that the artists would paint images related somehow to the festival on fifty oversized fibreglass guitars instead of on large banners. Fifteen of those guitars would then be transported to the festival grounds for display during the actual event.

Ironically, the announcement of Streets Alive saluting the folk festival did not sit easily with the Mariposa board of directors. At the time, the City of Orillia did not give any kind of funding to the festival. In fact, the city charged rent for the park and incidental costs, such as turning on and off the city water supply in Tudhope. President Catherine Brennan took issue with the city's funding of Streets Alive to the tune of $10,000. She sent a letter to the city council where she made it known that the folk foundation supported the guitars project and even allowed use of the MFF logo. Mariposa was not, however, a partner and was not receiving any of the funding that had been earmarked for Streets Alive. Council was confused and needed that clarification. Mayor Ron Stevens asserted that he understood that but Councillor Ralph Cipolla had believed the two arts organizations were taking part in a joint venture and sharing the money being doled out by the city. Both Catherine Brennan and Leslie Fournier had to set things straight with council and those who paid attention to city council business.

Brennan's letter was written partially out of the bitterness that had grown in the Mariposa organization when it came to funding. Federal and provincial grants were available each year to support the foundation, but municipal support lagged far behind. In fact, the "nickel and diming" actions of the city toward the festival were a major cause of resentment. Board members had often mumbled, "Maybe we should move to Barrie." Or Toronto. Or Bracebridge. Or somewhere with some ongoing local financial support. One board member went so far as to call a city councillor in Barrie to see if there was interest in having Mariposa return to that city. Considering what an economic driver the festival was for Orillia, such feelings of disgruntlement were justified.

The problems with finances and the city were not the only ones facing the festival. Like the proverbial duck, Mariposa *looked* peaceful. But while all seemed calm on the water's surface, beneath the waves Mariposa paddled frantically. There were undercurrents of distrust, disagreement, and dissatisfaction among the organizing team and especially on the board of directors.

Personality clashes were nothing new to this foundation, as in virtually every team, business, and venture. During the 70s Estelle Klein had not always agreed or gotten along with people in the Mariposa organization. Several times she'd left on lengthy vacations to recharge and recover from the stress of not only running the festival but also dealing with the people around her. So it was with modern Mariposa. The groups who managed the organization in the 80s and 90s had certainly had their rows and battles as well. The acrimonious split between Mariposa in the Schools and the mother foundation was a good case in point.

Over the years not all relationships between the board and the public, or the board and the volunteers, went smoothly either. For instance, when the festival returned to Orillia in 2000, one of the directors had been placed in charge of the Emporium, the festival's on-site store. He was an honest, dedicated, and hardworking individual who had devoted sizable portions of his time to Mariposa, yet he did not appear to have the necessary managerial skills when it came to handling people. His idiosyncrasies were tolerated for a few years, but eventually his welcome wore thin. His yelling at volunteers — in front of customers, no less — led to a decision by other board members to remove him from the post. The repercussions were predictable, and he resigned from the foundation and festival. His accusation that the rest of the board was a "star chamber" would have been humorous if it had not been said with much anger and spite.

Other schisms existed in the background of the festival. A predictable annual turnover of personnel at the various volunteer positions due to personal reasons could be expected. But every year it seemed that someone was leaving the board or FOG due to a perceived or real problem. Some alleged that they weren't getting the support from the board that they expected. There were too many hassles with handling all the logistics of what was in many ways a "working" board. It took up too much of the members' time. Sometimes it was just a case of burnout, thanks to the hours devoted to Mariposa. Many were the excuses.

Every year some board members were unhappy with the leadership of the day. However, early in 2010 things seemed to come to a head. While things were civil in public, many catty comments went back and forth in emails and phone conversations among board members. A few board meetings had some rather feisty exchanges over the direction and control of the festival itself.

That winter, a cabal of several board members secretly approached former president Chris Lusty and asked him to come back to the board with the promise that he would be elected president immediately after the annual general meeting. At the 2010 AGM a partially new slate of officers was elected, including Lusty, whose nomination came from the floor of the meeting and was a surprise to some. It was something of a *coup d'état*. The president at the time, Catherine Brennan, was replaced by Lusty in the subsequent vote for the presidency that was held at the end of the meeting. It was the result of a lot of inside politics, but some of the people who'd been running the festival the last couple of years were astonished. Understandably, resentment lingered as did some antagonism. Brennan, who'd been with the organization since 1992, did not attend the festival that July, tacitly withdrew from all meetings, and resigned from the board later that year.

Meanwhile, the planning went on. Pam Carter and her FOG team dealt with the nuts and bolts of the festival while the artistic committee went to work on securing the names for the roster.

With much to celebrate, the artistic budget was increased substantially and a lot of big names were hired, many of historical importance. Gordon Lightfoot was the natural choice as the major headliner. Ian and Sylvia Tyson (but with their own backup bands) were both brought back in a salute to the festival's initial lineup. There was much hoping and wishing that the two, who'd rarely performed together since the early 70s, would do something remarkable as a duo once again at the festival. Murray McLauchlan, with his long history at Mariposa, was hired. Ninety-year-old Oscar Brand, a headliner at the 1962 festival and a participant in many others, agreed to come from New York City to play a single concert. Long-time favourites such as David Francey, Chris Smither, Dave Gunning, Chris and Ken Whiteley, Catherine MacLellan, and the Downchild Blues Band were hired. Up-and-coming acts included Little Miss Higgins, the Métis Fiddler Quartet, Matt Andersen, Elliott Brood, Jason Collett, and Zeus. Serena Ryder, a rising star on the Canadian pop charts, was selected as the Saturday night headliner. Serena had played Mariposa while still in her teens and had returned often through-out the previous decade, once even as a "surprise guest." With each appear-ance, she loomed larger and larger on the music scene.

The reality of the festival business was that it felt necessary to have big names in order to draw the crowds. Yet it's impossible to say for sure that this is true. Audiences had come to expect good music and a good time at Mariposa, no matter who the final mainstage act was each night. In yearly audience surveys, the headliner was ranked well down the list of things people appreciated and wanted, yet having well-known names on the marquee assured attention would be paid to the festival advertising. In the surveys, interestingly, the general atmosphere, the artisans, Folkplay, and the workshop performances ranked higher in importance than the headliner.

One group not invited to participate was the Travellers, the stars of the 1961 festival. Jerry Gray still kept the band name alive and while the person-nel had changed, the group's banjo player felt — perhaps rightfully — that his act should have been included in the roster. He approached the artistic committee via email, asking that the Travellers be added to the fiftieth anni-versary lineup. That request put the artistic team in somewhat of a quandary.

Sid Dolgay, who'd been a Traveller until 1964, had helped to launch Mariposa and was an iconic presence at the festival each year. He'd worked as a board member and part of the artistic committee at one time, and though he was well into his eighties, a member of the honorary board of advisors. He was one of those initially inducted into the Mariposa Folk Festival Hall of Fame in 2005. Sid had always championed Mariposa and became openly emotional when speaking of its importance in his life. Each year at the festival since 2007 there had been a "This Land Is Your Land" workshop, hosted by Sid and celebrating the music and multicultural nature of Canada. But he and Jerry Gray were not on good terms, and Sid deeply resented the fact he'd been shunted out of the Travellers years before. I knew this, and when the Travellers were being considered — for their historical importance more than for their musical ability — I had lunch with Sid and broached the idea.

"Well, if Jerry Gray is coming to the festival, I won't!" Sid said emphatically.

It was certainly a dilemma. Option one meant excluding the historically important band. Option two meant excluding the festival's greatest cheerleader. I opted for the former. Complicating the whole affair was Sid's urgent plea that Jerry not be told the exclusion was due to Sid's insistence.

Jerry was told, much to his dismay, that the Travellers were not invited to Mariposa in 2010. Further complicating the issue, Jerry contacted his old pal Oscar Brand with the offer to accompany him during Oscar's solo concert. Oscar agreed, but when Sid found out, he was livid and repeated his threat to not come to the festival. I had to phone Oscar at his New York home and ask that Jerry not be part of his show. Oscar conceded and Jerry was told, in effect, not to show up. It was a sad and bitter episode.

In the leadup to the festival, a few creative tricks were attempted with varying degrees of success.

An arrangement had been made to facilitate camping. While the city strictly resisted the idea of allowing camping at Tudhope, a new "family event park" called Burl's Creek had opened about sixteen kilometres south of Orillia. They could provide camping for Mariposa ticket holders, provided there was an event going on in their park. (Thank you, silly local bylaws!) The artistic committee arranged for the Métis Fiddler Quartet to put on a concert on Thursday night for the few campers who'd arrived the day before the festival. The group was well-received but few campers registered. The same thing was attempted the next year but without much success again, so that venture was eventually axed.

Another local connection made by the festival was with the Stephen Leacock Museum in Orillia. The museum works much the same way that the Mariposa Folk Festival does. Both need to engage in partnerships in order to please the granting bodies, so it was a friendly marriage of convenience when the artistic committee arranged to put on a series of afternoon concerts at the Leacock Museum, only a few hundred metres down the road from Tudhope Park. Billed as a free gig, it was a way to offer a thank-you to locals in Orillia and provide a different venue for festival patrons. Mike Stevens, Ohbijou, and Elliott Brood all played there to small, satisfied crowds. This was the second year that a gateless, unticketed event was held on the grounds of the great author's summer home. It didn't necessarily garner new audiences but certainly offered some variety and a change of scenery.

That year a third attempt was made at running an arts-related school in the days leading up to the festival. Mariposa once again partnered with Orillia's Lakehead University campus, and the plan was to offer creative arts workshops on things like photography, songwriting, printmaking, puppetry, and singing. The undertaking had a couple of purposes. It was hoped that it would bring in new people who would partake in the arts classes and then attend the festival. Hopefully these folks would spend their money in Orillia, thereby adding something to the local economy. And on the nobler side of things, such classes were part of fulfilling the festival's mandate of encouraging folk arts in Canada. Unfortunately, many of the classes did not have enough registrants to be feasible. While such planning worked at events like Goderich's Celtic Roots Festival and the Winnipeg Folk Festival, it never seemed to gain traction in Orillia.

A glossy fiftieth anniversary magazine was produced. Rare photos, first-hand accounts, and in-depth interviews with legendary performers told the story of the Mariposa Folk Festival. It was a powerful and interesting piece of work, but it met with only fair to middling success in the Emporium. (Each subsequent year the Emporium sold the remainder of the magazine stock at ever-reduced sale prices!)

The actual festival that year was a major success by nearly any standard. From the opening night until the final bows on Sunday, nearly everything seemed to go well. Even the brief misty rain failed to dampen spirits that weekend. The lingering smell of straw, laid down over mud and wet patches, left the backstage area smelling like a barnyard, but the prevailing attitude was, "hey, at least it's not raining now." The daytime workshops, the artisan village, the community partners in attendance, the food venues, and the beer tent all seemed to hum along smoothly and offer enough variety, entertainment, and interest that organizers could honestly say that there was something at Mariposa for everyone.

Ruth Jones-McVeigh made the trek from her home in Ottawa and was effusive in her praise of the fiftieth incarnation of her baby. "I honestly wasn't too surprised that the first one was a success, but to ask me if I could visualize myself being there 50 years from now with an audience ten times as big, no I could not have imagined that…. I'm overjoyed and I think it's wonderful" (as quoted in the *Orillia Packet and Times*, July 12, 2010). The eighty-three-year-old founder kept up a hectic schedule as she caught up with old acquaintances and took in many of the musical offerings over the weekend. That Saturday, she cut a huge anniversary cake and served it to passing festival patrons.

Friday night was a mixed bag on the mainstage. It began with Matt Andersen, Dan Mangan, and the Wooden Sky and culminated with a very Beatles-sounding Zeus (from nearby Barrie, Ontario), first appearing alone and then backing Jason Collett, a singer-songwriter from Toronto and former member of the ensemble Broken Social Scene. The youth market was being served. The music was a bit more rocking than your usual folk music might be, but the emphasis on songwriting seemed to meet Mariposa standards.

During the daytime on both Saturday and Sunday the very young and their families were also being served. Renowned kids' entertainers Sharon and Bram, and poet Dennis Lee, of *Alligator Pie* fame, entertained the surprisingly large crowds of families and children at the Folkplay stage.

The weekend's workshops offered all one could ask for at a festival. Hearkening back to Estelle Klein's original concept, the workshops had over the years been at least as interesting as what was going on over at the mainstage. The 2010 festival was no different, as so many great combinations took place amid the shaded stages overlooking Lake Couchiching. A number of workshop ideas from the past were recycled, but with new lineups. For example, from 1977 there was one titled "Fiddle Evolution." Jean Carignan and John Allan Cameron had been two original participants in that workshop; the newer version included Chris McKhool, Gordie MacKeeman, and the Métis Fiddler Quartet. These individual musicians each brought their distinctive backgrounds to the stage and were able to show the crowd the differences in style between Québécois, Cape Breton, Métis, and the jazz and world music sounds that can be produced by a fiddle.

Mike Ford, Mike Stevens, Jason Collett, and Michael Johnston began the Saturday workshops with songs based on the Hank Snow–themed "I've Been Everywhere." Later in the afternoon, a folk superstar lineup graced the Estelle Klein stage where Murray McLauchlan, Sylvia Tyson, Dan Mangan, and Serena Ryder knocked it out of the ballpark with their unique skills in a workshop called "Songwriters Extraordinaire." The Barnfield Stage featured clog dancing and traditional folk dancing for some audience participation. The Whiteley Brothers, Matt Andersen, Rick Fines, Suzie Vinnick, and Little Miss Higgins thrilled those in attendance with their collective take on a revisited 1979 workshop called "The Seven Deadly Sins." Over at the Interactive Stage, festivalgoers could take part in steel drum playing, poetry writing, watercolour painting, a gospel singalong, basket making, and even some belly dancing. In keeping with some of the left-leaning political views expected from the aging hippie demographic, former Communist Party of Canada leader George Hewison sang about "Labour and Song." The Sultans of String, Liziwe Mahashe, and Alejandra Ribera were part of the world music offerings that year. Sherry Lawson and her brother Mark Douglas, members of the local Ojibwa community at Rama First Nation, presented entertaining and informative storytelling. James Gordon, a performer from Guelph, Ontario, drove his homemade houseboat the *Eramosa Belle* to the site and once again offered it up as a stage where the likes of David Francey, Mose Scarlett, and Dave Gunning sang out over the water of the bay. Such was the variety to be had on the side stages. A late-afternoon "Celebration of the Music of Oscar Brand" featured the ninety-year-old legend along with James Gordon, Sid Dolgay, and special guest Josh White Jr. It was a lovely tribute to the man who'd written the Canadian classic "Something to Sing About." It certainly was.

A Saturday night blues theme in the beer tent provided the drinkers in the Mariposa crowd some extremely talented acts. Chris and Ken Whiteley and guitar whiz Matt Andersen appeared alongside harmonica virtuoso Mike Stevens. Little Miss Higgins, Suzie Vinnick, and Rick Fines all provided variations of blues music. The Downchild Blues Band closed the bluesy evening in the pub.

The Downchild Blues Band holds legendary status as one of the best blues bands in Canada. They'd been performing for decades by that point and had played Mariposa in the past. The band was thoroughly professional in many ways. However, their hiring had caused much rancour at the board level. While I was on vacation in Florida that January, the president hired the band (without my knowledge) at a rather extravagant fee. I was not happy to have been circumvented and I made it known.

The band caused further friction once they got to the festival. When the band arrived to play their one and only appearance — closing the beer tent on Saturday night — one member of the band was extremely upset with me (in my role as artistic director) because there was no washroom backstage. The port-a-potties were less than sixty metres from the beer tent stage, and I felt it was something he should have been able to deal with. Annoyed by his complaints, I asked, with characteristic sarcasm, if he wanted me to carry one of the toilets over and place it beside the stage. Then I walked away. Needless to say, I didn't go back to see the band perform, and they didn't send me any flowers on Valentine's Day. Neither did Mariposa's president.

Over on the mainstage, the audience thrilled to the multicultural sounds of Sultans of String; the modern yet traditional Québécois tunes of Les Tireux d'Roches; the brilliant songs of Catherine MacLellan and her superbly tight band; the zany fiddling of Ashley MacIsaac; and the rather frenetic set of Serena Ryder, dancing and whirling about the stage, singing in her powerful, unique voice.

Mariposa had been witness to Serena's long and steady rise to fame. First hired in 2002 as a teenager, Serena had returned to the festival a number of times. She'd also played a winter Mariposa in Concert event to a standing-room-only (SRO) audience. Each time she played, she came away with new fans, won over not only by her incredible vocal powers but also by her songwriting ability. And even when she covered other people's material (such as her 2006 hit "Good Morning Starshine"), she gave it a new and often improved twist. By Mariposa's fiftieth anniversary, she had risen to such stature that she was an obvious choice to headline one of the nights of the festival. She was a Mariposa success story, starting out as an unknown at the festival and developing international renown. She was a drawing card, and although she was receiving a fee commensurate with that drawing power, we determined her higher fee was worth it to ensure her presence at the festival.

Sunday evening's mainstage show began with the Whiteley Brothers. Both had played the festival in the early 70s as young men in the Original Sloth Band. Now Ken, looking like an emaciated Santa Claus, joined his brother to give the audience a sample of outstanding and versatile musicianship. Murray McLauchlan offered up his usual articulate, insightful, and tuneful songs. Sylvia Tyson played her solo material and then, near the end of Ian Tyson's set, joined him on stage.

It was an arrangement only the two of them had known about. Ian turned to the wings late in his set and called up his ex-wife and ex-partner, giving the audience seated out front a musically spine-tingling thrill.

Seeing Sylvia Tyson reunite with Ian late Sunday night for a beautiful rendition of "Four Strong Winds" brought tears to Ruth Jones's eyes. She was not alone. As the two folk icons sang together, many in the audience reacted the same way. So, too, did that night's stage host, smiley-voiced CBC personality Shelagh Rogers. As the duo reconnected and harmonized on the Canadian classic — Peter Gzowski called it Canada's second national anthem — Shelagh turned to me with tears welling in her eyes.

For the audience there was a special treat in store that few expected. The marketing and promotion of the fiftieth festival had included information that there would be a "special guest act" appearing on Sunday night. People throughout the park speculated about who that might be. Would it be Joni Mitchell? Leonard Cohen? Not Neil Young, surely? It turned out to be the two leaders of Canada's favourite country-rock band Blue Rodeo, Greg Keelor and Jim Cuddy. The duo hopped on stage, sandwiched on the bill between Ian and Sylvia and Gordon Lightfoot, and with just their two acoustic guitars they ran through a fabulous rendering of Blue Rodeo's best-known songs. The park patrons were awestruck.

Finally, Gordon Lightfoot, the hometown boy and a living legend to all Canadians, took to the stage with his two accompanists, Terry Clements and Rick Haynes, and sealed the night with a smattering of his great songs, including "The Canadian Railroad Trilogy" and "The Wreck of the Edmund Fitzgerald." The audience could hardly have asked for more talent on stage that night. Indeed, the weekend was so laden with talent that former headliner David Francey was relegated to side-stage concerts during the day!

Performers do not always enthuse about where they play. Most have served their time in seedy bars or mildewed church basements, and it's uncommon for a singer to praise a bar or country hall. But with Mariposa — and this was especially true at the special fiftieth anniversary — many of the artists talked about how great the site, the stages, the sound, and of course the audiences were.

"It has a great feel," said Sylvia Tyson. "It's good to see old friends still at it and still going strong" (as quoted in *Orillia Today*, July 15, 2010).

Catherine MacLellan, writing in a PEI tourism newspaper called *The Buzz*, gave a glowing account of her time at Mariposa. She related how she and her band had enjoyed the after-party, jamming with the likes of the Breakmen, Ashley MacIsaac, and Elliott Brood, singing songs, and drinking tequila. She also revelled in the way that she and her mates were programmed in workshop situations:

> The great thing about these type of folk festivals is how bands and songwriters are thrown together on stages to see what will happen when element combine. Our first work-shop ended with a rowdy bluegrass version of Nirvana's "All Apologies," led by Madison Violet. Our second workshop of the day was in the beer tent doing a double bill with the Grass Mountain Hobos. It was so fun and we had the crowd wrapped in our PEI-themed banter and songs.... We got along so easily and understood each other on a very basic level, in a gut way, like family. (August 2010, 7)

Several Larrivée guitars had been donated to the festival in 2010. Amber McGarvey, a volunteer and the granddaughter of co-founder Pete McGarvey, had gone to each of the performers that year, including Lightfoot and the Tysons, to get autographs on each acoustic model. Highly valued without the autographs, the guitars took on extra prestige with all those signatures. Valued at over $3,000 each, two of the instruments were raffled off at the 2011 festival while a third was kept for the archives. Another model was later sold on eBay with the money going to support the festival.

The board of directors basked in the glow of a successful festival that year. The crowds were bigger than they'd ever been in Orillia, and the bank account, while not overwhelming, was in the black. Mariposa stood on solid ground. Praise was effusive from the media, the audience, and the performers alike. The sponsors were generally happy with their treatment and presence. The federal and provincial governments were happy with how the grant money had been spent. A feeling of confidence and security seemed to settle over the organization, and there was a general sense that the celebratory festival had been extremely successful. The fiftieth anniversary would be a hard act to follow in the years to come.

CHAPTER FIFTEEN
The Modern Era

AFTER THE SUCCESS OF THE FIFTIETH anniversary Mariposa Folk Festival in 2010, any subsequent incarnation was likely to suffer in comparison. It would not be easy to generate as much excitement and interest in years that followed. Most lineups could not compare in either depth of talent or historical importance. Yet every year after that landmark event the festival generated its own special stories and excitement, and the Mariposa Folk Foundation became more deeply rooted in the community and remained a sustainable, stable entity.

With the financial success of the 2010 festival, money was available to hire staff, if only on a part-time basis. While über-volunteer Bernie Haley still held down the fort almost daily at the downtown Orillia office, the organization's street presence could not truly function on the back of a single volunteer — at least, it wasn't good business to function that way. A new part-time office manager was hired. The Orillia District Arts Council still shared the space, and there would now be someone in the Mariposa Folk Festival office during most business hours. The MFF manager was expected to look after clerical duties for the festival and foundation. She had to, at times, look after ODAC business, but in a reciprocal arrangement the ODAC staff often answered the phones for Mariposa, too. There was feeling of co-operation between the two groups.

Part of the reason for having an office in downtown Orillia was to have a year-round visual presence. Located across from the gorgeous new public library and the 120-year-old landmark, the Orillia Opera House, the office was also the site of board meetings, press conferences, and sporadic concerts, and it provided space for other groups in town. Some of the space at the back of the office housed archival files, leftovers from the Emporium, boxes of festival supplies, and some of the more climate-sensitive electronic equipment. Even some of the leftover liquor ended up in boxes at the back of the downtown unit.

In 2011 the foundation office moved to new space in Orillia's "arts district," a city block favoured by art galleries, an art store, and the city's art and history museum. This was a unilateral decision, precipitated when the City of Orillia granted the Orillia District Arts Council free office space, and the ODAC moved out of the shared space on Mississaga Street.

On the financial side of things, for years former president Ted Duncan had gotten up to speak at annual general meetings about the need for some financial security in the form of a rainy-day fund. Board member Michael Slan took up the idea and, with a great deal of perseverance and determination, managed to eventually convince the foundation to set aside money in a sustainability fund. With an attorney's eye for detail, Michael managed to oversee the eventual accumulation of almost $250,000 in the fund. The rationale for both Ted's and Michael's thinking was that the event was "one rainy weekend away from going bankrupt."

Several other festivals had suffered that very fate. Summerfolk in Owen Sound, for example, a festival comparable in size and style, nearly bit the dust after one of their August weekends was inundated with rain. (Former artistic director Don Bird often refers to his old festival "Summersoak.") Only a frantic plea for financial help from the Georgian Bay community had saved it from collapse, and it took the festival years to recover. Mariposa itself had dodged that bullet several times in the past. The 1990 Mariposa festival, in particular, was one such heart-breaking year. Stanfest in Canso, Nova Scotia, was completely cancelled in 2014 because of the unexpected Hurricane Arthur. It was simply a matter of good governance to build a financial cushion in case of disaster. (In a gesture of support for their comrades on the east coast, the Mariposa board sent a cheque to help the Canso festival in its time of financial crisis.)

During the early winter months of 2011 the foundation held a "think tank" to poll stakeholders and outsiders on directions for the festival. President Chris Lusty announced to the local media that the foundation was looking for input from the public with regard to its vision for the festival.

It was probably wise to assess what outsiders thought of the event and its general direction. Invitations went out to interested parties such as former board members, city councillors, volunteers, and sponsors. A meeting was convened at Lakehead's new satellite campus in Orillia's west end. It was expedited by one of the men who'd brought the festival back to Orillia in 2000, Gord Ball, a professional facilitator. After a day-long series of discussions and group analysis, a picture of what the public liked and wanted was then available to the board of directors to integrate into their long-term planning. While there was a long list of positive ideas and suggestions, the board of directors examined the list and came away with three they chose to focus on: an awareness of and respect for the environment; making an effort to involve youth; and broadening the definition of folk. As with so much of the thinking that comes out of symposia, it was easier said than done.

Since the early days back in Orillia, planning sessions had been a key part of the board of directors actions. Periodic all-day retreats had helped the directors focus on what was needed, what should be eliminated, and what could be implemented. Between 2007 and 2016, the board held four such retreats, aimed at assessing both the past and the future of the foundation. In 2014, for example, they came to the conclusion that the festival and foundation should stay the course and build in small, measurable increments.

The greening initiatives that had begun under the watch of father–son team Warren and Aaron Howes began to pay dividends beyond their practical environmental impact. Since MFF could brag that less than 15 percent of the waste from the festival ended up in the area's landfill, both the government and businesses took notice. The Orillia Chamber of Commerce gave the festival an achievement award ("The Green Award") for what had been accomplished by the move to compost food resources at each festival. In 2015 the Ontario government recognized the value of such eco-friendly activity and gave the festival one of its annual awards. By then Ryerson University in Toronto was an active partner in studying the impact of Mariposa's greening initiative, and the general feeling was that Mariposa was a provincial leader in this kind of work. The waste diversion of sending over 80 percent of the festival's detritus to recycling and composting was impressive by any standards, and Mariposa's success story was told over and over again.

As the festival moved into its second decade in Orillia, it still looked remarkably vital, despite the ever-increasing amount of grey hair in the audience. Then again, there were also lots of young families bringing their children to the Folkplay area each year, a good indicator that the festival was keeping a core audience of middle-aged and more youthful patrons. The festival weekends took on a familiar and comfortable feel. Many of the patrons and performers described the wonderful vibe of each event.

Just prior to the festival in 2011 the Premier's Awards for Excellence in the Arts honoured Mariposa with a nomination. The awards are given out by Ontario government to recognize outstanding achievement and contribution to arts and culture in the province by an individual or group. Poet Dennis Lee, composer R. Murray Schafer, the Blyth Theatre Festival (theatre), Hot Docs, and dancer Menaka Thakkar were some of the other nominees. A resource centre called Vtape won that year, but it was nevertheless a prestigious and deserving accolade for Mariposa just to be nominated. Almost the same week, the fiftieth anniversary magazine, *50 Years of Mariposa*, which had been produced by the local weekly, *Orillia Today*, won a first-place award from the Ontario community newspaper association.

The festival in 2011 built on the success of the previous year's work. Josh Ritter headed the youth-oriented Friday night that also included Yukon Blonde, the Beauties, and Jim Bryson with the Weakerthans band on the mainstage. Saturday night saw Emmylou Harris return to the Mariposa mainstage as the weekend headliner. John McDermott, often critiqued as a "soft seat" crooner, put on a good show and dove into his workshop appearances like an old folk-festival pro. Being backed by two former Mariposa performers, Jason Fowler and Brian MacMillan, had probably helped McDermott prepare for the weekend. As the "special secret guest appearance" artist, Ron Sexsmith appeared just prior to Harris and even joined Harris on a beautiful rendition of Lucinda Williams's song "This Sweet Old World."

Sunday night was dedicated to singer-songwriters — the backbone of Mariposa's lineups throughout its history. Amelia Curran, Garnet Rogers, Ron Hynes, and Lunch at Allen's (Murray McLauchlan, Marc Jordan, Cindy Church, and Ian Thomas) gave the audience their musical take on love and nearly everything else in this world. Then legendary Peter Yarrow (one-third of Peter, Paul and Mary), gave his solo show with a rousing finale of "Blowin' in the Wind."

I thought it unusual, but it is perhaps telling that Peter Yarrow was not in demand for media attention that year. Roots Music Canada was a website that presented performances and interviews with folk acts from across

Canada and the U.S., and the brainchild of broadcaster Andy Frank and musician David Newland. During the 2011 festival, Newland and Frank recorded informative chats with many of the performers for the Roots Music Canada website. When I asked if they wanted to have some time with Peter Yarrow, both of the interviewers quickly declined. It seemed an odd decision given that Yarrow had been active on the folk/roots scene since the folk revival days and had been a contemporary of Bob Dylan, Phil Ochs, Joan Baez, and Pete Seeger. He'd even walked with Martin Luther King during the civil rights marches of the 60s. Were they snubbing an old-timer whose time they figured had come and gone? Perhaps it was simply a lack of regard younger folkies had for historical figures. Whatever the case, time marches on, even for folk singers.

That year we attempted an acoustic stage with absolutely no amplification for the first time since the festival was back in Orillia. Named in honour of Ruth Jones-McVeigh, the festival founder, it met with mixed success. While there was an appeal because of its "get in close to the performer" vibe, the noise from clattering golf carts and the general festival noise at times hampered the performances. Non-amplified acoustic guitars or fiddles and un-mic'ed voices simply cannot carry outdoors, especially amid a country-fair atmosphere. For future festivals we kept the name of the stage ("Ruth") but abandoned the acoustic idea, considering it a noble but failed experiment.

During the autumn of 2011 the festival took on a new initiative that, in some ways, grew into a battle with the Orillia city council and certain local residents. Audience camping had been a feature of the festival since Innis Lake in the mid-60s. At Molson Park in Barrie it had been an important part of the overall vibe as well. Yet in the years since Mariposa's return to Orillia, camping had never been something the festival could use as an attraction to sell tickets. There had been a half-hearted attempt to use a farmer's field outside of town in 2001, but that was completely unsuccessful and a logistical nightmare. The only people who were allowed to camp on site in the early years at Tudhope Park were the electrical crew and the overnight security volunteers. Then a few of the artisans were allowed to camp for the purpose of guarding their wares. Finally, after continual pushing from veteran organizers like Gerry Hawes and Catherine Brennan, the festival board applied officially to make camping a part of the Mariposa experience. Tudhope is a big park — over twenty-eight hectares — with lots of space to accommodate hundreds of campers.

Some of the board's directors, especially those who were from out of town, needed a brief history lesson regarding Orillia and Tudhope Park. The park had been donated to the Town of Orillia in 1928 by the wealthy Tudhope family, makers of carriages and early automobiles, with the proviso that it be "for park purposes only." Yet over the decades the town had allowed the grounds to become just that, a campground called "Barnfield." By the late 1980s the facilities and the clients who frequented the park had made the campground not only an eyesore but also a constant source of trouble. Police had to be called almost nightly throughout the camping season. Orillians were happy that the park reverted to open space in the 90s, and any move to reintroduce tents and visitors from out of town was generally frowned upon. Many residents of nearby Couchiching Point, Museum Drive, and MacIsaac Drive were adamant that the park never again allow camping.

So it was a major step when Pam Carter, on behalf of the board of directors, approached city council in November of 2011 with a proposal to allow audience camping at the park in 2012. The festival needed the revenue; there were not enough hotel rooms for visitors; and since council was allowing Ride for Sight, the other big summer weekend tenant of the park, to have camping in 2012, Mariposa should get a chance to try it. In January the council voted overwhelmingly to allow camping, and by the time the festival rolled around for 2012, a team of volunteers (led in part by Gerry Hawes) had organized the campers into zones. There were no drunken campers staggering into the lake, no noise to wake the park's neighbours, and no destruction of Tudhope facilities. It could hardly have been more peaceful. The furor from local residents quickly dissipated, and from then on the festival was able to offer a camping alternative to ticket buyers.

This was not the only battle that the festival faced with the city. Since the return to Orillia, the city had charged the festival $400 per day for use of Tudhope Park. In the fall of that 2011 out of the blue — with no consultation — the city decided to nearly quadruple that daily fee. The actual letter from the city stated, "it looked like the festival could afford it." President Chris Lusty took up the organization's case with the media, emphatically stating that the festival brought national attention to the town and attracted over twenty thousand people to Orillia over the course of each festival weekend. Indeed, MFF had even funded repairs and upgrades in the park to the tune of over $70,000. Lusty also pointed out in a *Packet and*

Times letter to the editor that the festival donated thousands of dollars worth of free tickets, put on free shows for Orillians, hired local talent, brought arts education to town — all on the backs of volunteers. Lusty emphasized that the City of Orillia looked upon Mariposa as simply a renter of space rather than a cultural and community partner. Eventually — and this took a couple of years to change — council decided that a sponsorship of the city's largest annual event might be wise, and they came aboard with a substantial annual sponsorship. It was large enough that the City of Orillia became one of the festival's major sponsors. It helped that the new mayor and council were predominantly supporters of tourism in general and the festival in particular.

The 2012 festival featured a stellar lineup of folk-rocker Billy Bragg, Canadian superstar Jann Arden, and South Africa's renowned musical hero Johnny Clegg. Young poet Shane Koyczan was the unexpected hit of the Friday night with his touching and personal verse — "Astonishing," according to John Swartz in the *Orillia Packet and Times*.

Headliner Jann Arden, 2012.

As I was chatting with Koyczan the next day near the mainstage, a festival patron enthusiastically approached us. "I just wanted to tell you," he said to Koyczan, "that I'm a high-school English teacher, and I have used some of your poetry in my classes. I'm going to do it even more in the future!"

o o o

And an old friend showed up unexpectedly once again.

Behind the mainstage and the green room, at the performer, VIP, and volunteer entrance into the park, the FOG team always assigned security volunteers (wearing T-shirts labelled "Access"). A young man, perhaps not even twenty years old, stood there to check for correct wrist-bands or identification to ensure people entering by these gates were indeed supposed to be coming this way. A nondescript Pontiac pulled into the parking lot, and an older gentleman, a septuagenarian, got out and walked toward the gate.

"I'm sorry sir, but I can't let you in," stated the young access volunteer.

A tall man with a "Board of Directors" badge around his neck tapped the young volunteer on the shoulder and said, as calmly as possible, "It's okay. That's Gordon Lightfoot." Michael Slan, the board's lawyer, had seen Lightfoot approaching and was there to greet him. The young volunteer stepped back and the famous singer was allowed into the park.

Lightfoot was naturally welcomed into the green room area and told me that his daughter Ingrid wanted to see Jann Arden perform, so they'd made the drive up from city. Then, almost as an aside, Gordon said, "I've brought my guitar. Would you like me to play a tune? But I don't want to upstage Jann."

I went to Jann's dressing room and knocked on the door.

"Gordon Lightfoot is here and is willing to do a song or two but he doesn't want to upstage you. Would you mind if he played something before you come on?"

"Hey, it's fucking Gordon Lightfoot," said Jann, with a huge smile. "He can play all night if he wants to!" Her enthusiasm was typically Canadian, characteristically humorous, and definitely adoring of our greatest song-writer. Jann took the stage afterwards with her ultra-professional band and delivered a fantastic and memorable concert.

o o o

The festival was in good shape all round as it moved on to the 2013 season. Early in the process the organizers named Arlo Guthrie as the Sunday night headliner. Having a reputable folkie name like his helped to spur ticket sales, especially before Christmas. Kathleen Edwards and Bahamas, two young and also reputable performers, were slated for Friday night. An unusual choice for the Saturday night headline act was Randy Bachman who was most famous as a member of the Guess Who and then Bachman–Turner Overdrive. A rocker through and through, Randy was backed by the Sadies, one of Canada's most skillful folk bands. The choice of Bachman was more a tribute to his skills as a Hall of Fame songwriter than for any connection he'd ever had with the Canadian folk music community.

Randy has a quirky and dry sense of humour. I accompanied him backstage with a photographer who wanted a picture of Bachman and the Sadies. Randy complied. The photographer led us to a large slab of quarried limestone near the backstage area. Dryly, Randy looked at the rectangular piece of stone and commented to the few of us assembled there, "Oh, so this is where they buried Gordon Lightfoot."

o o o

Although the lineup was great and attendance was good, the festival had to deal with several difficult issues in 2013.

During more than a dozen years back in Orillia, Mariposa had never had many alcohol problems: no drunken patrons staggering to their cars or into the lake, no belligerent ticket holders razzing the artists, no children in the pub area, no underage drinking. It had become routine for the FOG chair to secure liquor licences for the three areas where booze was to be sold — the pub, Alice's, and the green room.

In 2013 FOG chair Pam Carter applied for (and received) the licences in March. Out of the blue in May the Alcohol and Gaming Commission of Ontario (AGCO) called Pam to demand a meeting regarding the licence

Gordon Lightfoot.

application. That was the year that camping was fully implemented for the public. According to the police, the camping element changed the climate of the festival.

Pam explained,

> We were advised that we would be required to increase on-site OPP from two at the Pub and two roaming to four at the Pub and four roaming. We would be required to have four private security at the Pub and two each at Alice's and the Green Room. Lastly, we were required to have six volunteers at the Pub and three each at Alice's and the Green Room. All bags would have to be checked upon entrance into the licensed areas. If patrons refused they would be denied entrance. An in/out count was to be maintained.

The police would not be doing any bag checks so extra private security — already a huge expense to the event — would have to be hired. As ticket holders entered the fenced-off pub area, for instance, they were met with a crowd of police and security people. The police looked like they were armed to the teeth, and the security people wanted to check every purse and knapsack. To some folks it was intimidating, not to mention unnecessary. In addition to all of that, the extra cost of policing and security fees ran to over $15,000, an unexpected hit on the festival's budget that year.

The fencing that had worked so efficiently over the past dozen or so years was also deemed to be "insufficient." Double rows of fencing had to surround the licensed areas with a wide moat between the two fences. (In case someone tried to pass a beer from the licensed area to someone outside the area. Really?) And if the festival opted to have all of Tudhope Park licensed, the entire shoreline of the festival (at least a kilometre of waterfront) would have to be fenced. Picture that! And at that point the one-sided "negotiations" with the AGCO became heavy-handed. If Mariposa chose not to hire extra security and the AGCO felt the "situation was unsafe," they could — and would — pull the special occasions permit and licence. That was unfathomable for Mariposa; the sale of beer, wine, and coolers goes a long way to paying the bills of the festival weekend. The local AGCO rep had not been aware that the licences were already granted. Yet a week after the meeting, Pam received a call from the Toronto AGCO advising her that if Mariposa did not comply immediately, the licences to sell liquor would be revoked.

The festival had little choice, according to Pam, so organizers complied.

> The result of the additional security doubled the security budget, something we had not planned for. Patrons found it oppressive and thought that there must have been a terror threat or at least the suspicion of a motorcycle gang on its way. When we [Mariposa] questioned why other events that took in our area that summer didn't have the same amount of security we were advised that they would be brought up to the same standard. Central Ontario was setting the benchmark for the rest of the province.

What the Ontario Alcohol and Gaming Commission did not seem to realize was that Mariposa volunteers attend other events around the province each summer. At one particularly large and comparably sized event, there were no paid-duty police officers or hired security in view. In fact, organizers of the event admitted that they had not been required by their local AGCO officials to bulk up on security or police presence. It was rather disheartening and a source of resentment for the Mariposa organizers to think that they alone had been centred-out to beef up protection from all those (non-existent) drunks and rabble-rousers. Yet the MFF people were also not ready to throw another organization under the bus to make the point of fairness to the police.

Close to home, the annual Ride For Sight celebration of motorcyclists who raise money to fight blindness took place only a few weeks prior to the Mariposa Folk Festival at Tudhope Park. That event was licensed to use the entire park, but the organizers were not told to fence off the shoreline, nor were they required to have an excessive number of police officers present during the event. Puzzling, to say the least.

As one of the most peaceful public events imaginable, all of this over-the-top security planning and its added costs made for a rather absurd scenario at the actual festival. Nevertheless, relations between the police and the organization and between the police and patrons remained amicable and respectful.

Another issue was complimentary ticket sales demanded by city council. Since Mariposa's return to Orillia in 2000, the mayor and council were each given pairs of comp tickets to visit and enjoy the festival each year. With relations between the foundation and the city at their nadir in 2013, however, a decision was made at the board level to give the city (meaning the council and staff) a small number of free passes based not on political entitlement but on the town's contribution as a sponsor. One councillor phoned the festival office, angrily demanding his free tickets the week before the festival, but he was told that a new procedure was in place, and he'd have to see if any of the five or so passes sent to city hall were yet to be claimed. It was petty on the part of MFF but drove home the point that the municipality needed to treat its premier annual event in a less shoddy fashion. The passes for council were reinstituted the following year and relations between the city and the foundation have never been better, especially since that particular slate of councillors were all turned out of office in the election that fall.

o o o

The festival in 2014 saw good weather, and a good crowd, and presented a strong artistic lineup. Ani DiFranco, Dala, and Feist all made triumphant returns to Mariposa. World music fans got an eclectic mixture with Conjunto Chappottín, a big band from Cuba, as well as Niamh Ní Charra from Ireland, the Imbayakunas from Ecuador, and the Pacific Curls, a Maori trio from New Zealand. Rosanne Cash was the Sunday headliner and did not disappoint. Intriguing and unique performers like Trevor Gordon Hall, JoJo Worthington, Seryn, Zydeco Loco, the Barr Brothers, Birds of Chicago, and Ennis added much musical variety to the program. Singer-songwriters, the foundation of all Mariposa rosters, included veteran Dar Williams, Aboriginal star Keith Secola, and multi-talented Tim Chaisson.

o o o

The crowds were good and the performances were wonderful in 2014, but as with any festival there were a few "hiccups," including some issues with some of the acts. This is par for the course when dealing with performing artists and something any artistic director knows to expect. What follows is a bit of "inside baseball," but it gives a picture of what producers such as the Mariposa Folk Festival face when dealing with professional musicians.

Big-name acts tend to be represented by agents and managers. The performers have certain needs and are very precise about what they require — or desire. These demands are spelled out in "riders" that are attached to the contracts signed when the acts are hired. Technical riders lay out what sorts of microphones, amplifiers, and lighting the performers require to do their show. Most are fairly easy to accommodate. There are other kinds of riders also, such as hospitality riders — information specifying the food, drink, lodging, etc. that the performer demands. At times, the so-called hospitality riders might cause an artistic director to pull out his or her hair.

The most quirky rider I ever came across in my years as artistic director came from a young artist who'd managed to work her way up to headliner status. It included the following: eight cans of Guinness on ice (cans only, no bottles); two bottles of a specific Irish whiskey; two bottles of red wine; four bottles of vitaminwater; six bottles of premium, locally brewed India pale ale; six bottles of Stella or Heineken on ice; one bottle of Grey Goose or Absolut vodka ("on even numbered days") or one bottle of gin ("on odd numbered days"); two large bottles of tonic and two large bottles of soda water; two lemons and two limes; whiskey glasses; forty-eight bottles of spring water; two bunches of bananas ("fully ripe and ready to eat"); three ready-to-eat avocados; a fruit basket containing a variety of apples, grapes, and oranges; one loaf of multi-grain sliced bread; sesame or rice crackers; rice cakes; cold cuts — 250 grams of roasted turkey breast and 250 grams of roasted ham; mustard; a container of baba ghanouj; a container of hummus; salsa; two bags of purple corn chips; one bag of kettle chips ("salt and vinegar only"); a clean kettle; organic instant oatmeal; two brands of tea; honey; clean mugs or large coffee cups; plates and cutlery ("no plastic"); a pack of nine-volt batteries; ten sheets of blank paper; two Sharpie markers; a clean large mirror; and ten white hand towels.

You can only look at a list like that and laugh. Some provisions are put in simply to see if the producer (MFF) is reading all the contractual details (hence the well-known anecdote about a demand for all the red M&M's to be removed from a star's backstage candy supply). To fulfill every detail in a rider like the one above would be both tedious and expensive.

For years Sandy McAllister looked after the performers' dressing-room needs at Mariposa, picking and choosing from the riders what to place on their tables. There were never complaints with that compromise. Ironically, the bigger the stars, the less they seem to ask for in terms of hospitality. Lightfoot, Arlo Guthrie, and Peter Yarrow, for instance, did not ask for any kind of special treatment beyond what the festival deigned to offer them. And that was the approach that the festival had taken with artists: do what can be done with limited resources, and try to offer enough hospitality to make them comfortable while they spend a few hours in a dressing room. But don't go all out and buy enough stuff to house and feed an entire band for a week or more!

o o o

One major focus that year was accessibility. Special locations at the mainstage were mapped out and roped off for wheelchair access. A large-print festival schedule was made available at the information booth. Volunteers were trained to properly come to the aid of those needing assistance.

In the age of social media, it was crucial that the festival keep in touch and stay as up to date as possible. Patrons were invited before, during, and after the festival to visit sites such as Flickr, Facebook, Twitter, and Pinterest — in addition to the www.mariposafolk.com website — to keep up with all the news and images of the festival. A blog, written mostly by Gerry Hawes, was available with interviews, stories, and opinions. Videos were constantly being uploaded to YouTube, giving access to the festival experience to people anywhere in the world.

By 2015 the festival seemed to be cruising along — not that it was smooth and effortless (anything but!). Yet the organization was well led, the volunteer team seemed to be working in sync, and it was generally felt that the festival was meeting the needs of its audience. The City of Orillia had finally come on board and offered a generous grant. The sponsors continued with their ongoing support as well. Tweaks to the festival experience, such as the accessibility improvements and anti-smoking rules, made the site more pleasant for many patrons. The production company and technical crews were, by now, finely oiled machines delivering nearly faultless sound and lighting.

However, one ominous shadow was cast by interlopers in the vicinity. Burl's Creek, the event park fifteen kilometres south of Orillia, had been bought and was being transformed into a new kind of venue. Millions of dollars were spent on renovations to the site as it was revamped to include an audience bowl that could accommodate seventy thousand patrons. Space was also being provided for thousands of campers. The folks from the deep-pocketed Bonnaroo Music and Arts Festival in Tennessee arrived with both fanfare and controversy, announcing they'd be holding a monstrous new festival called "WayHome" two weeks after the Mariposa weekend. The headliners for the inaugural event included Neil Young, Modest Mouse, Hozier, the Sheepdogs, the Decemberists, Kendrick Lamar, alt-J, and other big-name rock, rap, and pop acts. Openly making it known that they didn't care if they made money, the organizers at Burl's Creek brought in huge crowds to see the well-known names. It helped that they had millions, literally, to spend on an artistic budget, compared with Mariposa's modest artistic budget, which hovered around $200,000.

The audience was made up of primarily twenty- and thirty-year-olds who camped or travelled from around Southern Ontario to hear a style of music very different from what was offered at Mariposa. Despite the fact their ticket prices were nearly 50 percent higher than the Orillia folk festival, the younger crowd more readily related to what they consider "their music." And the entertainment dollar can only go so far. It was hardly feasible for that young demographic to pay $150 for Mariposa *and* pay over $250 for WayHome two weeks later. Something had to give. On top of that, Burl's Creek also became home to the country music spectacle "Boots and Hearts" in early August. Again, tens of thousands showed up to see their favourite country music acts at exorbitant cost. How many of that audience might have attended Mariposa? It was difficult to gauge, but most MFF board members began to feel that the mega-festivals could hit smaller entities like Mariposa hard.

Soldiering on, the MFF team put on a festival in 2015 that stayed the course. All varieties of folk music genres were available for the taking: singer-songwriters like Eric Andersen, Mary Chapin Carpenter, Jimmy Webb, Irish Mythen, and Leonard Cohen's son, Adam; world music names like Peruvian star Lucho Quequezana and Zimbabwe's song/dance troupe Black Umfolosi; poets and storytellers like Dan Yashinsky and Toronto's poet laureate George Elliott Clarke; Aboriginal bluesman George Leach; francophone variety with Ariko and Réveillons; the tuneful folk rock of Reuben and the Dark; the alt-country feel of Doug Paisley; bluesmen Rick Fines and Rev. Robert B. Jones; the traditional approach of Jayme Stone's Lomax Project; humour from Cheryl Wheeler; Celtic dash from Poor Angus, the East Pointers, and RUNA; reggae from Taj Weekes and Adowa; dance, participatory activities, and kids' music…. It was a folk potpourri, as one would expect.

One downside was the performance of Lucinda Williams. Long recognized as a premier songwriter, she had performed at Mariposa in the 90s. Lucinda was the Saturday night headliner. She arrived on stage after a lengthy delay, launched into a hard-rocking set, and seemed more than a little surly, grumbling and cursing into the microphone. Long-time festival volunteer Peter Monahan muttered, "If we'd wanted AC/DC, we'd have hired AC/DC!" Many festival patrons picked up their chairs and began to leave, only to be taunted by the singer in a slurring and mumbling voice. It was not one of her better moments — or Mariposa's, for that matter. From her attitude, one might have assumed that bad-tempered audience members had been throwing rotting tomatoes toward the stage.

In 2015 a slo-pitch game was organized for Sunday afternoon at the impressive Jerry Udell Diamond, part of the Tudhope Park complex. It added yet another interesting element to an already jam-packed weekend event. "Fans Versus Bands" was the cry, and a trophy was supplied by Wood Hog, who played the festival that year as a member of the Ever-Lovin' Jug Band.

Adam Cohen's closing performance on Sunday night that year was a standout. He delivered great songs, talked with the audience like they were in his living room, and made a number of new fans with his profoundly professional approach. It was as good a performance as I could have expected from anyone I'd ever hired, yet it almost didn't happen.

About twenty minutes before Cohen was slated to go on stage, his manager came to the trailer that the Mariposa organizers use as a headquarters.

"Where's the tequila?" asked the manager, rather brusquely.

"What are you talking about?" I said.

"The Patrón Silver. It's in his rider. They pass around the bottle just before going on stage. It's their routine and ritual."

"I don't supply alcohol," I said.

"Well you'd better get some, or Adam doesn't go on."

I gulped and said I'd see what I could do.

Luckily, the MFF treasurer Ian Brown was in the trailer and had overheard the conversation. I shrugged my shoulders; I wasn't sure what to do. I wasn't going to be able to magically make booze appear. Ian said, "I can get you some tequila," then he exited the trailer and disappeared into the night. About ten minutes later he reappeared with a small mickey of tequila. It seems miracles can happen!

As luck would have it, Ian knew of an unopened bottle of Cazadores tequila at his girlfriend's house near the festival. He sped over to pick it up and brought it back in record time to save the day. I don't know whether the manager ever figured out how I came up with high-grade alcohol on a Sunday night in Ontario, but thank goodness for an efficient festival treasurer.

Everyone got what they wanted: the crowd went away happy and the 2015 festival ended on a positive note.

o o o

The 2016 festival encountered a number of challenges. A new, tiny folk festival had been planned for April in Orillia, there were mega-festivals close to Mariposa on the calendar, and a host of other entertainment opportunities around Central Ontario all conspired to cut into the limited budget people have for leisure activities. We also wondered if some audience burnout played a factor. Beyond all that, it seemed possible that the capricious nature of modern day musical tastes had begun to affect the Mariposa vibe.

The skyrocketing cost of artistic talent was a factor limiting who could be brought in as headliners. One simple example: we had an opportunity to hire John Prine for the 2016 festival, but his fee for a one-night appearance would have been approximately half of the entire artistic budget. Many performers who might have been headliners at affordable prices only a few years before were now asking for fees that were totally out of our range — remember, Mariposa is a small weekend festival run mostly by volunteers. As CD and recording sales diminished, the live performance fees rose proportionately. Big-name "folk" acts such as Mumford & Sons or the Avett Brothers were asking for money in the neighbourhood of $250,000 or more a night! So many performers were beyond the limited budget of a relatively small festival like Mariposa. Eventually, the Good Family (a combination of the Good Brothers, the Sadies, and their extended families), the Milk Carton Kids, and Rita Coolidge were secured as headliners, but it was quite a task to pull together an affordable lineup that would entice ticket buyers.

Despite the financial and artistic challenges that Mariposa had to face that year, the organizers managed to pull things together and put on another event. However, on the first night of the 2016 festival the weather turned nasty, and it felt like a replay of ten years earlier. Only a couple of the main-stage acts were able to complete their sets before an ominous dark cloud transformed into an ugly downpour. Patrons fled to their cars as the production crew scrambled to secure the sensitive electronic equipment on stage.

Some lessons had been learned from the debacle of 2005. Backstage, president and organizing chair Pam Carter quickly conferred with the team of firefighters who were in charge of whether or not the show could continue. Following a carefully written "disaster plan" that had been put together by the board and the FOG team, the mainstage was shut down and, following the example of the 2005 festival, a few of the headline acts, including closer Rita Coolidge, moved over to the covered beer tent and delivered altered versions of the shows they'd planned. Again, it felt like a happy ending to a near-disaster.

It was a case of "the show must go on," and most of the audience was pleased with what transpired. Such is the nature of outdoor summer events, and one must be aware of such possibilities when purchasing tickets. The contingency planning worked well. No one was injured, no equipment was destroyed by rain, and although a few people ended up wet and chilled, things turned out reasonably well. The rest of the weekend was rain-free and the final concert, which featured the Milk Carton Kids on the mainstage, was a happy surprise for both old and new folkies in the main festival bowl. The crowd left smiling at the Milk Carton Kids' humour and their Simon & Garfunkel–like harmonies.

Gordon Lightfoot paid another visit to the park for a couple of reasons. In October of 2015 the City of Orillia unveiled a beautiful statue of the singer in Tudhope Park. It depicts Orillia's most famous native son sitting and playing his guitar with a halo of maple leaves surrounding him. The leaves represent the songs on *Gord's Gold*, Lightfoot's greatest hits album. The long-range plan is for more leaves, with a similar motif, to be planted along the section of the Trans-Canada Trail — known locally as the Lightfoot Trail — that winds along Orillia's waterfront.

Gord had attended the initial unveiling in October and was now back for the unveiling of a leaf for "Black Day in July" at the festival. The event had been coordinated so that the ceremony would take place during the Mariposa Folk Festival.

Gordon came for the statue presentation but also to take in a number of performances. He was effusive in his praise for what he saw. "There was magic this past year," he stated in an interview after the festival. "There were so many good moments. I always get an emotional lift at Mariposa. It has a life of its own and will go on for a long time. It's one of the best-known festivals on the planet — internationally recognized."

o o o

In the end the 2016 Mariposa Folk Festival experience was not all that different from being at, say, the 1978 festival on the Toronto Islands, the 1987 festival at Barrie's Molson Park, or even Innis Lake in 1966. Take a time machine and go back to Caledon or Olympic Island or any of the other venues where Mariposa has been set up and, except for the fashion and perhaps the average audience age, you'd be hard pressed to see a lot of difference in the demeanour of the festival. The positive and laid-back vibe, the acoustic-based music, the artisans and children's areas — all of it would seem familiar. Perhaps that is the nature of folk festivals. Perhaps it's simply the nature of folk music and those who love this kind of sound.

When the Mariposa Folk Festival began in 1961, folk music was one of the most popular genres of popular culture. It played on the radio of the day and filled the record stores. Consequently, crowds came by the thousands to Mariposa. In the late 60s and through the 70s, that type of music — especially in the hands of singer-songwriters — maintained a foothold in the public's taste and record-buying habits. As the 80s and 90s came along, with CDs and music videos on TV, the genre began to fade into the background, and so too did the audience for a time. At the dawn of the twenty-first century there was a renewed interest in acoustic, homegrown music and likewise a renewed interest in hearing it live and in person. People came to Mariposa — maybe not in the same numbers as in earlier decades but certainly in a way that sustained interest in the festival scene.

Mariposa had grown up, so to speak, with the baby boom generation. Or was it vice versa? As that demographic cohort aged, so too did the festival. Cultural changes were reflected in the festival. The styles of clothing changed over the decades. The different attitudes toward social activism were reflected in actions and stances over the years. Looking at the audience, one could see the change from single young people to young couples with kids, to grandparents bringing their grandchildren. Even the music changed in terms of its style and delivery. Early in the festival's history the focus was on traditional music. Then that focus shifted to songwriters penning and singing their own material. Gradually world music, Aboriginal, and francophone, and even jazz and rock music influenced what could be heard on a Mariposa stage. Yet through all those changes, much remained familiar and the same.

Mariposa, in large part due to the remarkable leadership of people like

Estelle Klein, had developed a format and vibe that carried it around the province — from Orillia to Innis Lake to the Toronto Islands to Molson Park and eventually back to Orillia. That format was copied and imitated by festivals all over Canada and the United States. The festival became a favoured destination of not only audiences but also performers. In many other ways MFF has throughout its history been a leader, an innovator, and an influencer. Mariposa played a role in wider acceptance of music that might not have been considered folk music at one time, and the festival was instrumental in bringing children's music to the fore. In addition to showcasing some of the most famous and best musicians in the world, it also fostered the development of young, emerging performers. It was a leader in establishing what we at one time called "Canadian content."

Despite the ever-changing events in the world around us and the advances in technology, each Mariposa has a familiarity that tells you where you are and why you're there. Will that feeling endure? We can only hope so.

Notes

INTRODUCTION: FOLK MUSIC AND FOLK FESTIVALS

1. *Mariposa: Under a Stormy Sky*, directed by Bay Weyman and Robert Lang (Toronto: Lyric Film and Video, 1991).

CHAPTER ONE: IN THE BEGINNING

1. Linda Page-Harpa and Bill Usher, eds., *For What Time I Am in This World: Stories from Mariposa* (Toronto: Peter Martin, 1977), 178.
2. The Newport Folk Festival was founded in 1959 by George Wein. The first board of directors included Pete Seeger, Oscar Brand, Theodore Bikel, and Albert Grossman — all prominent movers and shakers in the folk revival of the late 50s and early 60s. Newport later became famous for events such as "Dylan going electric" in 1965.
3. Ruth Jones-McVeigh, "Mariposa Folk Festival Origins: The Accurate Story" (unpublished manuscript, 2010).
4. Ruth Jones, "Operational Notes" (unpublished journal, 1961).
5. Ruth Jones McVeigh, "My Impression of a Folk Music Festival," *Mariposa '90: The Festival of Roots Music* (Orillia, ON: Mariposa Folk Foundation, 1990), 17.
6. Page-Harpa and Usher, eds., *For What Time I Am in This World*, 180.
7. Ibid.
8. The duo is called the Tu-Tones in festival advertising although their one LP is called *The Two Tones at the Village Corner*.
9. Nicholas Jennings, *Before the Gold Rush* (Toronto: Viking Books, 1998), 46.
10. Page-Harpa and Usher, eds., *For What Time I Am in This World*, 181.

CHAPTER TWO: YEAR THREE ... CHAOS!

1. Pete McGarvey, "From Melody to Melee," *Mariposa Folk Festival* (Orillia, ON: Mariposa Folk Foundation, 2001), 7.

2. Randy Richmond, *The Orillia Spirit: An Illustrated History of Orillia* (Toronto: Dundurn Press, 1996), 104.

3. Author's note: I was a nine-year-old entrepreneur myself. On the Monday after the festival, my cousin and I scoured the area between the two railway lines and rounded up $80 worth of beer bottles. At two cents apiece on the returns, that was a substantial number of empties!

4. Both the Newport Jazz Festival and the Newport Folk Festivals were banned from that city for two years. As you will see, the Mariposa Folk Festival was banned from Orillia for a much longer period of time.

CHAPTER THREE: THE INNIS LAKE YEARS

1. CKFH was owned by famous sports broadcaster Foster Hewitt. According to many sources, Hewitt rarely interfered with the programming on his station. That perhaps explains why Ferris was able to play many songs, such as Buffy Sainte-Marie's "Universal Soldier," that were banned from other radio playlists.

2. Page-Harpa and Usher, eds., *For What Time I Am in This World*, 183.

3. Ibid., 184.

4. Ibid.

5. Frank Matys, "50 Years of Mariposa," *Orillia Today*, 2010, 16.

6. Page-Harpa and Usher, eds., *For What Time I Am in This World*, 186.

7. Randall A. Ferris, "Wasn't That a Time!," *The 25th Anniversary Mariposa Folk Festival: Official Program* (Orillia: Mariposa Folk Foundation, 1985), 25.

8. Page-Harpa and Usher, eds., *For What Time I Am in This World*, 187.

9. Ibid., 188.

10. Ibid.

11. Ibid., 190.

12. Ibid., 192.

13. Buddy Guy with David Ritz. *When I Left Home* (Philadelphia: Da Capo Press, 2012), 185.

CHAPTER FOUR: TORONTO ISLAND YEARS, 1967–1971

1. Page-Harpa and Usher, eds., *For What Time I Am in This World*, 194.

2. Murray McLauchlan. *Getting Out of Here Alive: The Ballad of Murray McLauchlan* (Toronto: Viking Books, 1998), 207.

3. Page-Harpa and Usher, eds., *For What Time I Am in This World*, 196.

4. Ibid.

5. Ibid., 197.

6. Ibid.

7. The "blind Canadian singer" was most likely Freddy McKenna, a regular on the popular CBC-TV show *Don Messer's Jubilee*.

8. *RPM* was a music industry publication that featured song and album charts for Canada. It operated between 1964 and 2000.

CHAPTER FIVE: THE MEMORABLE 1972 FESTIVAL

1. Dave Bidini, *Writing Gordon Lightfoot: The Man, The Music, and the World in 1972* (Toronto: McClelland and Stewart, 2011), 85.

2. Ibid., 145.

3. Page-Harpa and Usher, eds., *For What Time I Am in This World*, 199.

4. Ibid., 201.

5. As quoted by Howard Druckman, unpublished document, 14 June 1990, Mariposa Folk Festival Fonds, Clara Thomas Archives, York University.

6. Page-Harpa and Usher, eds., *For What Time I Am in This World*, 201.

7. Bidini, *Writing Gordon Lightfoot*, 207.

8. Page-Harpa and Usher, eds., *For What Time I Am in This World*, 201.

9. Ibid.

CHAPTER SIX: THE TORONTO ISLAND YEARS: THE 70s

1. Page-Harpa and Usher, eds., *For What Time I Am in This World*, 203.

2. As quoted in Sija Tsai, "Mariposa Folk Festival: The Sounds, Sights, and Costs of a Fifty-Year Road Trip" (Ph.D. diss., York University, 2013), 127.

3. Page-Harpa and Usher, eds., *For What Time I Am in This World*, 203.

4. As quoted in Tsai, "Mariposa Folk Festival," 116.

5. Clay Eals, *Steve Goodman: Facing the Music* (Toronto: ECW Press, 2007), 384.

6. Garnet Rogers, *Night Drive: Travels with My Brother* (Brantford, ON: Tickle Shore, 2016), 252.

CHAPTER SEVEN: THE DECLINE AND NEAR FALL OF THE MARIPOSA EMPIRE

1. Interestingly, when the folks at Mariposa made known that there wouldn't be a summer festival in 1980, a group of enterprising individuals put together the "Toronto Folk Festival" and staged it at both Hanlan's Point on the island and

at Harbourfront. It only survived one year, losing a great deal of money and suffering the indignity of failing to pay all the artists.

2. With new records out, David Amram was still going strong in 2016 at age 85, and he made an appearance at the Mariposa Folk Festival in Orillia.

3. Daryl Auwai, "Here We Go Again," *Mariposa Fall Festival*, (Orillia, ON: Mariposa Folk Foundation, 1980), 3.

4. Matys, "50 Years of Mariposa," *Orillia Today*, 10.

CHAPTER EIGHT: THE BARRIE MOLSON PARK YEARS

1. Lynne Hurry and Rob Sinclair, "History of the Mariposa Folk Festival" (unpublished manuscript, 1997).

2. Lynne Hurry, "Welcome to the 30th Anniversary of the Mariposa Folk Festival," *Mariposa '90: The Festival of Roots Music* (Orillia, ON: Mariposa Folk Foundation, 1990), 9.

3. *Mariposa Notes: Festival Issue* (Orillia, ON: Mariposa Folk Foundation, 1984), 4.

4. The name was a historical tip of the hat to explorer Samuel de Champlain. Champlain had implemented *l'ordre de bon temps* as a means to keep his men active and enthusiastic during the long winters at Port Royal. Champlain had also spent the winter of 1615 in Huronia, only a few kilometres from the Barrie area. A world-famous statue to Champlain standing in Orillia's Couchiching Beach Park was the object of some of the hijinks at the infamous 1963 Mariposa Festival.

5. *Mariposa Notes* 4, no. 5 (1984): 3.

6. *The 25th Anniversary Mariposa Folk Festival: Official Program*, (Orillia, ON: Mariposa Folk Foundation, 1985), 32.

7. The OCFF grew and has evolved, changing its name to Folk Music Ontario in 2012. As of 2016 the organization consists of twenty-one member festivals, thirteen organizational members, and approximately 129 individual members.

8. *Mariposa Notes*, no. 12 (1990): 2.

9. *Mariposa: Under a Stormy Sky*, directed by Bay Weyman and Robert Lang (Toronto: Lyric Film and Video, 1991).

10. Don Cullen had been a stage host and had played a number of roles in festivals over the years. In 2006 Don was honoured with induction into the Mariposa Hall of Fame alongside Ian and Sylvia Tyson. One of the stages at Mariposa each year is called the "Bohemian Embassy Stage," a tribute to Don and his contributions.

CHAPTER NINE: A RETURN TO TORONTO IN THE 90s

1. *Mariposa Notes* 8, no. 2 (1992): 1.

CHAPTER TEN: CHASING MARIPOSA

1. Tim Lauer, "Chasing Mariposa" (unpublished manuscript, n.d.), 1.
2. Ibid., 2.
3. Ibid.
4. Ibid., 3.
5. Ibid., 4.
6. Gord Ball, "The Mariposa Folk Festival Rises Again: Back Home in Orillia in the Year 2000" (unpublished manuscript, 2010), 2.
7. Lynne Hurry, "President's Message," *Mariposa Festival By-the-Shore at Cobourg* (Orillia, ON: Mariposa Folk Foundation, 1996), 2.

CHAPTER ELEVEN: WELCOME HOME MARIPOSA

1. A councillor from nearby Oro-Medonte Township was advocating through the media for the event to be staged at the ODAS park fairgrounds site, well outside the city boundaries. No trees, no water … enough said!

CHAPTER TWELVE: MARIPOSA GETS ITS MOJO BACK

1. Lightfoot as the headliner ensured a good crowd. Orillians love their hometown boy! The fact that it was a benefit performance is even more important to note. His generosity to Mariposa cannot be understated.
2. The actual Mariposa Folk Foundation was still in debt. FestO had been set up as a separate entity with its own constitution so that the organizers from Orillia did not take on the debt that had amassed in Toronto.
3. Charitable Alliance Corporation, *Business Plan for the Development of a Comprehensive Revenue Generation Program* (November 2001).
4. By way of comparison, by 2015 over 62 percent of the festival audience came from Central Ontario, that is, within forty kilometres of Orillia (Mariposa Folk Festival Audience Survey, 2015).

CHAPTER THIRTEEN: CONSOLIDATION IN ORILLIA

1. Jowi returned with the Six String Nation guitar a few years later, set up a booth, and encouraged Mariposa audience members and volunteers to have their picture taken with the iconic "axe."

2. Baker took his water station that he'd invented for MFF to the next level. He appeared on the TV series *Dragon's Den*, where all five Dragons asked to buy into his concept. The water stations began appearing at other festivals and events all across North America, including Barack Obama's 2012 inauguration in Washington, D.C.

Bibliography

BOOKS

Amram, David. *Upbeat: Nine Lives of a Musical Cat.* Boulder, CO: Paradigm, 2008.

Bidini, Dave. *Writing Gordon Lightfoot: The Man, the Music, and the World in 1972.* Toronto: McClelland and Stewart, 2011.

Cohen, Ronald D. *Rainbow Quest: The Folk Music Revival & American Society, 1940–1970.* Boston: University of Massachusetts Press, 2002.

Collins, Maynard. *Lightfoot: If You Could Read His Mind.* Toronto: Deneau, 1988.

Dunaway, David King and Molly Beer. *Singing Out: An Oral History of America's Folk Music Revivals.* New York: Oxford University Press, 2010.

Eals, Clay. *Steve Goodman: Facing the Music.* Toronto: ECW Press, 2007.

Einarson, John, with Ian and Sylvia Tyson. *Four Strong Winds: Ian and Sylvia.* Toronto: McClelland and Stewart, 2011.

Guy, Buddy, with David Ritz. *When I Left Home.* Philadelphia: Da Capo Press, 2012.

Jennings, Nicholas. *Before the Gold Rush.* Toronto: Viking Books, 1997.

McLauchlan, Murray. *Getting Out of Here Alive: The Ballad of Murray McLauchlan.* Toronto: Viking Books, 1998.

Page-Harpa, Linda, and Bill Usher, eds. *For What Time I Am in This World: Stories from Mariposa.* Toronto: Peter Martin, 1977.

Richmond, Randy. *The Orillia Spirit: An Illustrated History of Orillia.* Toronto: Dundurn Press, 1996.

Rogers, Garnet. *Night Drive: Travels with My Brother.* Brantford, ON: Tickle Shore, 2016.

Wynn, Jonathan R. *Music City: American Festivals and Placemaking*. Chicago: University of Chicago Press, 2015.

OTHER SOURCES

Billboard Magazine
The Buzz (Charlottetown, PE)
Globe and Mail
Mariposa Folk Festival programs
Mariposa Newsletter
Mariposa Notes
Orillia Packet and Times
Orillia Today
Ottawa Citizen
Toronto Star
Toronto Telegram
Winnipeg Tribune

Ball, Gord. "The Mariposa Folk Festival Rises Again: Back Home in Orillia in the Year 2000." Unpublished manuscript, last modified 2010.
Hurry, Lynne, and Rob Sinclair. "History of the Mariposa Folk Festival." Unpublished manuscript, last modified 1997.
Jones, Ruth. "Operational Notes/Journal." Orillia, ON: Unpublished journal, 1961.
Jones-McVeigh, Ruth. "Mariposa Folk Festival Origins: The Accurate Story." Unpublished manuscript, last modified 2010.
Lauer, Tim. "Chasing Mariposa." Unpublished manuscript, date unknown.
MacDonald, Michael. "This Is Important! Mitch Podolak, the Revolutionary Establishment and the Founding of the Winnipeg Folk Festival." Master's thesis, Carleton University, 2006.
Matys, Frank. "50 Years of Mariposa." *Orillia Today*, 2010.
Tsai, Sija. "Mariposa Folk Festival: The Sounds, Sights, and Costs of a Fifty-Year Road Trip." Ph.D. diss., York University, 2013.

FILM

Mariposa: Under a Stormy Sky. Directed by Bay Weyman and Robert Lang. Toronto: Lyric Film and Video, 1991.

Image Credits

62　Leo Harrison, 1969, ASC05770, Toronto Telegram fonds, F0433, Clara Thomas Archives, York University.

63　A. Rengendanz, 1974, ASC05933, Mariposa Folk Foundation fonds, F0511, Clara Thomas Archives, York University.

65　Betts, 1970, ASC06255, Toronto Telegram fonds, F0433, Clara Thomas Archives, York University.

66　Photographer unknown, 1971, Mariposa Folk Foundation fonds, F0511, Clara Thomas Archives, York University.

68　Betts, 1970, ASC06240, Toronto Telegram fonds, F0433, Clara Thomas Archives, York University.

69　Photographer unknown, Mariposa Folk Foundation fonds, F0511, Clara Thomas Archives, York University.

72　Photographer unknown, 1975, ASC05925, Mariposa Folk Foundation fonds, F0511, Clara Thomas Archives, York University.

75　Photographer unknown, 1975, ASC04746, Mariposa Folk Foundation fonds, F0511, Clara Thomas Archives, York University.

78　Photographer unknown, 1978, ASC05958, Mariposa Folk Foundation fonds, F0511, Clara Thomas Archives, York University.

80　Reg. Towers, 1969, ASC05785, Toronto Telegram fonds, F0433, Clara Thomas Archives, York University.

83　B.I. Chertkoff, ASC05322, Mariposa Folk Foundation fonds, F0511, Clara Thomas Archives, York University.

87　Photographer unknown, 1977, Mariposa Folk Foundation fonds, F0511, Clara Thomas Archives, York University.

92　(top) Paul Till, 1978, ASC05883, Mariposa Folk Foundation fonds, F0511, Clara Thomas Archives, York University.

92　(bottom) Jim Mys, 1974, ASC05876, Mariposa Folk Foundation fonds, F0511, Clara Thomas Archives, York University.

94　Photographer unknown, 1977, ASC05948, Mariposa Folk Foundation fonds, F0511, Clara Thomas Archives, York University.

97　(top) Photographer unknown, Mariposa Folk Foundation fonds, F0511, Clara Thomas Archives, York University.

97　(bottom) Photographer unknown, 1977, Mariposa Folk Foundation fonds, F0511, Clara Thomas Archives, York University.

109　Dave Williams, 1975, ASC05910, Mariposa Folk Foundation fonds, F0511, Clara Thomas Archives, York University.

113　Photographer unknown, Mariposa Folk Foundation fonds, F0511, Clara Thomas Archives, York University.

138   Photographer unknown, Mariposa Folk Foundation fonds, F0511, Clara Thomas Archives, York University.

140   Photographer unknown, 1999, Mariposa Folk Foundation fonds, F0511, Clara Thomas Archives, York University.

146   Photographer unknown, Mariposa Folk Foundation fonds, F0511, Clara Thomas Archives, York University.

169   Mariposa Folk Foundation, 2004.

173   Ron Hill, 2007.

203   Adam Mullins, 2012.

206   Adam Mullins, 2012.

Index

Deer Life
Ron Sexsmith

Deryn Hedlight was not having a very good day and it was about to get much worse. He'd read stories of witches as a boy, but never believed for a second they were true. That is, until an unfortunate hunting accident turns his world upside down. An honest mistake, it would seem, leads to an altogether unexpected transformation. But poor Deryn isn't the only wronged character tied up in these gloomy circumstances and sinister forces.

Deer Life tells the story of a kind-hearted boy from Hinthoven and his mother's undying love. It's a wicked fairy tale of witchcraft, bullying, revenge, and a mysterious bowler hat. Mostly though, it's all about patience, friendship, and heroism where you least expect it.

Strange Way to Live
Carl Dixon

Carl Dixon's journey through the twists and turns of a music performer's life began in Northern Ontario, where his boyhood dreams, shaped by the 1960s, collided with a new musical culture.

Though Carl's road was rocky, it was still paved with gold. It has led from his early days with hard rockers Coney Hatch to tours and lasting friendships with huge acts like Iron Maiden. The ups and downs were meteoric. Carl became a member of the legendary bands The Guess Who and April Wine and then faced the hardest test of all: a horrific auto collision in Australia that left him in a coma, barely clinging to life.

Strange Way to Live follows Carl's progress, never faltering and sometimes comical, toward musical glory. Blind determination can lead one to some strange places. Carl's took him through some of the biggest, smallest, and weirdest scenes in this vast country, and from the glory days of Canadian rock to the present day.